EFFECTIVE LEADERSHIP AT MINORITY-SERVING INSTITUTIONS

Strong, effective, and innovative leadership is critical for institutions of higher education, especially for Minority-Serving Institutions (MSIs). Indeed, research and examples have shown leadership instability among some types of MSIs, while discussions and research on effective leadership for other MSIs is noticeably absent from the extant literature. In this volume, noted experts, researchers, and leaders discuss opportunities and challenges for leadership across the full range of MSIs, while creating a dialogue on leadership models and best practices. Chapters explore issues at Historically Black Colleges and Universities (HBCUs), Hispanic Serving Institutions (HSIs), Tribal Colleges and Universities (TCUs), and Asian American and Native American Pacific Islander Serving Institutions (AANA-PISIs). This book helps higher education and student affairs scholars and administrators unpack contemporary leadership issues and strategies, and synthesizes best practices to help MSI leaders increase the effectiveness and sustainability of their institutions.

Robert T. Palmer is currently Interim Chair and Associate Professor in the Department of Educational Leadership and Policy Studies at Howard University, USA.

Dina C. Maramba is Associate Professor of Higher Education at the Claremont Graduate University, USA.

Andrew T. Arroyo is Associate Professor of Interdisciplinary Studies, Co-Director for Learning Communities, and Program Director for the Career Pathways Initiative at Norfolk State University, USA.

Taryn Ozuna Allen is Assistant Professor of Educational Leadership and Policy Studies at the University of Texas at Arlington, USA.

Tiffany Fountaine Boykin is Assistant Dean of Student Services at Anne Arundel Community College, USA.

John Michael Lee, Jr. is Vice Chancellor for University Advancement at Elizabeth City State University, USA.

EFFECTIVE LEADERSHIP AT MINORITY-SERVING INSTITUTIONS

Exploring Opportunities and Challenges for Leadership

Edited by
Robert T. Palmer, Dina C. Maramba,
Andrew T. Arroyo, Taryn Ozuna Allen,
Tiffany Fountaine Boykin, and
John Michael Lee, Jr.

Routledge
Taylor & Francis Group
NEW YORK AND LONDON

Saginaw Chippewa Tribal College
2274 Enterprise Drive
Mt. Pleasant, MI 48858

First published 2018
by Routledge
711 Third Avenue, New York, NY 10017

and by Routledge
2 Park Square, Milton Park, Abingdon, Oxon OX14 4RN

Routledge is an imprint of the Taylor & Francis Group, an informa business

© 2018 Taylor & Francis

The right of Robert T. Palmer, Dina C. Maramba, Andrew T. Arroyo, Taryn Ozuna Allen, Tiffany Fountaine Boykin, and John Michael Lee, Jr. to be identified as the authors of the editorial material, and of the authors for their individual chapters, has been asserted in accordance with sections 77 and 78 of the Copyright, Designs and Patents Act 1988.

Library of Congress Cataloging in Publication Data
A catalog record has been requested for this book

ISBN: 978-1-138-21172-8 (hbk)
ISBN: 978-1-138-21174-2 (pbk)
ISBN: 978-1-315-45229-6 (ebk)

Typeset in Bembo
by Taylor & Francis Books

CONTENTS

List of tables   viii
Foreword   ix
Preface   xiii
Acknowledgments   xvi

1 Exploring the Need for Leadership at Minority-Serving
   Institutions   1
   Robert T. Palmer, Andrew T. Arroyo, Dina C. Maramba,
   Taryn Ozuna Allen and Tiffany Fountaine Boykin

PART I
Historically Black Colleges and Universities (HBCUs)   19

2 HBCUs: Valuable – Yet Substantially Impaired – Institutions   21
   Kofi Lomotey and Megan Covington

3 Student Affairs Administrators: A Catalyst for HBCU
   Transformation   46
   Edward M. Willis and Andrew T. Arroyo

4 Avoiding Forced Turnover(s): Best Practices for HBCU
   Senior-Level Executive Recruitment   65
   William J. Broussard and Adriel Hilton

5 Paul Quinn College: Servant Leadership in Action 81
Marybeth Gasman, Amanda Washington Lockett, and Levon Esters

PART II
Hispanic-Serving Institutions (HSIs) 91

6 Being a Culturally Responsive Leader at a Hispanic-Serving
Institution Community College 93
Magdalena H. de la Teja

7 Accelerating Student Success Through Bold Leadership 112
Joseph I. Castro and Isaac M.J. Castro

8 The Evolution of Hispanic-Serving Institutions: Past, Present,
and Future 125
Laura J. Cortez

PART III
Tribal Colleges and Universities (TCUs) 137

9 Tribal College and University Leadership: Overcoming
Challenges through Service and Collective Leadership 139
Ginger C. Stull and Marybeth Gasman

10 Tribal Colleges and University Leaders: Warriors in Spirit and
in Action 150
Cheryl Crazy Bull

PART IV
**Asian American and Native American Pacific Islander-
Serving Institution (AANAPISIs)** 167

11 Leadership is More Than a Checklist!: Exploring Leadership at
AANAPISI Community Colleges 169
Loretta P. Adrian, Kathi Hiyane-Brown, and Naomi Okumura Story

12 AANAPISI Leadership: Perspectives from the Field 186
*Robert T. Teranishi, Cynthia M. Alcantar and
Robert A. Underwood*

13 Setting the Stage for Change: Emerging Knowledge on
Leadership at MSIs 199
*Andrew T. Arroyo, Dina C. Maramba, Robert T. Palmer,
Tiffany Fountaine Boykin and Taryn Ozuna Allen*

Afterword: Twenty-first Century Leadership at Minority-Serving
Institutions   208
Ivory A. Toldson

Contributors   211

Index   *223*

TABLES

6.1 Number of Hispanic–Serving Institutions   97

6.2 Post-secondary enrollment by race/ethnicity and school type (2013)   98

FOREWORD

One thing I have learned as an administrator entering my eighteenth year in higher education is to live in truth. Not only is it important for your reputation, but it is good professionally. I must admit that I did not want to write this preface. I was just too busy. With the start of a new semester unfolding, evaluating tenure and promotion portfolios of faculty, preparing for classes, and my own writing projects – not to mention just trying to enjoy life, I just did not feel that I had the time or the energy for even one additional thing.

After logging on to a popular social media site and reading a post about the high number of historically Black colleges/universities (HBCUs) Presidents who had left their positions less than five years after assuming their posts, I began to reconsider that position. The affected institutions included two very public and protracted "tug of war" like struggles between the President and board of Trustees at two large public HBCUs, one in Florida and one in Alabama. So, when I picked up the manuscript by Robert Palmer et al. and read the preface and the chapters within the context of these high-profile leadership battles, it became very clear why this book is needed.

For whatever reason, be it personal aggrandizement, sense of efficacy, logical progression, or the desire for more money, entry level administrators long for the day of becoming a dean, vice president, provost, or president of an institution. The irony is that though they desire to reach such positions they dare not express it openly as if by so doing, it would automatically disqualify them. As such, most express anything but a willingness to ascend to leadership. I am reminded of a faculty member who detested the thought of being a leader at her university, and often referred to leaving the classroom for administration as entering the "dark side." In fact, she had all the qualities and the temperament needed to be an outstanding administrator. Luckily, her provost saw her skills and mentored her to become a very successful provost in her own right.

Colleges and universities, especially Minority-Serving Institutions (MSIs), often having to operate with limited resources, are amazing places – swarming with highly energetic and engaging people who are extremely complex, ranging from individuals like faculty members who by their training are precocious and opinionated about nearly everything to alumni of the institution who often have a glorified obsession with how things used to be. The reality is that most individuals, even those associated with the institution, do not understand what it fully takes to lead these complex organizations nor what the requirements are to move from a faculty member to a provost or from a coordinator to a vice president of student affairs. While the job descriptions read easily on paper, and the persons in these positions make it look easy on the surface, the reality is that these positions are very difficult – professionally, personally, and emotionally.

As an administrator who has served in both predominantly White institutions (PWIs) and MSIs, the challenges that currently beset MSIs are both similar and distinct from PWIs. MSI administrators, even more than their counterparts at PWIs, are often challenged by Boards who do not thoroughly understand boards' proper role. Although trustees have fiduciary and oversight responsibilities for their respective institutions, their roles should not extend to the daily operation of the campus. It has been suggested that such board member tampering is the case in both the Alabama and Florida situations. According to the Association of Governing Boards, the essence of a board is to promote the institution, support the leadership, and assist in advancing the mission of the college/university financially.

MSI Presidents and Vice Presidents are often not just leaders on the campus, but also in the communities in which their campus resides, such as being a member of the local rotary or serving on various community-based boards. He/she becomes the de facto spokesperson for all things related their persona – from their gender to race. For example, President Dwaun Warmack of Harris-Stowe State University in Saint Louis, Missouri became a national figure – appearing on nearly all the major news networks and meeting with several key politicians – during the Michael Brown shooting and protests in Ferguson, Missouri.

Linked to this is the "constancy" that comes with serving as a leader at a MSI. The "fish bowl" syndrome is the reality at most institutions, but typically it is reserved for the face of the institution – the President. At PWIs, especially those that are mid to large in size, administrators can hide in the numbers. Such opportunities do not exist for administrators at MSIs. In short, you are always on – from worship on Sunday to dinner at a restaurant on Wednesday to grocery shopping on Saturday. This constant scrutiny often forces administrators into virtual isolation – only associating with a small group of individuals, such as immediate family, trusted friends/mentors, and close colleagues in similar positions at other institutions.

I am reminded of what C.K. Gunsalus said about being a college administrator: "There are always 'people problems'." He asserts and I can attest that this is probably the most difficult part of being a leader. The phrase "People Problems" encompasses anything from a disgruntled faculty member who desires to be promoted even though he/she has not met all the criteria, to an irate student who is upset with the Bursar because the institution will not allow him/her to return because of an outstanding bill. It is these types of problems that land on the desk of leaders at MSIs. Although these things happen at PWIs, rarely do they make it to the attention of the leadership. Nearly all my colleagues complain about having to deal with issues that rise to their level that could easily be handled by a frontline administrator. Why do people bypass the chain of command and take things straight to the Vice President, Provost, or the President? They do not think the frontline leaders will give them the answer they want? They do not accept the initial answer of another administrator? They feel that by making a compelling argument to the executive leadership they will get the answer that they want? But whatever their reasons, this process distracts MSI leaders from focusing on the critical issues facing their institution.

And, though we cannot change the people factor problem, might I suggest some approaches to consider as you engage in this work: Be Confident in who you are; Be Resolute in your values; Be Strategic in your actions; Be Customer focused; Be Nimble; Be Willing to take calculated risks; Be Open to listening to your team; Be Connected; and Be Mindful of those who have been at the institutions.

Leadership is important amid the changes that are taking place with the landscape of higher education. It is predicted by educational scholars that the number of MSIs, especially HBCUs, will be substantially reduced by 2025. While this dire prediction has not been met by alumni and others positively, many of these institutions are challenged with limited endowments, high tuition costs, the effects of integration, outdated missions and curriculums, and low enrollments and graduation rates. In many stances, the contributors to this work challenge current and future leaders to look beyond traditional frames of leadership that rely on hierarchical and status quo strategies.

Palmer et al.'s book is designed to provide individuals with an understanding of higher education as a field of practice, while probing more deeply into issues of MSIs. In addition to its unique emphasis, the distinctive challenges facing HBCUs, Hispanic Serving Institutions (HSIs), Tribal Colleges and Universities (TCUs), and Asian American and Native American Pacific Islander-Serving Institutions (AANAPISIs), this book emphasizes the interaction and opportunities that could exist among these institutions with the "right" leadership. This book will help its readers to appreciate and understand the multiple perspectives that may be needed in higher education leadership.

The challenges that MSIs face require that administrators not only adapt to change but also understand the historical mission, the culture, human capital, politics, resources, and issues that beset these institutions, as well as possessing a vision of MSIs for the twenty-first century. While some might dispute the assertions and strategies made in these chapters, what cannot be debated is the imperative to strengthen "our" institutions by well preparing individuals for leadership to understand the issues, through generating and applying knowledge, to advance the role of MSIs in supporting the public good, and to improve institutional practices. This book aims to accomplish this mission through its various chapters.

In closing, I am reminded of the words of the greater educator, Horace Mann, who said, "One should be afraid to die until they have made a difference in the World." Truly one can have no greater impact on individuals than through education; therefore, we need you to read, reflect on, and reimagine how you can help lead MSIs through the twenty-first century.

Said Sewell, Ph.D.
Provost and Vice President for Academic Affairs
Lincoln University of Missouri

PREFACE

This edited volume is divided into four sections pertaining to Minority-Serving Institutions (MSIs). The first section focuses on Historically Black Colleges and Universities (HBCUs), followed by a section on Hispanic-Serving Institutions (HSIs), Tribal Colleges and Universities (TCUs), and Asian American and Native American Pacific Islander Serving Institutions (AANAPISIs). Chapter 1, "Exploring the Need for Leadership at Minority-Serving Institutions," by Robert T. Palmer, Andrew T. Arroyo, Dina C. Maramba, Taryn Ozuna Allen, and Tiffany Fountaine Boykin, provides an overview of MSIs and discusses the contribution that this volume makes to the literature on leadership for MSIs. This chapter moves the book into section one, which is on HBCUs. Chapter 2, "HBCUs: Valuable – Yet Substantially Impaired – Institutions," is by Kofi Lomotey and Megan Covington. In it, the authors use personal and other documented illustrations to discuss some of the significant strengths as well as the profound challenges of HBCUs. Most importantly, they propose opportunities and strategies for the leadership of HBCUs to address the myriad challenges that impact these institutions.

In Chapter 3, "Student Affairs Administrators: A Catalyst for HBCU Trans-formation," Edward M. Willis and Andrew T. Arroyo argue that student affairs administrators provide leadership for an array of programs and services, which cultivates myriad skills including a keen awareness of the student experience, student development, crisis management, fundraising, fiscal management, innova-tion, and relationship building. The authors assert that these skills position student affairs administrators to serve as effective institutional leaders. They note that recently HBCUs have appointed experienced student affairs administrators to the presidency (e.g., Walter Kimbrough – Dillard; Dwaun Warmack – Harris-Stowe; and Kevin Rome – Lincoln University, Missouri). In this chapter, the authors challenge the traditional trajectory of the presidency by exploring the selection of student affairs administrators to serve as catalysts for HBCU transformation. In Chapter 4, "Avoiding Forced Turnover(s): Best Practices for HBCU Senior-Level Executive Recruitment," William Broussard and Adriel Hilton examine an unconsidered negative consequence of high turnover rates for HBCU executives – the career derailments of senior-staff level administrators and cabinet members who are also terminated when HBCU presidents resign or are terminated. The authors identify strategies for talent recruitment for HBCU presidents, which offer incentives and protection for leadership staff in a tumultuous employment climate.

In Chapter 5, "Paul Quinn College: Servant Leadership in Action," Marybeth Gasman, Amanda Washington Lockett, and Levon Esters examine servant leadership as demonstrated by Michael Sorrell, President of Paul Quinn, and how it has resulted in a transformative culture for the small, private HBCU. Chapter 6 focuses on HSIs. Specifically, in this chapter – "Being a Culturally Responsive Leader at a Hispanic-Serving Institution Community College" – Magdalena H. de la Teja explores the attributes of effective leadership within HSI community colleges. Specifically, the author discusses what these leaders will confront and shares recommendations to help support leaders of HSI community colleges. In Chapter 7, "Accelerating Student Success Through Bold Leadership," Joseph Castro and Isaac Castro focus on how servant leadership has helped institutional stakeholders embrace the goal of student success at Fresno State, a university that is recognized as both an HSI and AANAPISI.

In Chapter 8, "The Evolution of Hispanic-Serving Institutions: Past, Present, and Future," Laura Cortez provides an analysis of Hispanic-Serving Institutions by discussing their past, present, and future impact. The author concludes her chapter by offering specific recommendations for institutional leaders at HSIs. Chapter 9 focuses on TCUs. Specifically, in this chapter, "Tribal College and University Leadership: Overcoming Challenges through Service and Collective Leadership," Ginger Stull and Marybeth Gasman focus on Native American leadership practices as they relate to TCUs. This chapter in particular, discusses how Indigenous Ways of Knowing and historic leadership approaches to Native American schooling have provided a backdrop to contemporary TCU leadership. In Chapter 10, "Tribal Colleges and University Leaders: Warriors in Spirit and in Action," Cheryl Crazy Bull discusses how leaders of Tribal colleges must be warriors. Specifically, this chapter emphasizes how leaders of TCUs must use all the resources they can access to ensure the survival of their institutions so that their people may prosper and their Tribes can thrive.

Chapter 11 focuses on AANAPISIs. In this chapter, "Leadership is More Than a Checklist!: Exploring Leadership at AANAPISI Community Colleges," Loretta Adrian, Kathi Hiyane-Brown, and Naomi Okumura Story review recent theories and research on leadership excellence and cultural competency and they analyze survey and interview results from successful leaders of AANAPISIs across the country. They also identify and discuss the critical elements and factors that influence successful AANAPISI leadership. In Chapter 12, "AANAPISI Leadership: Perspectives from the Field," Robert Teranishi, Robert Underwood, and Cynthia Alcantar describe the unique institutional characteristics of AANAPISIs and the role and function of leadership in advancing these institutions. This chapter concludes with advice, recommendations, and strategies regarding effective leadership for AANAPISIs. In the final chapter – Chapter 13, "Setting the Stage for Change: Emerging Knowledge on Leadership at MSIs" – Andrew T. Arroyo, Dina C. Maramba, Robert T. Palmer, Tiffany Fountaine Boykin, and Taryn Ozuna Allen synthesize the emerging knowledge on leadership at MSIs that have emerged from this edited volume.

ACKNOWLEDGMENTS

Robert T. Palmer dedicates this book to his colleagues in the School of Education in general and the Department of Educational Leadership and Policy Studies (ELPS) in particular at Howard University. He would also like to dedicate this book to Jehovah God for HIS love, support, mercy, and kindness. He would like to acknowledge Ms. Barbara Boakye and Mr. Chase Frazer – Graduate Assistants in ELPS who reviewed research articles, policy reports, and book chapters, which informed the writing of Chapter 1.

Andrew T. Arroyo wishes to dedicate this book to Mr. Edward M. Willis, Dr. Sandra J. DeLoatch, Dr. Stacey Franklin Jones, and Mr. Eddie N. Moore, Jr. for mentoring and providing him leadership opportunities at Norfolk State University.

Dina C. Maramba wishes to acknowledge her colleagues in the School of Educational Studies at Claremont Graduate University and the unconditional support from her family and friends. She is also thankful to her co-editors who made this project a very positive professional and intellectual collaborative experience.

Taryn Ozuna Allen wishes to thank her co-editors and she dedicates this book to her family.

Tiffany Fountaine Boykin: I would like to express my gratitude to my co-editors. It is truly an honor and privilege to work among such talented individuals who have committed their research efforts to examining Minority-Serving Institutions. Thank you for continuing to serve as trailblazers in advancing success agendas for students, particularly those from underrepresented and underserved communities.

My work is dedicated to those who believed I never would,

And, to my loving husband who always said that I should,

And, to my beloved Morgan State University – she reminded me that I could do anything.

1

EXPLORING THE NEED FOR LEADERSHIP AT MINORITY-SERVING INSTITUTIONS

Robert T. Palmer, Andrew T. Arroyo, Dina C. Maramba, Taryn Ozuna Allen and Tiffany Fountaine Boykin

Although Minority-Serving Institutions (MSIs) are comprised of diverse institutional types, which have distinctive histories, missions, and characteristics (Conrad & Gasman, 2015; Cunningham, Park, & Engle, 2014; Gasman, Nguyen, & Conrad, 2015), they share common threads (Conrad & Gasman, 2015; Gasman et al., 2015). For example, MSIs, which consist of Historically Black Colleges and Universities (HBCUs), Hispanic-Serving Institutions (HSIs), Tribal Colleges and Universities (TCUs), Predominantly Black Institutions (PBIs), and Asian American and Native American Pacific Islander Serving Institutions (AANAPISIs), serve high populations of students who are first-generation college students, come from low socio-economic backgrounds, and who are dependent upon financial aid to access and persist through higher education (Flores & Park, 2013). There are currently 650 MSIs and they enroll 3.6 million students at the undergraduate level, which is 20% of all undergraduate students (Conrad & Gasman, 2015; Gasman et al., 2015).

On average, MSIs are more affordable than many Predominantly White Institutions (PWIs), but they are also underresourced despite serving students who arguably need more financial and academic support to help attain their baccalaureate degrees (Cunningham et al., 2014; Gasman et al., 2007). MSIs are noted for doing more with less (Conrad & Gasman, 2015). For example, despite lacking funding parity (Palmer & Griffin, 2009), 2011–12 data revealed MSIs awarded more than 540,000 undergraduate degrees and certificates, which comprised almost 16% of all degrees and 32% of all credentials awarded to minority students at the undergraduate level (Cunningham et al., 2014). MSIs disproportionately graduate the nation's teachers, doctors, dentists, and judges of color (Gasman, 2008). They have been particularly lauded for their success in graduating minority students with degrees in science, technology, engineering, and mathematics (STEM). Given that many MSIs provide cultural nourishment, facilitate a sense of role modeling, and provide an environment inside and outside the classroom that helps to cultivate students' self-efficacy, particularly in areas related to success in STEM, Palmer, Maramba, and Gasman (2012) argued MSIs should be viewed as exemplars for helping to increase the achievement of minority students in this discipline.

Another commonality that MSIs share is a lack of research on a multitude of issues pertaining to students, faculty, and staff. This is true when it comes to leadership[1] in general and the presidency specifically. While this list is nowhere near exhaustive, there has been a paucity of research around HBCU leadership. For example, HBCU researchers have explored the preparation process for HBCU presidents (Freeman & Gasman, 2014), characteristics of effective leadership for HBCU presidents (Freeman, Commodore, Gasman, & Carter, 2016), and the challenges that impinge upon the success of HBCU presidents (Freeman & Gasman, 2014; Ricard & Brown, 2008; Stewart, 2014; Watson, 2013). Despite this research, scholarship on HBCU leadership in general, and the presidency specifically, is sparse (Freeman & Gasman, 2014; Freeman et al., 2016).

Moreover, research on leadership at other MSIs has received even less focus. Knowing that leadership serves as the linchpin to the success and sustainability of organizations generally, and colleges and universities specifically (Hurtado, Milem, Clayton-Pedersen, & Allen, 1999), discussing leadership at MSIs is critical given the important role they play in educating the future of our nation – historically marginalized students (Transforming Leadership at MSIs, 2015). According to a report on transforming leadership at MSIs, "MSIs need high performing leaders to assist them in overcoming historic barriers, supporting new populations, confronting complex financial constraints, and forging new visions of their evolving roles" (Transforming Leadership at MSIs, 2015, p. 15). This statement is consistent with our rationale for conceptualizing this book.

With this in mind, this book serves several purposes. First, it provides insight into some of the challenges MSI presidents may face. Second, it creates dialogue on leadership models and best practices for MSIs. Third, it synthesizes best practices for MSI leaders to help MSI leaders increase the effectiveness of their institutions. Having established the relevancy of this book, the subsequent sections of this chapter will better contextualize the need for this volume by providing an overview of the aforementioned MSIs and reviewing the literature on leadership in MSIs. This chapter will first focus on HBCUs, followed by HSIs, TCUs, PBIs, and AANAPISIs.

Historically Black Colleges and Universities

Historically Black Colleges and Universities (HBCUs) are classified as educational institutions founded prior to 1964 to provide access to education for Blacks (Gasman, 2008). These institutions were founded with the assistance of White philanthropists, the American Missionary Association, the Freedmen's Bureau, and Black churches (Nichols, 2004). Cheyney University and Lincoln University, both located in Pennsylvania, were some of the first HBCUs to be established before the Civil War. The Morrill Act of 1890, which required states to establish separate land grant colleges for Blacks if they were precluded from attending existing land grant schools, played a vital role in the development of HBCUs. Specifically, this legislation resulted in the creation of 19 HBCUs in the Southern states (Brown, 2002). Today, there are 105 HBCUs and they enroll approximately 11% of Black students (Gasman, 2013). These institutions are comprised of a rich tapestry of colleges and universities, including public, private, two-year, four-year, selective, and open (Gasman, 2013).

Research has shown that HBCUs have made and continue to make significant contributions to society and to advancement for Blacks specifically (Nichols, 2004; Palmer & Wood, 2012). For example, not only have they provided a gateway to help Blacks advance into the middle class, but they have also produced important leaders, such as Dr. Martin Luther King, Thurgood Marshall, Diane Nash, and Stokely Carmichael, all of whom had a profound impact on the Civil Rights Movement (Nichols, 2004; Palmer & Gasman, 2008). HBCUs are credited for disproportionately graduating Black students who earn bachelor degrees and matriculate into graduate or professional schools (Palmer, Hilton, & Fountaine, 2012). In fact, in 2012, HBCUs awarded nearly 19% of baccalaureate degrees to Black students (Lomax, 2014). Though some may question the relevancy of these illustrious institutions (e.g., Riley, 2010) HBCUs have proven their importance not only by their outcomes, but also by their impact on Black students during their enrollment. Indeed, HBCUs facilitate and engender Black students' self-efficacy, cultural connectiveness, psychological wellness, and racial uplift (Palmer, 2008; Palmer & Gasman, 2008; Nichols, 2004).

While HBCUs are labeled as historically Black institutions, they have always welcomed students, faculty, and staff from diverse racial and ethnic backgrounds (Arroyo, Palmer, Maramba, & Louis, 2016; Gasman & Nguyen, 2015). In fact, some of the first students to attend Howard University were the daughters of the founder, Olive O. Howard, a White man (Gasman & Nguyen, 2015). Nevertheless, upon their founding until the 1950s, the population of HBCUs was nearly 100% Black. Over the years, however, particularly beginning in the 1980s, the racial and ethnic diversity of HBCUs has increased (Nichols, 2004). According to the Center for Minority-Serving Institutions (CMSIs) as well as data from the National Center for Educational Statistics (2013), Black students currently make up about 76% of the student population at HBCUs while Native Hawaiians, Native Americans, Asian Americans, Latino/as, and Whites comprise, respectively, 0.08%, 0.3%, 1.5%, 3.7%, and 11% of the students enrolled in HBCUs (Palmer, Arroyo, & Maramba, 2016).

Without a doubt, HBCUs are vital institutions. Despite their relevancy, the instability in presidential leadership is one aspect that threatens their survival (Gasman, 2012; Stewart, 2014; Watson, 2013). In 2012, at least 20 "HBCU presidencies were either vacant or recently filled" (Stewart, 2014, para. 1). More-over, Freeman and Gasman (2014) explained 42% of presidents at HBCUs hold their positions for four years or less. The rapid turnover in HBCU leadership has played out recently. For example, the president of Jackson State University (JSU), Carolyn Meyers, who was appointed in 2011, was asked to resign by the gov-erning board because of concerns of how she spent JSU's cash reserve (Diverse Staff, 2016). Moreover, the president of Florida A&M University, Elmira Mangum was voted out by the Board of Trustees in 2016. Mangum had faced constant criticism from the Board since she was hired, and some surmised that her gender was one of the reasons for this (Commodore, 2016; Gasman, 2016; Stewart, 2014).

Furthermore, Willie Larkin, who was appointed the ninth president of Grambling State University in 2015, resigned a year later – in 2016 – amid reports that the University of Louisiana System Board of Supervisors was going to fire him. It is important to point out that Larkin was the third president that Grambling had lost in less than two years (Stuart, 2016). In addition, Gwendolyn Boyd, president of Alabama State University (ASU), was removed by the governing board (Davis, 2016). Similar to her counterpart, Elmira Mangum, some believe that Boyd's gender played a role in the challenges she experienced with the governing board at ASU (Gasman, 2016). In fact, when she assumed the role of presidency in 2014, there was a clause in Boyd's contract that prohibited her from having a potential lover spend the night (Rivard, 2014). This clause was unprecedented and there is tremendous doubt that such a stipulation would have been included in her contract if she were a man.

Scholars have characterized the frequent turnover in HBCU leadership as problematic and deeply troubling (Esters et al., 2016; Freeman & Gasman, 2014; Freeman et al., 2016; Gasman, 2012; Watson, 2013). Some scholars have cited factors such as the recycling of ineffective presidents, being micromanaged by the governing boards, lacking fundraising experience, having a dearth of experience running large, complex organizations, alleged fiscal mismanagement, and poor retention rates as problems that contribute to the instability of HBCU presidents (Freeman & Gasman, 2014; Freeman et al., 2016; Gasman, 2012; Schexnider, 2013; Watson, 2013). To help mitigate some of these factors, there have been articles, reports, studies, and organizations formed to help increase the leadership efficacy of those at the helm of HBCUs. For example, CMSIs published a report in 2016, which detailed critical skills that HBCU presidents should possess in order to be effective leaders in the twenty-first century (Esters et al., 2016). Some of the skills mentioned in this report included the importance of HBCU presidents' understanding of local, state, and federal policy, particularly around areas of funding, using data in their decision making processes, and being familiar with the accreditation process and promoting student engagement. The report also underscored other important skills, such as the willingness of HBCU presidents to develop collaborative partnerships with other MSIs and PWIs, as well as having an expertise in fundraising and institutional finance. Another critical quality that HBCU presidents should possess, the report suggested, is the ability to maintain communication with a variety of stakeholders, such as business, community, and governmental officials, as well as developing a positive relationship with the Board of Trustees.

Freeman et al. (2016) added to the discourse on effective leadership for HBCU presidents. Specifically, through an analysis and qualitative responses from current HBCU presidents, trustees, and presidential consultant firms, they developed a list of essential skills for HBCU presidents to attain in order to be successful in their positions. Interestingly, but not surprisingly, many of the skills listed in their study echo those that Esters et al. (2016) discussed. For example, similar to Esters and colleagues, Freeman et al. discussed the importance of HBCU presidents being skilled at fundraising, communicating with policymakers, having a sense of the political landscape, developing positive relationships with the governing board, and demonstrating a willingness to collaborate. Moreover, Freeman et al. emphasized the critical nature of HBCU presidents making data driven decisions and understanding the accreditation process as well as valuing student engagement. One skill that Freeman and colleagues mentioned that was not articulated in Esters et al.'s report was the significance of HBCUs using social media. They noted that although many HBCU presidents used social media less than presidents at PWIs, many of the HBCU presidents they interviewed saw the value of using this type of media.

In sum, leadership instability is a significant problem at HBCUs, which threatens the future of these venerable institutions. Women presidents at HBCUs, in particular, seem to encounter a lot of challenges and resistance from governing boards (Gasman, 2016), which is one factor that exacerbates the instability among HBCU presidents. While there is some research on HBCU leadership and some organizations may provide workshops on leadership development (e.g. United Negro College Fund, Thurgood Marshall College Fund, and Hampton's Executive Leadership Summit), much of the extant literature on HBCU leadership has discussed the problems that hinder the success of HBCU presidents rather than characteristics that facilitate their successful outcomes. Chapters in this volume on MSI leadership seek to provide HBCU leaders, particularly those at the presidency, with models, examples, and best practices that have yielded success for college leaders at HBCUs. Specifically, four chapters in this volume are focused on the HBCU context and they explore a range of topics, such as the impact of servant leadership at Paul Quinn College to providing best practices to help HBCU presidents propel their institutions forward.

Hispanic-Serving Institutions

Unlike HBCUs that were established to provide educational opportunities to Blacks due to the blatant racist conditions of the United States, the majority of

Hispanic-Serving Institutions[2] (HSIs) on the US mainland emerged out of changing demographic trends, and they became federally recognized in 1992 (Gasman & Conrad, 2013). HSIs are colleges and universities (i.e., two-year, four-year, and nonprofit institutions) that have an enrollment of 25% or more of Hispanic students enrolled at the undergraduate level, on a full-time basis (Nellum & Valle, 2015; Núñez, Crisp, & Elizondo, 2016; Núñez, Hoover, Pickett, Stuart-Carruthers, & Vázquez, 2013). There are 409 HSIs in the United States and Puerto Rico (Núñez et al., 2016) and 296 emerging HSIs, (Núñez et al., 2016), which are defined as "institutions that are approaching HSI statuses, with between 15% and 25% Hispanic enrollment" (Núñez et al., 2013, p. 81). Given the continuously changing demographics of the United States, which are primarily driven by the growth in the Latino population, more institutions are certain to be classified as HSIs or emerging HSIs (Núñez et al., 2014). HSIs play a critical role in facilitating access to higher education for Latinos and providing a pathway to degree attainment (Gasman & Conrad, 2013). While they comprise about 12% of all colleges and universities in the higher education system, they educate 60% of Hispanic students in the United States and Puerto Rico (Garcia & Okhidoi, 2015; Nellum & Valle, 2015).

Most HSIs are two-year institutions and the majority are located in 15 states with high populations of Hispanics. A larger proportion of HSIs function as open access institutions and 12% of four-year HSIs (14% on the mainland) are designated as doctoral granting institutions (Núñez et al., 2013). Federal funding for HSIs did not come until 1994, when HSIs were eligible for funding under Title III of the Higher Education Act (HEA) (Núñez et al., 2014). When the HEA was reauthorized in 1998, funding for HSIs was included under Title V (Part A) (Nellum & Valle, 2015), also known as the *Developing Hispanic-Serving Institutions program* (Núñez et al., 2014). "Title V authorizes eligible institutions to apply for institutional development and planning grants in order to improve and expand their capacity to serve Hispanic and low-income students" (Núñez et al., 2014, p. 7). When the HEA was reauthorized in 2008, HSIs became eligible for Title V (Part B), which expanded funding to graduate education for Hispanics and other low-income students at HSIs (Núñez et al., 2014). While the federal government has devoted more resources to HSIs over the years, given the changing demographics and the growing number of HSIs, federal appropriations are not able to keep pace with the number of HSIs eligible for funding (Nellum & Valle, 2015).

Given that the majority of HSIs were not founded with the specific intent to educate Hispanic students, the voices of Hispanic and other underrepresented students may be absent from the curricula of HSIs (Garcia & Okhidoi, 2015). To this extent, Garcia and Okhidoi (2015) encouraged that all institutions, HSIs in particular, to make ethnic studies courses, such as Chicana/o Studies, part of the general education courses all students take to graduate. They recommended that ethnic courses should be made into a department at the institution. This would enable such a department to have more influence and power on campus. Finally, they also advocated that HSIs as well as other institutions encourage other academic units on campus to address multicultural issues within their courses. Garcia and Okhidoi advised that their recommendations are particularly important for federally funded HSIs. They indicated that the proposal request for HSI competitive grants places more value on the creation of STEM programs or the retention of STEM students and little emphasis on providing culturally relevant curricula for students.

Interestingly, as noted in the aforementioned discussion, research on HSIs has explored topics such as the founding and mission of HSIs (Laden, 2004; Núñez et al., 2013), funding (Nellum & Valle, 2015), and the experiences of Hispanic students in HSIs (e.g., Conrad & Gasman, 2015; Contreras, Malcolm, & Bensimon, 2008; Garcia & Okhidoi, 2015; Nelson Laird, Bridges, Morelon-Quainoo, Williams, & Salinas Holmes, 2007; Núñez & Bowers, 2011). However, while there may be organizations, such as the Hispanic Association for Colleges and Universities and *Excelencia* in Education, that provide workshops to help develop leaders for HSIs, research on leadership (e.g., Cortez, 2015; Santiago, 2006), especially presidential leadership at HSIs, is limited. Despite this, some research has shown that one of the challenges HSI leaders may encounter is understanding the needs of their students (Cortez, 2015). This is because, in many instances, while the institution may have a large percentage of Hispanic students enrolled, the administration and faculty may be largely White (Contreras et al., 2008) and not fully understand the lived realities of their students. Moreover, some research suggests that HSIs may find it challenging to embrace their new identity (Contreras et al., 2008). Both of these issues have important implications for leadership and require the involvement of leaders at all levels of the institutions to be engaged (Transforming Leadership at MSIs, 2015). In light of the lack of research on leadership at HSIs, this book makes a major contribution to the literature in this area. Specifically, three chapters in this book focus on leadership at HSIs. One chapter is by a president of a two-year HSI, another chapter is by a president of a four-year, public HSIs, and the third chapter offers recommendations to executive leaders of HSIs. These chapters offer rich, critical insight into the challenges faced by executive leaders and discuss leadership strategies that have played a vital role in the sustainability of these institutions.

Tribal Colleges and Universities

Similar to HBCUs, Tribal Colleges and Universities (TCUs) were created with the specific intent of providing educational experiences to the Indigenous population. The first tribal college – Navajo Community College – now named Dine College, was established in 1968 (Stull, Spyridakis, Gasman, Samayoa, & Booker, 2015). Prior to the establishment of this institution, formalized education for Indigenous students focused on cultural alienation and assimilation, which was carried out by European colonists and later, the US government (Stull et al., 2015). Given the historical social barriers faced by Native students and recognizing that traditional colleges and universities were not serving students sufficiently, tribal leaders started a movement to create "tribally self-determined postsecondary education" (Nelson & Frye, 2016, p. 2).

Since the creation of the first tribal college, 37 TCUs have been created, 34 of which are accredited by mainstream accrediting bodies (Stull et al., 2015). These colleges and universities enroll a growing population of students, which currently total about 28,000 students, made up of Indigenous and non-Native students (Stull et al., 2015). TCUs are located on or close to reservations and they offer students culturally relevant curricula as well as a host of other services, such as childcare, GED tutoring, computer training, and financial literacy (Stull et al., 2015). Each TCU reflects the culture of the founding tribe and functions to meet the particular needs of the Tribal community. TCUs offer various degrees, such as master's, bachelor's, associates, and certificate programs in a variety of fields. Collectively they offer four master's programs, 46 bachelor's programs, 193 associate degrees, and 119 certificates in a multitude of fields (Stull et al., 2015).

While MSIs in general are underfunded, this is particularly true for TCUs. According to a report by the American Council on Education, state and local governments have no obligation to fund TCUs (Nelson & Frye, 2016). Moreover, in most cases, states do not provide funding for non-Native residents, who account for 20% of the students enrolled in TCUs (Stull et al., 2015). These institutions receive a significant proportion of their total revenue from federal sources "averaging between 71% and 74% at two and four-year TCUs, respectively" (Nelson & Frye, 2016, p. 3). Federal funding for TCUs emanates from the Tribally Controlled College or University Assistance Act (TCCUAA) of 1978. While TCUs receive federal funding under TCCUAA, the actual dollar amount allocated to these institutions is far from equitable. For example, in 2015, TCUs were supposed to receive $8,000 per Native student. However, they received $6,355 per student (Nelson & Frye, 2016). Also, unlike mainstream institutions, given their limited funding, TCUs are forced to rely more on competitive grants to help augment their operating budgets.

Another factor contributing to the lack of funding for TCUs is their inability to raise tuition and fees given the population they serve. TCUs receive less than 9% of their total revenue from tuition and fees. Despite this, they provide tuition waivers and discounts to help students with their education. The majority of students attending TCUs face significant economic barriers and many TCUs do not participate in federal student loan programs. To this end, TCUs are committed to keeping tuition and fees low so as to not prevent students in their tribal communities from accessing these important institutions. Similar to HSIs and PBIs, the research on leadership at TCUs is limited. Nevertheless, it is clear that factors, such as the need to advocate for more funding while maintaining affordable tuition, and a continued need to focus on cultural connectiveness, provide important implications for leaders of TCUs (Transforming Leadership at MSIs, 2015).

This book, along with important reports (e.g., Boyer, 2014; Stull et al., 2015) and organizations (e.g., the American Indian Higher Education Consortium and American Indian College Fund) makes an important contribution to the area of leadership at TCUs. Two chapters in this volume delineate different forms of leadership for TCU presidents. One chapter underscores the importance of service and collective leadership for TCU leaders. This chapter also examines what institutional leaders at other MSIs could learn from TCU presidents. The second chapter delineates how leadership of TCUs is undergirded by spirituality, cultural values, and customs of the Indigenous people. The chapter concludes with important challenges and opportunities for TCU presidents.

Predominantly Black Institutions

The establishment of Predominantly Black Institutions (PBIs) is similar to the emergence of HSIs in that they are based on a concentration of students from a specific demographic group attending a college or university. More specifically, PBIs emerged from the reauthorization of the Higher Education Act of 2008 and they must meet the following criteria: (1) enroll at least 40% of Black students; (2) have an enrollment of at least 1,000 students at the undergraduate level; and (3) serve at least 50% low-income or first-generation degree seeking undergraduate students.

Most PBIs are two-year colleges and research on these institutions is lacking significantly. PBIs tend to be concentrated in the South, Midwest, and East and they enrolled nearly 300,000 undergraduate students in the fall of 2013 (Post-secondary National Policy Institute, 2015). While most PBIs enroll more than 50% of Black students, at least nine enroll 75% of Black students. Generally, after Black students, White, and in some cases, Hispanics are the second largest racial groups enrolled in PBIs (Postsecondary National Policy Institute, 2015). Given their status as PBIs, these institutions are eligible for competitive grants and formula grants (Postsecondary National Policy Institute, 2015). The initial grant is designed to support PBIs in establishing or strengthening programs in the following areas: (a) science, technology, engineering, and mathematics; (b) health education; (c) internationalization or globalization; (d) teacher preparation; and (e) improving education among Black males. The latter funding is used to enhance efforts to serve low- and middle-income Blacks in higher education. Funding from the formula grant also allows PBIs to implement efforts or initiatives that help expand higher education opportunities for this student demographic as well (Postsecondary National Policy Institute, 2015).

While PBIs face much of the same challenges as their MSI counterparts (i.e., a large population of first-generation, low-income, and Pell eligible students), there is not any research that specifically discusses leadership at PBIs. Similar to their HSI counterparts, one of the challenges that leaders of PBIs may face is serving a large portion of low-income minority students while the faculty, staff, and administrators at these institutions may not be reflective of this student demography. Moreover, another challenge that leaders at PBIs may face is fundraising to help augment the financial support they receive from the competitive grant in order to help support their students or implement special initiatives to support their academic achievement. Complicating this factor is that not all PBIs that apply for funding through this grant receive it. And, when a PBI does receive such funding, it is limited in duration. Finally, similar to HSIs, PBIs may not fully embrace their new institutional identity, which may be harmful to student growth and learning. While we highlight PBIs in this chapter, we do not directly extend or contribute to the discourse on leadership at these institutions. Future research needs to be more intentional about conducting meaningful research – not just on leadership, but on a range of issues – on PBIs because they are often not included in scholarly discussions in reports, peer-reviewed journal articles, and books on MSIs.

Asian American and Native American Pacific Islander Serving Institutions

Similar to HSIs and PBIs, Asian American and Native American Pacific Islander Serving Institutions (AANAPISIs) are institutions that have a concentration of students from a specific demographic community enrolled. More specifically, AANAPISIs are institutions classified as having 10% of Asian American and Pacific Islander students (AAPIs) in attendance (Gasman & Conrad, 2013; Pak, Maramba, & Hernandez, 2014; Teranishi, 2012). AANAPISIs were designated as MSIs in 2007; the struggle, however, to attain such a designation occurred incrementally and encountered some challenges (Pak et al., 2014). One of the challenges is that there are many who view Asian Americans through the prism of the Model Minority Myth, which perpetuates the idea that Asian Americans are a homogenous group who are talented in mathematics and science and heavily invested in succeeding academically (Gasman & Conrad, 2013; Pak et al., 2014; Teranishi, 2012).

Educational researchers have worked to combat this perception by underscoring the wide array of diversity among AAPI students as it relates to poverty rates, educational attainment, and college attendance and persistence (CARE, 2010). For example, the AAPI community is made up of 48 ethnic subgroups, such as South Asians, Southeast Asians, East Asians, and Pacific Islanders (CARE, 2010), and these individuals speak more than 300 languages (Gasman & Conrad, 2013). Research has shown that among AAPIs, Southeast Asian Americans (SEAAs) and Pacific Islander students have some of the highest poverty rates. In terms of educational attainment, there are high rates of SEAA and Pacific Islander students with less than a high school education and they are critically underrepresented in higher education (Maramba & Palmer, 2014; Palmer & Maramba, 2015; Teranishi, 2012). Pointing out the within-group differences among AAPI students helps to dismantle the Model Minority Myth and call attention to the fact that like all college students, AAPI students need guidance and support to access and successfully complete a higher education degree (Maramba, 2011).

Another factor that serves as a challenge to the promulgation of AANAPISIs is existing data on AAPIs make it hard to understand the concerns of underserved AAPI ethnic groups. A report by the White House Initiative on Asian Americans and Pacific Islanders not only shined light on the lack of education, community, and social needs for AAPI communities; it also recommended a federal designation of colleges and universities that served AAPI students (Pak et al., 2014). Congressman Robert Underwood played an important role in this process by proposing an amendment to adjust the Higher Education Act of 1965 to provide funding for postsecondary institutions that served AAPI students. Underwood's amendment was revised by David Wu, another Congressman, and later, senators Barbara Boxer and Daniel Akaka. It eventually came to be known as the Asian American and Pacific Islander Serving Institutions Act (Pak et al., 2014).

According to Pak and colleagues (2014), "the official designation of the AANAPISI federal program was instituted in 2007 as part of the College Cost Reduction and Access Act of 2007" (p. 89). One of the major functions of the AANAPISI program is to provide grants to colleges and universities that serve AAPI students. Institutions must first apply to the AANAPISI grant program to be considered an AANAPISI. In order to be considered an AANAPISI and to be eligible for grant funding that accompanies such a designation, colleges and universities, as indicated, must have at least 10% of AAPI students and at least 50% of students must be low-income (Pak et al., 2014). In 2009, the Congressional Research Service determined that 116 institutions met the specification to be classified as an AANAPISI (Gasman & Conrad, 2013), while Teranishi (2012) noted that in 2011, 52 institutions were designated as AANAPISIs. Given that the AAPI population is the second fastest growing population in the United States (Teranishi, 2012), it is likely that more institutions will be eligible for the AANAPISI grant program, and therefore, will be classified as an AANAPISI. For example, it is estimated that the AAPI population in America will grow from its current standing of 17 million (White House Initiative on Asian Americans and Pacific Islanders, 2014) to 40 million by 2050 (Teranishi, 2012).

AANAPISIs are critical for at least three reasons (Teranishi, 2012). First, they call attention to the diversity within the AAPI communities and recognize that certain ethnic communities face unique challenges accessing and completing higher education. Second, AANAPISIs provide resources and programs, such as first-year experience programs, academic and personal counselors, and tutoring, which help to improve postsecondary education completion rates for AAPI and low-income students. Finally, AANAPISIs serve as important sites for responding to the challenges and needs of AAPI students (Teranishi, 2012). Despite the fact that AANAPISIs comprise less than 3% of higher education institutions, they enroll over 25% of all AAPI students at the undergraduate level (Gasman &

Conrad, 2013). Most AANAPISIs are two-year colleges and they have shown success in increasing college participation and degree completion among AAPI students (Gasman & Conrad, 2013).

Though there are some organizations, such as the AAPI Association for Colleges and Universities (APIACU) that offers leadership guidance to AANAPISIs, similar to some of the other MSIs discussed in this chapter, research on leadership at AANAPISIs is limited. Notwithstanding, leaders at AANAPISIs may encounter similar problems as other leaders at MSIs, such as lacking culturally relevant curricula, not fully embracing their new institutional identity, faculty, staff, and administrators who may not understand the lived realities of AAPI students, and the need to fundraise to help augment the funding provided by the AANAPISIs competitive grant – if they were awarded such funding.

While there is a dearth of leadership research on AANAPISIs, this volume makes a contribution to this area with two chapters. For example, one chapter discusses leadership in the context of AANAPISIs that are community colleges while the other chapter contextualizes effective leadership for AANAPISIs. Both of these chapters are critical in that they help us to understand leadership challenges and potential for AANAPISIs.

Conclusion

This chapter has examined research on leadership, particularly presidential leadership, at MSIs. Before discussing the literature on leadership at these important institutions, this chapter provided an overview of the MSIs discussed in this chapter. It further revealed that although there is a dearth of literature on leadership at HBCUs, specifically executive leadership, most of the literature has highlighted the instability among HBCU presidents. Indeed, a recent article in *The Chronicle of Higher Education*, similar to others (e.g., Freeman & Gasman, 2014; Watson, 2013), Kimbrough (2016) noted that the leadership vacuum at HBCUs places these institutions in peril.

Despite this, there has been some discussion on the challenges that encumber MSI presidents. These challenges range from a lack of funding, to a lack of culturally relevant curricula and leaders at the executive level and throughout the institution that may not fully understand or care about the lived realities of the student demographic they are intended to serve. Given that they were intended to specifically serve their student demographic, some of these challenges may be less problematic for HBCUs and TCUs and more apparent to HSIs, PBIs, and AANAPISIs. Moreover, while MSIs serve low-income, first-generation students, which has challenged their graduation and persistence rates, HBCUs in general have received the most criticism over their graduation rates. Since many state systems of higher education are moving toward performance based funding, presidents at MSIs must comply with the criteria, even though some aspects of the criteria do not consider the unique institutional context of MSIs and the populations they serve. This serves as another challenge to MSI leaders. Indeed, while there are commonalities in some of the challenges that leaders at MSIs face, chapters in this volume will not only provide greater discussion on the challenges encumbering leaders at specific MSI designations (i.e., HBCUs, HSIs, PBIs, TCUs, and AANAPISIs), but they will also provide models, examples, and best practices that MSI leaders could use to help foster the growth and development of their institutions. In this regard, this edited volume makes a significant contribution to the literature on leadership at MSIs in general and the presidency of MSIs specifically.

Notes

1   In a study that Palmer and Freeman conducted with 20 HBCUs leaders, they found that leadership at HBCUs is comprised of not only the presidents, but also other members of the institutions (i.e., students, department chairs, and other officials at the institution). Notwithstanding, in this edited volume, we are primarily focused on executive leadership, particularly the presidency of MSIs.
2   The following institutions on the US mainland were founded specifically to provide a college education to Latinos: National Hispanic University (California), St. Augustine's College (Illinois), Boricua College (New York), Eugenio Maria de Hostos Community College (New York), Northern New Mexico College (New Mexico), and Colegio Cesar Chavez (Oregon) (Nuñez, Hurtado, & Calderón Galdeano, 2014)

References

Arroyo, A., Palmer, R.T., Maramba, D.C., & Louis, D. (2016). Exploring the efforts of HBCU student affairs practitioners to support non-Black students. *Journal of College Student Affairs Research and Practice*. Retrieved from http://dx.doi.org/10.1080/19496591.2016. 1219266

Boyer, P. (2014). Tribal Colleges and Universities program. Retrieved from http://native sciencereport.org/wp-content/uploads/2016/06/TCUP-Leaders-Forum-report.pdf

Brown, C.M. (2002). College desegregation and transdemographic enrollments. *The Review of Higher Education*, 25, 263–280. Retrieved from http://dx.doi.org/10.1353/ rhe.2002.0009

CARE (National Commission on Asian American and Pacific Islander Research in Education) (2010). *Federal higher education policy priorities and the Asian American and Pacific Islander community*. New York: USA Funds.

Commodore, F. (2016). Figuring out the future of FAMU: Lessons learned. *HBCU Lifestyle*. Retrieved from http://hbculifestyle.com/the-future-of-famu/

Conrad, C., & Gasman, M. (2015). *Educating a diverse nation: Lessons from minority serving institutions*. Cambridge, MA: Harvard University Press.

Contreras, F.E., Malcom, L.E., & Bensimon, E.M. (2008). Hispanic-Serving Institutions: Closeted identity and the production of equitable outcomes for Latino/a students. In M. Gasman, B. Baez, & C. Turner (Eds.), *Interdisciplinary approaches to understanding Minority-Serving Institutions* (pp. 71–90) New York: SUNY Press.

Cortez, L.J. (2015). Enacting leadership at Hispanic-Serving Institutions. In A.-M. Núñez, S. Hurtado, & E. Calderón Galdeano (Eds.), *Hispanic-Serving Institutions: Advancing research and transformative practice* (pp. 136–152). New York: Routledge.

Cunningham, A., Park, E., & Engle, J. (2014). Minority serving institutions: Doing more with less. *Institute for Higher Education Policy*. Retrieved from www.ihep.org/sites/default/files/uploads/docs/pubs/msis_doing_more_w-less_final_february_2014-v2.pdf

Davis, K. (2016). ASU Board suspends Gwendolyn Boyd. *Montgomery Advertiser*. Retrieved from www.montgomeryadvertiser.com/story/news/2016/11/04/asu-board-suspends-gwendolyn-boyd/93287082/

Diverse Staff (2016). Jackson State University president Carolyn Meyers resigns. *Diverse Issues in Higher Education*. Retrieved from http://diverseeducation.com/article/88600/

Esters, L.T., Washington, A., Gasman, M., Commodore, F., O'Neal, B., Freeman, S., Carter, C., & Jimenez, C.D. (2016). *Effective leadership: A toolkit for the 21st-century historically Black college and university*. Philadelphia, PA: Penn Center for Minority Serving Institutions.

Flores, S.M., & Park, T.J. (2013). Race, ethnicity and college success: Examining the continued significance of the minority-serving institution. *Educational Researcher*, 42(3), 115–128.

Freeman, S. Jr., & Gasman, M. (2014). The characteristics of historically Black colleges and university presidents and their role in grooming the next generation of leaders. *Teachers College Record*, 116, 1–34.

Freeman, S. Jr., Commodore, F., Gasman, M., & Carter, C. (2016). Leaders wanted! The skills expected and needed for a successful 21st century historically Black college and university presidency. *Journal of Black Studies*, 47(6), 570–591.

Garcia, G.A., & Okhidoi, O. (2015). Culturally relevant practices that "serve" students at a Hispanic Serving Institution. *Innovative Higher Education*, 40, 345–357. doi:10.1007/s10755-015-9318-7

Gasman, M. (2008). Minority-Serving Institutions: A historical backdrop. In M. Gasman, B. Baez, & C.S.V. Turner (Eds.) *Understanding Minority-Serving Institutions* (pp. 18–27). Albany: SUNY Press.

Gasman, M. (2012, April 12). Vacancies in the Black College presidency: What's going on? [Web log post]. Retrieved from *The Chronicle of Higher Education* Innovations blog: http://chronicle.com/blogs/innovations/vacancies-in-the-black-college-presidency-whats-going-on/32204

Gasman, M. (2013). *The changing face of Historically Black Colleges and Universities*. Philadelphia, PA: Penn Center for Minority Serving Institutions.

Gasman, M. (2016). HBCUs' self-imposed leadership struggles. *Inside Higher Ed*. Retrieved from www.insidehighered.com/views/2016/09/02/boards-hbcus-should-not-micromanage-their-presidents-essay

Gasman, M., Baez, B., Drezner, N., Sedgwick, K., & Tudico, C. (2007). Historically Black Colleges and Universities: Recent trends. *Academe*, 93, 69–78.

Gasman, M., & Conrad, C.F. (2013). *Minority serving institutions: Educating all students*. Philadelphia, PA: Penn Center for Minority Serving Institutions, Graduate School of Education, University of Pennsylvania.

Gasman, M., & Nelson, B. (2011). How to paint a better portrait of HBCUs. *Academe*, 97(3), 24–27.

Gasman, M., & Nguyen, T. (2015). Myths dispelled: A historical account of diversity and inclusion at HBCUs. In R.T. Palmer, C.R. Shorette., & M. Gasman (Eds.), *Exploring diversity at Historically Black Colleges and Universities: Implications for policy and practice* (pp. 5–15). San Francisco, CA: Jossey-Bass.

Gasman, M., Nguyen, T., & Conrad, C.F. (2015). Lives intertwined: A primer on the emergence of minority serving institutions. *Journal of Diversity in Higher Education*, 8(2), 120–138.

Hurtado, S., Milem, J., Clayton-Pedersen, A., & Allen, W. (1999). *Enacting diverse learning environments: Improving the climate for racial/ethnic diversity in higher education.* Washington, D.C.: The George Washington University.

Kimbrough, W. (2016). Trump's election is an opportunity for HBCUs, if they can take it. *The Chronicle of Higher Education.* Retrieved from http://www.chronicle.com/article/ Trumps-Election-Is-an/238421

Laden, B.V. (2004). Hispanic-Serving Institutions: What are they? Where are they? *Community College Journal of Research and Practice*, 28, 181–198.

Lomax, M. (2014). Strengthening Minority Serving Institutions: Best practices and innovations for student success. The US Senate Committee on Health, Education, and Labor Pensions. Testimony of Dr. Michael Lomax. Retrieved from http://www.help. senate.gov/imo/media/doc/Lomax1.pdf

Maramba, D.C. (2011). The importance of critically disaggregating data: The case of Southeast Asian American college students. *AAPI (Asian American Pacific Islander) Nexus Journal: The Role of New Research Data, & Policies for Asian Americans, Native Hawaiians & Pacific Islanders*, 9(1–2), 127–133.

Maramba, D.C., & Palmer, R.T. (2014). The impact of cultural validation on the college experiences of Southeast Asian American students. *Journal of College Student Development*, 55(6), 515–530.

National Commission on Asian American and Pacific Islander Research in Education (2010). *Federal higher education policy priorities and the Asian American and Pacific Islander community.* New York: USA Funds.

Nellum, C., & Valle, K. (2015). Government investing in Hispanic serving institutions. American Council on Education. Center for Policy Research and Strategy, Minority Serving Institution Series, Washington, D.C. Retrieved from www.acenet.edu/news-room/Pages/Hispanic-Serving-Institutions.aspx

Nelson, C.A., & Frye, J.R. (2016). Tribal college and university: Tribal sovereignty at the intersection of federal, state, and local funding. American Council on Education. Center for Policy Research and Strategy, Minority Serving Institution Series, Washington, D.C. Retrieved from www.acenet.edu/news-room/Documents/Tribal-College-and-University-Funding.pdf

Nelson Laird, T.F., Bridges, B.K., Morelon-Quainoo, C.L., Williams, J.M., & Salinas Holmes, M. (2007). African American and Hispanic student engagement at Minority Serving and Predominantly White Institutions. *Journal of College Student Development*, 48(1), 39–56.

Nichols, J.C. (2004). Unique characteristics, leadership styles, and management of Historically Black Colleges and Universities. *Innovative Higher Education*, 28, 219–229.

Núñez, A.-M., & Bowers, A.J. (2011). Exploring what leads high school students to enroll in Hispanic-Serving Institutions: A multilevel analysis. *American Educational Research Journal*, 48(6), 1286–1313.

Núñez, A.-M., Crisp, G., & Elizondo, D. (2016). Mapping Hispanic-Serving Institutions: A typology of institutional diversity. *The Journal of Higher Education*, 87, 55–83. doi:10.1353/jhe.2016.0001

Núñez, A.-M., Hoover, R.E., Pickett, K., Stuart-Carruthers, A.C., & Vázquez, M. (2013). Special issue: Latinos in higher education and Hispanic-Serving Institutions: Creating conditions for success. *ASHE Higher Education Report*, 39(1), 1–132. doi:10.1002/aehe.20007.

Núñez, A.-M., Hurtado, S., & Calderón Galdeano, E. (2014). Why study Hispanic Serving Institutions. In A.-M. Núñez, S. Hurtado, & E. Calderón Galdeano (Eds.),

Hispanic-Serving Institutions: Advancing research and transformative practice (pp. 1–22). New York: Routledge.

Pak, Y., Maramba, D.C., & Hernandez, X.J. (2014). *Asian Americans in higher education: Charting new realities*. ASHE Higher Education Report Series 40(1).

Palmer, R.T. (2008). Promoting HBCUs: Black colleges provide a superior education; they just need to toot their horns a little louder. *Diverse Issues of Higher Education*, 24(26), 29.

Palmer, R.T., Arroyo, A., & Maramba, D.C. (2016). Exploring the perceptions of HBCU student affairs practitioners toward the racial diversification of Black colleges. *Journal of Diversity in Higher Education*. Retrieved from http://dx.doi.org/10.1037/dhe0000024

Palmer, R.T., & Gasman, M. (2008). "It takes a village to raise a child": The role of social capital in promoting academic success for African American men at a Black college. *Journal of College Student Development*, 49(1), 52–70.

Palmer, R.T., & Griffin, K. (2009). Desegregation policy and disparities in faculty salary and workload: Maryland's historically Black and Predominantly White Institutions. *Negro Educational Review*, 60(1–4), 7–21.

Palmer, R.T., Hilton, A.A., & Fountaine, P.T. (Eds.) (2012). *Black graduate education at HBCUs: Trends, experiences, and outcomes*. New York: Information Age Publishing.

Palmer, R.T., & Maramba, D.C. (2015). The impact of social capital on the access, adjustment, and success of Southeast Asian American college students. *Journal of College Student Development*, 56(1), 45–60.

Palmer, R.T., Maramba, D.C., & Gasman, M. (Eds.) (2012). *Fostering success of ethnic and racial minorities in STEM: The role of minority serving institutions*. New York: Routledge.

Palmer, R.T., & Wood, J.L. (Eds.) (2012). *Black men in college: Implications for HBCUs and beyond*. New York: Routledge.

Postsecondary National Policy Institute (2015). Predominantly Black Institutions: A background primer. Retrieved from www.newamerica.org/post-secondary-national-policy-institute/our-blog/predominantly-black-institutions-pbis/

Ricard, R.B., & Brown, M. (2008). *Ebony towers in higher education: The evolution, mission, and presidency of Historically Black Colleges and Universities*. Sterling, VA: Stylus.

Riley, J. (2010). Black colleges need a new mission. *Wall Street Journal*. Retrieved from https://www.wsj.com/articles/SB10001424052748704654004575517822124077834

Rivard, R. (2014). President's home or prison? *Inside Higher Ed*. Retrieved from www.insidehighered.com/news/2014/01/10/alabama-university-limits-presidents-love-life

Santiago, D.A. (2006). *Inventing Hispanic-Serving Institutions (HSIs): The basics*. Washington, D.C.: *Excelencia* in Education.

Schexnider, A.J. (2013). *Saving black colleges: Leading change in a complex organization*. New York: Palgrave Macmillan.

Stewart, P. (2014). The rise of the woman president. *Diverse Issues in Higher Education*, 31 (3), 26–28.

Stuart, R. (2016). Willie D. Larkin resigns after 1 year as Grambling State University president. *Diverse Issues in Higher Education*. Retrieved from http://diverseeducation.com/article/85087/

Stull, G., Spyridakis, D., Gasman, M., Samayoa, A.C., & Booker, Y. (2015). *Redefining success: How Tribal Colleges and Universities build nations, strengthen sovereignty, and persevere through challenges*. Philadelphia, PA: Center for Minority Student Institutions, University of Pennsylvania.

Teranishi, R.T. (2012). Asian American and Pacific Islander Students and the institutions that serve them. *Change*, 16–22.

Transforming leadership at Minority Serving Institutions (2015). Retrieved from https://lsa.umich.edu/content/dam/ncid-assets/ncid-documents/publications/Transforming%20Leadership%20Booklet.pdf

Watson, J.E. (2013). Education experts concerned about the future of HBCUs as leadership frequently changes. *Diverse Issues in Higher Education*, 30(18), 7.

White House Initiative on Asian Americans and Pacific Islanders (2014). Fact sheet: Naturalization matters to the AAPI community. Retrieved from https://sites.ed.gov/aapi/files/2014/02/2016-Final-AAPI-Naturalization-Fact-Sheet.pdf

PART I

Historically Black Colleges and Universities (HBCUs)

2

HBCUs

Valuable – Yet Substantially Impaired – Institutions

Kofi Lomotey and Megan Covington

Virtually all historically Black colleges and universities (HBCUs) offer unique benefits and strengths, particularly for Black students. Indeed, HBCUs accomplish much with little. These institutions also share several challenges. In fact, we argue in this chapter that HBCUs, collectively, are impaired or debilitated institutions. This condition, we contend, is not new, but as W.E.B. DuBois (1930) and others have argued, these institutions have been significantly challenged since their inception. Moreover, HBCUs, we posit, have both self-inflicted wounds and wounds that have been meted out from outside of the Black community.[1]

In this treatise, we contend that all students benefit from a culturally responsive education (Dee & Penner, 2016; Ladson-Billings, 1995; Ladson-Billings & Tate, 1995). Moreover, we believe that Black students at all levels, including higher education, have not received such an education. HBCUs, we argue, are not an exception in this regard; they, too, do not provide Black students with a culturally responsive education.

We first describe culturally responsive education. Then, we discuss some of the significant strengths as well as the profound challenges faced by HBCUs and their leadership. Most importantly, we propose opportunities and strategies to enable these institutions to continue to provide benefits to their students and to address the myriad challenges that impact them daily. We begin by defining culturally responsive education.

Culturally Responsive Education

Culturally responsive education entails learning and knowing about self, learning to think critically, learning to appreciate different worldviews, learning the stories and cultures of one's people and learning to work toward self-actualization. It enables students to (1) relate their educational experiences to their cultural realities at home and in their communities, (2) have some faculty who look like them, (3) see people in the texts who look like them, and (4) experience illustrations within the curriculum that reflect their reality. It fosters a group's self-interest. With culturally responsive education, the recipients are prepared to utilize their skills, expertise, and creativity in the interest of their group or people. It empowers a group and prepares them to use power responsibly. It insures the survival of a group; without culturally responsive education, a group is doomed. It also emphasizes leadership training in a realistic context. That is, the leadership training that a group would receive would provide preparation for serving existing or emerging roles in their own communities and in society. Culturally responsive education enables a group to fit into and serve their own communities as well as the larger society. In essence, it enables students to "see themselves in the curriculum" (Lomotey, 1989).

By way of illustration, Kofi Lomotey had the opportunity to play a vital role in the creation and development of the Black Studies program at Oberlin College when he was an undergraduate there in the early 1970s. At that time, he, along with others, argued successfully for a minor in Black Studies as opposed to a major. His rationale was that it is more important for students to major in chemistry, business, education or art – and master those disciplines. The role of the Black Studies minor, then, as he saw it, was to enable Black students to utilize those mastered disciplines in the self-interest of themselves and, correspondingly, of their people. In other words, Black Studies would enable them to answer questions like:

How can we use chemistry to develop the Black community?
How can we use business expertise to move Black people forward? and
How can we excel in language arts and tap our Black genius in order to help guide language arts for all?

Lomotey thought this was important because, the reality then – and the reality now – is that whether Black students are in predominantly White institutions (PWIs) or in HBCUs, they are taught the various disciplines in a manner that does not further their own self-interest, but rather furthers the interest of people and cultures other than their own; they are taught in a way that reinforces the interests of those in power.

In speaking of the Black experience, Mary McCloud Bethune (1963) defines culturally relevant education. She does so by providing illustrations of individuals who received such an education. She says:

We have had great men and women in the past: Frederick Douglass, Booker T. Washington, Harriet Tubman, Sojourner Truth, Mary Church Terrell.

We must produce more qualified people like them, who will work not for themselves, but for others.

(p. 150)

Bethune identifies leaders who focused their leadership skills toward addressing issues facing a group of which she was a member. She heralded them because they put their people before themselves. They understood that their work was intended to improve the circumstances of their people. They sought freedom, justice, and power for their people. Many would argue that, currently, HBCUs are not producing these great men and women to which Bethune refers in any significant numbers. Many would contend, and there is ample evidence to suggest, that HBCUs are not providing culturally responsive education for Blacks.

US society was and is one wherein people are discriminated against because of the color of their skin, the amount of money they have in the bank, their gender, their height, their religious views, their sexual orientation, their weight, their beauty, et cetera. Historically, because of these and other illegitimate forms of exclusion, many people, including Blacks, were at one time systematically left out of US higher education. Indeed, initially all institutions of higher education in the USA were established primarily for well-to-do White men. Later, when Black people were allowed into predominantly White male institutions, the educational experience was not equitable. Black students received less of everything: less classroom space, lower quality textbooks, and the least prepared instructors. Overall, human and material resources were far less available to Black students. In essence, historically, predominantly White colleges and universities did not provide culturally responsive education for Black people. It was not a part of the higher educational schemes devised for Black people. Then HBCUs came along.

At HBCUs, the curricula were flawed from the onset, as they were not constructed to perpetuate a Black worldview or to facilitate self-determination, self-discovery, and self-knowledge. These institutions, too, did not provide culturally responsive education; they were not equipped or designed to serve the interest of Black people.

People in power, by definition, seek to remain in power, in part, by facilitating the domination of other groups. In the schooling of Blacks in the USA, those in power only support curricula that will, by definition, prepare Blacks to serve the powerful. Culturally responsive education would insure that Blacks are being prepared to serve Black people.

Beginnings

Much of the initiative and certainly the majority of the money utilized in starting up most HBCUs came from powerful White philanthropists. Some were principled and truly sought quality higher education for Black people. But they were not the most persuasive ones. It was their associates, relatives, and colleagues whose motives ruled the day; they employed a strategy of transforming Black people into workers who labored in the interest of those in power. These seemingly benevolent and benign efforts were designed to alienate Black people from our roots and culture. While some Black religious groups did start some HBCUs, these efforts were few and far between.

These White philanthropists, who were not truly principled and who did not really seek culturally responsive education for Black people, had a plan. Their plan was not short term; it was long term. People in power – like those philanthropists – plan strategies for a century and beyond. According to Jim Anderson (1988), the focus of the architects of Black higher education was on schooling selected leaders to help those in power to develop "good citizens," who would then stay in their place. Clearly, the role of Black students was working in, supporting, and aiding in maintaining the status quo, which served the interest of those philanthropists and others who were in power.

These philanthropists did not want self-determination and equality for Black people. Even the Hampton-Tuskegee model, as Anderson (1988) points out, was not designed to benefit Black people. According to Anderson:

> authorities wanted Hampton-Tuskegee graduates as teachers because they were advertised as young Black men and women who "knew their place" and who were uncontaminated by the pompous ideals of classical liberal education.
>
> (p. 258)

Here we see evidence of the motives of these philanthropists when they established institutions of higher education for Blacks. In harmony with Anderson, William Watkins (2001) reflects on the thinking of those who were in power, "The Negro must be semieducated for semicitizenship. Black Americans would be junior partners in industrial America" (p. 175). Again, the role was not to lead at the highest levels, but instead, to provide inexpensive labor and to direct that labor to support the status quo. According to Randolph Edmonds (Anderson, 1988):

> college-bred Negroes, or [the] "talented tenth," were not being educated to think and act in behalf of the interests of Black people. Rather, they were internalizing a social ideology nearly indistinguishable from that of the philanthropists who helped finance Black higher education.
>
> (p. 277)

Watkins (2001) added:

> accommodationist education was politically constructed. It taught the cultural values of the ruling order. It aimed to shape an ideological outlook for an entire people. It taught conformity, obedience, sobriety, piety and the

values of enterprise. Heavy emphasis on teacher training guaranteed that the word would be spread ... the architects understood the great ideological possibilities of Black education. The curriculum was thus geared to social engineering as much as anything else.

(p. 182)

Again, the picture is clear; HBCUs were not designed to move Black people forward. Yet, many would argue, with plausible evidence, that these institutions have many positive attributes. We now discuss these attributes.

Strengths

All HBCUs have strengths and benefits, in spite of their relatively limited human and material resources. As Lomotey and Aboh (2009) stated:

HBCUs accomplish a remarkable feat every day. They have overcome a multitude of obstacles, financial instability, social ostracism, racism, disparaging news headlines, dilapidated buildings, underpaid faculty, and sometimes, the admission of [severely] underprepared students. From all accounts, HBCUs have been instrumental in training and rendering people of African descent in the United States more marketable.

(pp. 315–316)

These successes include preparing their graduates to be significantly more marketable than they might be otherwise. This occurs as a result of providing the undergraduate foundation for more Black teachers, physicians, dentists, lawyers, political leaders, and writers than any other higher education institutions. Colon categorizes the virtues of these institutions in five areas: (1) pedagogical (transforming students), (2) psycho-social (nurturing/caring), (3) cultural (repositories of culture), (4) economical (affordable), and (5) political (leadership laboratories) (Colon, 2000).

Doing More With Less

An historical by-product of systematic discrimination, HBCUs were established as institutions to educate Blacks as they were otherwise excluded from higher education institutions (Kim, 2002; Palmer & Gasman, 2008). Studies indicate that HBCUs tend to have far fewer institutional resources than PWIs (Gasman & Commodore, 2014). With less university faculty, the facilities, available academic programs, and opportunities for advanced study are often less available in HBCUs than in PWIs (Allen, Epps, & Haniff, 1991), thus impacting the educational experience of their students (Gasman & Commodore, 2014). In addition to having limited financial resources for students in need, HBCUs are often faced with the challenge of accommodating students who have received inadequate public schooling and who come from disadvantaged backgrounds (Kim, 2002).

Indeed, many HBCUs have shown positive educational outcomes. By way of illustration, Grambling State University has been noted for receiving inadequate state financial support to service high proportions of low-income students and still has one of the highest graduation rates among HBCUs (Townsend, 1994).

Significant research focuses on the ability of HBCUs to impact student outcomes, including future success, overall satisfaction, and career attainment (Allen, 1992). Additionally, HBCUs are well known for fostering environments in which students find a unique support system (Gasman, 2013). The recent Gallup–USA Funds Minority College Graduate Report (2015) shows that HBCUs are successfully producing larger quantities of Black students who are generally more satisfied and successful than Black students who graduate from other institutions. Additionally, Kim and Conrad (2006) purport that although the probability of a Black student obtaining a bachelors degree does not differ based on institution type, because HBCUs are underfunded and provide admission to students who would typically be inadmissible at other institutions, they have a greater impact on students than do PWIs.

HBCUs also have a longstanding history of producing iconic leaders in spite of scarce resources, including W. E. B. DuBois, Martin Luther King Jr., Reverend Jesse Jackson Jr., Ella Baker and Thurgood Marshall to name a few (Gasman & Commodore, 2014). Kim's (2002) study revealed that even with their limited academic resources, HBCUs are as effective in providing students with academic preparation as are PWIs. In fact, the authors noted that HBCUs appear to be more cost-effective in achieving their mission of educating Black students (Kim, 2002). Taken together, the resilience of HBCUs is shown through their consistent ability to produce better results with fewer resources (Gasman & Commodore, 2014).

Positive Campus Environments

In Fleming's (1984) study, she defines a supportive environment as a place in which students (1) have many opportunities for interaction with peers, faculty, staff, and counselors beyond the classroom; (2) are free to engage in extracurricular campus life, including holding leadership positions; and (3) feel a climate of academic development that allows them to grow (Fleming 1984). In this study, as in many others, the Black HBCU students felt more supported on these measures than did Black students at PWIs. More recently, researchers have continued to find a positive environment for Black students at HBCUs (Allen et al., 1991; Stewart, Wright, Perry, & Rankin, 2008), including one that fosters interpersonal relationships and social networking (Davis, 1991), wellness (Spurgeon & Myers, 2010), and a sense of family and brotherhood (Jett, 2013). HBCUs have been found to foster higher engagement levels with peers and faculty and greater levels of faculty diversity (Stewart et al., 2008). Additionally, Black students who attend HBCUs report that although their curriculum is rigorous, they are able to succeed as a result of the supportive environment (Flowers, 2002).

Between 1976 and 1994, there was a 71% increase in White student enrollment at HBCUs. As a result, there has been an added focus given to the experiences of these students. In a study conducted to investigate the experiences of White HBCU students, Hall and Closson (2005) found that unlike the hostile environment reported by Black students who attend PWIs, White students who attend HBCUs report a general sense of comfort. While White students who attend HBCUs have reported initial feelings of uneasiness toward attending, they found that these feelings were not their reality upon entrance to the environment, which they describe as supportive (Hall & Closson, 2005). In addition to the evidence that being the temporary minority is beneficial for White students, researchers also assert that exposure to non-Black students is beneficial in helping Black students disconfirm stereotypes, particularly for those students who come from highly segregated high school environments (Orfield, Frankenberg, & Lee, 2003).

Engagement With Peers and Faculty

As the atmosphere at universities often determines whether students persist to graduation, meaningful relationships with both peers and faculty are important. This is especially true for HBCU students who often come from disadvantaged backgrounds. A unique value of HBCUs is that with the higher concentration of Black faculty and administrators, students are provided distinct opportunities to interact with and receive mentorship from faculty and students who have backgrounds similar to their own (Stewart et al., 2008). HBCU professors and administrators are noted for being accessible and possessing a sincere willingness to form supportive relationships with students, as well as being empathetic and supportive to students and encouraging them to work to their maximum potential (Palmer & Gasman, 2008). Students at HBCUs tend to be invested more deeply in campus life, enjoy more intimate relationships with faculty and are more fully involved in campus organizations and activities (Redd 1998; Roebuck & Murty, 1993; Stewart et al., 2008).

Developmental theory shows that support from peers may facilitate academic motivation and performance within environments that are conducive to achievement-related outcomes (Gonzales, Cauce, Friedman, & Mason, 1996). Moreover, there is some support for strong peer networks resulting in healthy outcomes such as psychological development, motivation, and competence. Palmer and Gasman's (2008) study conducted with Black males at an HBCU indicated that peers were critical to student persistence, as they assisted Black males in developing the motivation and desire to become and remain academically successful. According to the authors, "by forming supportive relationships with other students, which facilitates perseverance and persistence toward the goal of graduation, peers provide a rich source of social capital" (Palmer & Gasman, 2008, p. 61).

Campus Diversity

Diversity has become a common buzzword in higher education. An aim of higher education institutions is to prepare students to function in an increasingly diverse society. To do this, it is imperative that students be exposed to diverse perspectives and people. Since their inception, HBCUs have employed faculty from a variety of ethnic backgrounds. Recent data from the National Center for Education Statistics (NCES), revealed that 56% of full-time faculty members across 99 HBCUs were Black, 25% were White, 2% Hispanic, and 10% Asian. This is in comparison to the national level where 79% of full-time faculty were White, 6% Black, 4% Hispanic, and 9% Asian or Pacific Islander (National Center for Education Statistics, 2011).

Faculty have indicated that the environment is much more collegial at HBCUs than at PWIs, expressed in various ways, from collaboration on academic work or grant proposals to participating in casual conversations or occasional lunches (Johnson, 2001). Additionally, a classic text written on the experience of non-Black faculty employed at HBCUs titled *Affirmed Action* indicates that being the minority race among Blacks in higher education creates some common realities of vulnerability that are beneficial. This text also provides evidence that all people have something valuable to contribute to higher education (Foster, Guyden, & Miller, 1999).

While PWIs typically have many challenges in providing students with the support needed to create inclusive environments and engage with diverse populations, HBCUs and other Minority-Serving Institutions (MSIs) in general are known for offering students a diverse campus and are noted for being havens for diversity and inclusion (Jewell, 2002). In fact, as HBCUs are home to the most racially and ethnically diverse faculty (Stewart et al., 2008), the inclusiveness, emphasis on community service, and student service could not be emulated by PWIs (Richardson & Harris, 2004).

While the student body at HBCUs is typically majority Black, it is important to acknowledge the diversity that exists at these institutions. According to a report by the Center of Minority-Serving Institutions, Black students make up approximately 76% of HBCU students, with 13% of HBCU students being White, 3% Hispanic, 1% Asian American, 1% biracial or multiracial, and 1% unknown. HBCUs are celebrated for providing an environment that is supportive and nurturing for all students. Additionally, diversity extends beyond just the racial and ethnic makeup of universities. Many HBCUs are made up of students from a wide variety of backgrounds, including first-generation, non-traditional, international, and LBGTQQ[2] from which students are able to learn (Palmer, 2015).

Cultural Focus

Freeman and Cohen place emphasis on the importance of cultural empowerment, defined as "the procedures through which a group of people develop a belief system in their capabilities – that is, their ability to achieve" (2001, p. 587). The authors assert that students who are culturally empowered are able to take pride in their own abilities as well as the accomplishments of others who share their culture. To some degree, HBCUs empower members of the Black community (Freeman & Cohen, 2001). According to the authors, this is done through various aspects of HBCUs, including the welcoming atmosphere, reinforcing of student sense of self, providing students with the tools needed to confidently confront racism through the existence of a welcoming atmosphere, and fostering of persona and professional development.

The curricula at HBCUs help to give Black students a sense of empowerment (Ginwright, 2004). In a Eurocentric environment in which Blacks are often portrayed negatively, a major strength of HBCUs is the increased opportunities to learn Black history. As HBCUs continue to fight to retain their missions of educating Black people, many HBCUs require that students take at least one Black history class and even US history classes include a component to which Black students who attend HBCUs can relate. It is important that cultural empowerment occur not only through the formal and informal curriculum, but also in teaching materials, counseling programs, and teaching strategies (Banks, 1993).

Where many institutions focus on preparing students to adapt to the teaching styles of the instructors, more often than not, some HBCU instructors place an emphasis on teaching in ways that students are best able to understand. The study conducted by Perna et al. (2009) has been noted as an illustration of this (Gasman & Commodore, 2014). In this study, the authors provide insight into the strategies for learning used by HBCUs to promote the success of Black women in graduate programs in STEM fields, including the fostering of both a competitive and supportive learning environment.

Community and Civic Engagement

Long before institutions realized the need for community and civic engagement offices and community and civic engagement became buzzwords in academia, HBCUs played a vital role in community involvement (Ehrlich, 2000; Gasman & Commodore, 2014). HBCUs are known for offering all students an opportunity to develop their skills and talents and training young people for service domestically and internationally in both the public and private sectors (Peace Corps, 2008). These institutions were deeply involved in their communities, particularly doing so to defend themselves against the consequences of segregation in the south, where most HBCUs are located (Gasman & Commodore, 2014). As many of their mission statements suggest, HBCUs have always been committed to community and civic engagement. During the Civil Rights Movement, many HBCU leaders, faculty, and staff played significant roles in training community members in the art of activism and civil disobedience (Gasman, 2007). Today, many HBCUs still uphold this commitment to community service by requiring students to complete community service hours for registration and graduation. For many HBCU students, this creates a commitment to the community that extends well beyond graduation from the college or university.

With an increased focus on the relationship between universities and communities and a move toward direct community engagement an initiative has emerged known as community based participatory research (CBPR) (Sydnor, Hawkins, & Edwards, 2010). Some argue that Black institutions have a longer and more stable model of community engagement (Sydnor et al., 2010). In fact, HBCUs have been cited as the top producers of Peace Corps volunteers, with Howard, Spelman, North Carolina A&T State University, and Texas Southern University among the top HBCU producers of alumni serving in the Peace Corps. HBCUs share a commitment to social justice and equality that is a major component of CBPR (Sydnor et al., 2010). Many of these institutions were created not only to meet students' educational needs, but also to be explicitly committed to providing and improving service to Black communities (Allen, Jewell, Griffin, & Wolf, 2007; LeMelle, 2002). The historical need to redress social inequity for individuals and communities still exists and continues to be addressed by HBCUs. We next discuss the challenges within HBCUs.

Challenges

Juxtapositioned with the strengths and benefits of these remarkable institutions are tremendous and longstanding challenges; HBCUs, we argue, are unhealthy at best. Colon (2016) speaks of the legacy of HBCUs being stifled from their beginnings:

> Then, as now, the HBCUs were stifled by: (1) woefully small institutional endowments, fractional state and federal appropriations and disparate private donor contributions; (2) dilapidated physical facilities; (3) ineffective, authoritarian and culturally insensitive administration; (4) inadequately pre-pared and poorly compensated teachers; (5) imitative and culturally irrelevant curricula; (6) racist textbooks; and (7) other hallmarks of the legacy of Black educational subordination.
>
> *(p. 271)*

Some of these challenges are internally generated and some are brought about as a result of external forces. Indeed the curricula at HBCUs were flawed from the onset, as these institutions were not designed to perpetuate a Black worldview or to facilitate self-determination, self-discovery, and self-knowledge for Black students. Other wounds inflicted primarily from outside include (but are not limited to): (1) underpaid faculty (Freemark, 2012; Snyder, 2013), (2) deteriorating buildings (Clement & Lidsky, 2011), and (3) institutionalized racism (Malveaux, 2013).

Some wounds that are primarily internally generated include: (1) poor financial management in the business office *and* in the financial aid office (Jacobs, 2015; Saffron, 2016; Scott & Hines 2014), (2) extremely high levels of nepotism (America, 2012; Carter, 2016), (3) autocratic leadership (AAUP, 2006; America, 2012; Scott & Hines, 2014), (4) the disproportionate admission of less prepared students (America, 2012; Rivard, 2014), (5) low retention and graduation rates (JBHE, 2014), (6) excessive micromanaging by management boards (America, 2012; Gasman, 2016; Rivard, 2014), and (7) (with some strong academic programs and some not so strong programs), few individuals who seem to be concerned with strengthening the academic programs (America, 2012).

For the most part, HBCUs continue to fail to provide culturally responsive education for Black people. Recall that culturally responsive education entails being prepared for meaningful leadership roles, having and using power responsibly and having assurances of the survival of one's group.

When we look at HBCUs today we observe that, for example, we have been unsuccessful, thus far, in raising money to augment the funding of these institutions. State funding decreases have hit HBCUs disproportionately. Between 2002 and 2012, 10 HBCUs lost more than 15% of their state funding, with these losses ranging from 15 to 89% (Toldson & Cooper, 2014). Fourteen HBCUs have endowments of less than $2 million (Toldson & Cooper, 2014). The combined endowments of all 105 or so HBCUs is about $1.6 billion. Alumni giving at HBCUs is a little under 10% (Robinson, 2012), compared to nearly 27% nationally (Council for Aid to Education, 2015). Of course, a number of factors come into play in bringing this set of circumstances into reality, not the least of which is the relatively low level of income and wealth within the Black community. In addition, in many instances board members of HBCUs are not selected because of their ability to personally *give* money to the institutions or *get* money from other sources for the institution. How many HBCU board members are senior level officers at major corporations? (Board selection at HBCUs is discussed elsewhere herein.)

Infrastructurally, HBCUs are not competitive: in their residence halls, their classrooms, and in their instructional programs (America, 2012; Gasman, 2014). These are the kinds of things that prospective students and their parents are comparing when they go from one campus to the next.

Again, HBCUs, to varying levels, are characterized by autocratic leadership, poor financial management, extremely high levels of nepotism, low retention and graduation rates, mediocre academic programs, and poor customer service.[3] While this argument may sound dangerously similar to that put forth by conservative columnist Jason Riley (2010) in the *Wall Street Journal*, the difference is that, while few would argue with Mr. Riley's description of HBCUs, we would differ with him in that his analysis fails to acknowledge the political, economic, racial, and other social issues that have brought us to this point in the development – or lack thereof – of HBCUs.

Autocratic leadership. This is a critical problem with many HBCUs. It starts at the board level where many boards seek to be intricately involved in the day-to-day operations of these institutions, rather than limiting their efforts to broad oversight and governance of these institutions. This challenge is exacerbated by the absence of board members who are able to "give or get" and who have inadequate business acumen. Essentially, they are usually unable to give the much-needed guidance to HBCU campus CEOs.

A fundamental issue here is the constant micromanagement of HBCU boards. At one institution, after an athletic director and a campus CEO had made the decision to retain a coach who had one year remaining on his contract, the board chair overruled them and fired the coach. Putting aside the inappropriateness of this act from a governance perspective, the fallout included having to pay the fired coach for an additional year while also hiring and paying a new coach at the same time – this with limited funds at the institution.

Poor financial management. This problem crops up in HBCU after HBCU regularly. The issue is in the business office with poor accounting as well as in the financial aid office. In one HBCU, a little more than 15 years ago, the administration misappropriated more than $25,000,000 in Title IV funding. After negotiating with the US Department of Education, a subsequent administration was fortunate to only have to pay the interest and penalties totaling $1.7 million. With limited business expertise and the absence of other qualities that could buttress efforts on HBCU campuses, the margin of error is extremely limited for these institutions where finances are concerned.

Nepotism. There is an argument to be made for hiring someone who is related to or who knows someone in power, *if the potential employee is competent in the area into which they are being hired.* There are instances on HBCU campuses where people are hired *solely* because they know or are related to someone in power – with no consideration for their ability to do the job for which they have been hired. On one HBCU campus, a *second-year assistant professor* was serving as an interim dean. During the search for the permanent dean a debate ensued on the search committee and the decision was made to not include the interim dean in the final pool. The next day the administration canceled the search and hired the interim dean as the permanent dean. In this instance the individual was the spouse of a senior campus administrator.

Low retention and graduation rates. It is not a secret that some HBCUs do a poor job of retaining and graduating their students. Of course, there are causative factors that have been historically outside of the control of administrators on these campuses.[4] Still the disparity between the current rates and where the rates should be is massive. After six years, on average, only three out of every 10 students graduate from HBCUs (Gasman, 2013). On average, six out of 10 students at HBCUs are retained to their second year. Only five HBCUs have first-year retention rates exceeding 80%. Indeed, at 11 HBCUs nearly half of all students leave prior to their second year (Toldson & Cooper, 2014).

Mediocre academic programs. Not unlike other institutions of higher education, HBCUs have some very good academic programs and some programs that are not so good. Regardless of the quality of the programs there seems to be insufficient or inconsistent interest in making the programs better at some HBCUs. This raises the question as to how much commitment there is on some HBCU campuses to making the academic programs stronger. The issue is twofold here. HBCUs must insure that their curricula are up-to-date and are preparing their students to fit into and serve the community and the world.

Poor customer service. This is a constant complaint on many HBCU campuses. It is as though staff forget that they are on campus to serve students. This is a problem in face-to-face interactions, in written communication, and also on the phone. Relatedly, many HBCUs are understaffed. When an employee is away from his or her station for whatever reason and for however long, if employees are not cross-trained, customers (read: students and others) do not get served. For example, in the registrar's office on many HBCU campuses, if a student wants a copy of his or her transcript and the person who normally prints transcripts is not in, the student is typically told to come back. Should not everyone in the registrar's office be able (and willing) to print transcripts when students (and others) need them? How might we address these challenges? We next address this question.

Opportunities and Strategies

Assumptions

Our discussion of challenges on HBCU campuses could be construed as a damning indictment of these institutions. In truth, we are truly concerned about their survival and benefit to the Black community and the nation and we are guardedly optimistic that they can be habilitated. We preface our discussion of opportunities and challenges with three assumptions.

The first assumption is that just as power relations impact our lives on a societal level, they also impact our interactions on campuses. Nobles (1978) defines power as the capacity to interpret reality and to persuade others that it is their reality. Spring (1991) extends this truism, stating that power is the capacity to control others and to avoid being controlled by others. There is substantial agreement that there are more powerful people in society and less powerful people. Similarly, there are more powerful people (e.g., usually governors, board members, and senior level central administrators) and less powerful people (e.g., usually faculty, students, and alumni) impacting what happens on HBCU campuses (and all institutions of higher education). These power relations, in fact, significantly impact the campus culture.

The second assumption, or truism, is that many, if not most, of the issues impacting HBCUs in a negative way also affect other institutions of higher education in the USA, including predominantly White colleges and universities. The impact is exacerbated on HBCU campuses by several factors, including the limited wealth of these institutions and self-inflicted wounds.

The third assumption is that students and faculty have extensive power that is, too often, unexercised. The power of students was demonstrated in the late 1960s and early 1970s when they demanded more Black studies programs, more Black faculty and more Black students (Edwards, 1970). Similar displays of power were exhibited in other instances, for example, in demands for Hispanic studies and women's studies programs. Students also demonstrated their power recently at the University of Missouri and elsewhere (Eligon, 2015).

College and university faculty by their sheer numbers have the potential to exercise power much in the way that K–12 teachers have demonstrated their power across the country for many years with work stoppages and other often effective strategies. We now move to a discussion of selected opportunities and strategies to improve the status of HBCUs.

Leadership

1. *HBCU communities should demand that when governors or legislatures appoint members to public HBCU boards, consideration should be given to the potential appointees' (1) general knowledge of the campus, (2) interest beyond personal concerns in terms of desiring to make the institution better, (3) ability to benefit the institution personally or through networking, and (4) general knowledge of higher education or a sincere expressed willingness to learn.* In far too many instances, politicians place individuals on public HBCU boards and they display very little commitment to the advancement of the institution and, in fact, do more disservice than service to the campus.

2. *HBCU communities should insist that their boards have on-going training through such organizations as the Association of Governing Boards (AGB) that have experience in providing professional development for new and less knowledgeable college and university board members.* Many HBCU board members have very little knowledge of how higher education operates and provide little value to the institutions in their critical roles. They do more damage than good to the institutions, in many instances.

3. *HBCU boards should give campus CEOs a chance.* The average tenure of an HBCU campus CEO is less than six years, and many are gone in as little as three years. Forty-two percent of HBCU presidents hold their positions for four years or less (Freeman & Gasman, 2014). Sixteen HBCUs had five or more CEO changes in the period from 2000 to 2013. That is five or more changes in leadership in 13 years. According to Toldson and Cooper (2014):

there is no universal consensus on how long a university president's tenure should be. However, too much turnover in leadership is widely considered to indicate problems with governance. Further, frequent and abrupt turnover in leadership harms stability in programs and the morale of personnel.

(p. 7)

Long time president of Wiley College, Haywood Strickland (2009), adds, "If you want to know when a college is heading down a slippery slope, I can tell you that it is when you change presidents every two, three, or four years. That's a sign that the college is going to have difficulties" (p. 2).

How can anyone be expected to move an institution forward (or even demonstrate that they are capable of moving an institution forward) in such a short period of time? It takes a year to figure out what is happening on a campus. It takes another year to begin to implement strategies, policies, and guidelines. Then it takes a third year to assess what you have done and make any necessary adjustments. To be sure, few HBCU presidents are given sufficient time to make much needed, lasting improvements. And the institutions suffer as a result.

4. *HBCU administrators should hire a competent, trusted leadership team, particularly in the business office.* According to Alexander (2008):

    in building a leadership team, appoint supremely competent persons who clearly understand that their role is to implement the institutional vision and plan. Complete the requisite background reviews and face-to-face interviews to confirm that potential team members will be loyal and trustworthy.

    (p. 30)

    If a campus CEO hires less than competent people around him or her, their jobs will not get done or the campus CEO will do them. (We are not sure which is worse.) If a campus CEO hires people who they cannot trust, they will never know whether what they tell them is the truth. That is a very difficult position to be in as a campus leader.

5. *HBCU leaders should model the behavior that they expect of others (i.e., faculty, administrators and students).* For faculty, model a focus on research, teaching, and service. For students, model a focus on academic excellence and goal selection and attainment. For administrators, model commitment, hard work, determination, and competence.

6. *HBCU leaders should involve others in decision making, where practical, and communicate decisions and the rationales for them.* It is not always possible to involve everyone in decisions that have to be made, but when it is possible and practical efforts should be made to do so. By doing this a leader can increase

the likelihood that people will develop a sense of ownership of the decisions and respond favorably to their implementation. When it is not possible to include (particularly affected) individuals, clear explanations should be given as to why the decision was made.

7. *HBCU CEOs should have a general knowledge of every administrative area of the institution.* One of the major responsibilities of the campus CEO is the regular evaluation of his or her direct reports (e.g., VP for finance, VP for academic affairs, VP for student affairs, etc.). If the campus CEO does not have a general understanding of each of these areas, how can he or she effectively evaluate the persons leading those positions?

8. *Seek clarity on your role.* Every constituency group has specific responsibilities and authority. The board is not responsible for hiring individual faculty members; they hire senior administrators who then, in turn, hire other faculty and staff. The alumni are not responsible for selecting an athletic director (or a football coach); that is the responsibility of the campus CEO. Administrators, for the most part, are not responsible for curriculum development; that is the domain of the faculty. Board members, administrators, faculty, alumni, and students should seek clarity on their areas of authority and responsibility and act accordingly.

Financial Management

1. *HBCU leaders should redouble efforts to raise money.* One of the biggest challenges on HBCU campuses is limited funding. While it is true that Black people, generally speaking, have less wealth than Whites, a much better job can be done in raising funds than what is occurring now. The evidence exists in the fact that some HBCUs do much better than others in raising funds. According to Gasman and Bowman (2011):

> Fundraising is the most important factor for the long-term sustainability of HBCUs. Institutions with substantial endowments and vibrant alumni giving programs are less likely to have problems with accreditation, student retention, leadership, and faculty satisfaction.
>
> *(p. 2)*

2. *HBCU leaders should minimize the gaps between faculty and administrative salaries.* Salaries of faculty at HBCUs are deplorable. They earn slightly more than one half of the national average for faculty salaries (Chronicle of Higher Education, 2011). This is compounded by the large gap between administrative and faculty salaries at these institutions. There will, invariably, be a gap between faculty and administrative salaries, but they can be made less substantial. This is important, in part, because, while there is almost always distrust and some level of antagonism between faculty and administration, it is exacerbated by unnecessarily wide gaps between faculty and administrative salaries.

Nepotism

1. *HBCU leaders should select employees based first on their sense of the potential employee's ability to do the job for which they are being hired.* Doing anything else invariably does (often unreparable) damage to the institution. In far too many instances failure to adequately consider the legitimate qualifications of a candidate has led to disastrous consequences on campuses.

2. *HBCU leaders should check the backgrounds of potential employees and use the information gleaned therefrom.* Too many people are hired on HBCU campuses who have been fired repeatedly on other campuses, for serious violations. It is hard to believe that this information is unknown when they are hired again, particularly with all of the information that is now available on the Internet. This applies to the hiring of campus CEOs as much as it applies to the hiring of custodial engineers. We are talking about sexual assaults, massive embezzling, and more. On one HBCU campus, a candidate was being considered for a vice presidency. He had held a comparable position before – six times, never for more than two years. That type of record should raise a red flag. In this particular case, the candidate was hired – and lasted for about two years with no substantial accomplishments (as had been the case in the first six instances).

3. *HBCU leaders should not move incompetent people around the campus from one position to another; they should fire them.* More often than not, if an individual is performing substantially below expectations in one position on a campus, he or she will do likewise in other positions on campus. There are, of course, exceptions, but they are few and far between.

Retention and Graduation Rates

HBCUs need to conduct a serious analysis of the human and material resources at their disposal. While we know of the tremendous success that these institutions have had with large numbers of underprepared students, data show that many more get lost in the shuffle. And these students who do not complete programs end up with massive educational debt. Once such an analysis of available resources is made, institutions need to then ascertain a realistic number of underprepared students that they can accommodate. That is, it may be that some HBCUs will need to further limit the number of underprepared students that they can accommodate unless they can increase the human and material resources at their disposal.

Academic Programs

1. *HBCU administrators should facilitate the regular assessment of academic and non-academic programs, including insuring that the curricula are culturally responsive while*

being intellectually robust. The point here is that HBCUs must be more intentional in ensuring that the curriculum contains information that enables graduates to be effective and efficient participants and encourages them to unselfishly serve meaningful roles in their own communities, in the larger society, and in the world.

2. *HBCUs should maximize students' opportunities for leadership experiences.* The term "talented tenth" refers to the approximately 10 percent of Black people who earn a bachelor's degree. These graduates, in many instances, have the opportunity to go into leadership roles in their communities, cities, counties, states, nation, and the world. The more opportunities that they have to exercise leadership and display leadership qualities in college, the better prepared they will be beyond graduation.

3. *HBCU faculty should insure that their classes and their programs are the best that they can be.* Aside from the students, faculty are the most important people on the campus. Indeed, the interaction between students and faculty is where "the rubber meets the road." Many faculty work hard in their classes and in their academic programs.

4. *HBCU alumni should be more concerned about academics and administration.* Many alumni at HBCUs are seriously concerned about athletics on the campus. This is great. It is good for campus spirit and usually fosters a healthy degree of competition and fun. There is an opportunity for alumni to put a comparable focus on the academics and administration of the tertiary institutions from which they have graduated.

Customer Service

1. *Everyone on HBCU campuses should seek to become socially active.* We live in a society wherein injustice continues to exist based upon illegitimate forms of exclusion. HBCUs are no different in terms of the existence of these injustices. As long as these injustices occur, every one on these campuses has a responsibility to challenge them and to work with others to seek change. Injustices against LBGTQQ students, faculty, or staff, for example, should not be tolerated by anyone on HBCU campuses. Be aware of what is happening around campus. There is always something happening on campus and many times it impacts you directly. Pay attention to what is occurring on your campus and, where possible and practical, get involved. For example, students should be concerned about controversies within the administration. Changes in leadership or campus policies impact students, faculty, alumni, and staff.

2. *HBCU faculty and administrators should make decisions in the interest of the campus and the students.* Colleges and universities operate to benefit their students and society at large. Accordingly, decisions that are made on these campuses should be made in the interest of students. On a practical level, when

making a decision, the question should be asked, will it benefit the students of today and tomorrow?

3. *HBCU administrators should listen to all constituency groups.* Faculty, staff, administrators, students, alumni, and board members each have a stake in the success or lack thereof of the campus. Accordingly, when practical, their voices should be heard, particularly when there are major decisions to be made that will impact the institutions into the future. Just because a decision rests with the campus CEO or with the board, does not mean that the views of other constituencies should not be solicited and considered when possible and practical.

No college or university is ideal. These opportunities and strategies, we believe, will make HBCUs better. These are, in many cases, obvious fixes. They will require a change in the campus culture and a change in power relationships on campus.

Final Thoughts

Lomotey and Aboh (2009) wrote:

> it is still important to ponder the extent to which HBCUs prepare their graduates to address the interest of people of African descent in their quest for liberation and/or equitable treatment in all areas of life. For example, while various HBCUs rightfully profess to prepare leaders for the Black community, the question, pregnant with relevance, remains: How and to where are HBCU graduates leading the masses of people in the United States and in the African world as a whole?
>
> ... while still very important, HBCUs remain a vehicle for the retention of people of African descent as second-class citizens with inequitable status in politics, economics (i.e., employment, income, and wealth), education and health.
>
> *(pp. 315, 317)*

The challenges facing HBCUs, if not addressed, will threaten their survival. Here is a description of HBCUs:

> Our college man today is, on the average, a man untouched by real culture. He deliberately surrenders to selfish and even silly ideals, swarming into semiprofessional athletics and Greek letter societies, and affecting to despise scholarship and the hard grind of study and research. The greatest meetings of the Negro college year like those of the White college year have become vulgar exhibitions of liquor, extravagance, and fur coats. We have in our colleges a growing mass of stupidity and indifference.
>
> *(DuBois, 1973, p. 67)*

DuBois offered that description of HBCUs at the June 1930 commencement exercises of Howard University. Many would argue that description is still relevant today. Indeed, many of the problems, issues, and challenges that we face in HBCUs are mere extensions of the problems, issues, and challenges that we have faced since the inception of these institutions. And that is our point. Just like public K–12 institutions and predominantly White colleges and universities were not intended to serve the interests of Black people, neither were many HBCUs. The result, then, is not an accident; it is by design.

There is a need for a revolution in the higher education of Black people. What do we mean by a revolution? We can attempt to change things slowly and insignificantly; that is a reform. Generally speaking, reforms in US education have not benefitted Black people. We can seek to change things rapidly and significantly; that is a revolution. We need a revolution to facilitate the provision of quality higher education for Black people.

Turning to DuBois (1970) again, he advised that, "a Negro University in the United States of America begins with Negroes … . it should be founded on a knowledge of the history of their people in Africa and in the United States, and their present condition" (p. 181). To be sure, this is not an apt description of the current status of the institutions that we call HBCUs. DuBois understood the need for revolutionary change.

Our final related point would be that people do not have revolutions staged for them; they stage them themselves. If a revolution is to occur in the higher education of Black people, it will have to be initiated by Black people. According to Frantz Fanon: "One cannot expect an oppressor to facilitate the liberating process of the oppressed" (Fanon, 1973, p. 3).

The question is: Are Black people, or more specifically, is the so-called Talented Tenth up to the challenge? We believe that they are. Edward Wilmot Blyden (1971) was clear on this also. He said, of the Talented Tenth, "Your places have been assigned you in the universe as Africans, and there is no room for you as anything else."

Also of counsel are the words of the late Jacob Carruthers (1994), who said:

> The crisis in Black education will not be resolved until Black intellectuals achieve intellectual freedom and reconstruct Black education on an African-centered foundation … . Schooling that was always intended to instill loyalty to and prepare us to serve a social order that oppresses us must be rejected and replaced with a liberating education.
>
> *(pp. 41, 51)*

These words of the late Carruthers were crystal clear here and need no clarification. He – like Blyden and DuBois – has given us our marching orders. Indeed, DuBois (1935) concurred, stating:

I have become curiously convinced that until American Negroes believe in their own power and ability, they are going to be helpless before the white world, and the white world, realizing this inner paralysis and lack of self confidence, is going to persist in its insane determination to rule the universe for its own selfish advantage.

(p. 333)

We close with the words of W.E.B. DuBois (1968), who, while credited with coining the term, the "Talented Tenth," speaks here in his autobiography about his sense that they had betrayed him.

Negroes of intelligence and prosperity had become American in their acceptance of exploitation as defensible, and in their imitation of American "conspicuous expenditure." They proposed to make money and spend it as pleased them. They had beautiful homes, large and expensive cars and fur coats.

(p. 239)

"It is still my hope," he continued, "that the Negro's experience in the past will, in the end, lead the majority of his intelligentsia into the ranks of those advocating social control of wealth, abolition of exploitation of labor, and equality of opportunity for all."

In spite of the fact that no institutions of higher education in the USA were designed to provide culturally responsive education for Black people, DuBois and others have implored us to re-develop HBCUs to address the needs of Black people's needs. We must do this for ourselves, for our children, and for our grandchildren. We must develop a plan for a century and beyond.

Notes

1 We are not oblivious to the fact that there are some challenges that are self-inflicted today, that may have initially been externally generated. That is, some challenges may have first been brought about from the outside and have been perpetuated, sometimes unwittingly or uncontrollably, from within. We focus herein on who we believe is most responsible/culpable presently.
2 Lesbian, bisexual, gay, transgender, queer, and questioning.
3 Certainly these realities exist on other campuses as they do on HBCU campuses. However, the focus of this chapter (and, indeed, this book) is on HBCUs. Also, the limited resources in HBCUs exacerbate the impact of these challenges. Our intent is to articulate these matters prior to exploring ways that they can be addressed if these institutions are to survive. We cannot talk about what HBCUs can and should be and do without a clear and honest understanding of where they are today.
4 It is important to keep in mind that many HBCUs admit students who are first generation, heavily dependent upon financial aid, and given the issue of unfair access to a quality education in K-12, many may be underprepared for a college education. Nevertheless, HBCUs do a good job of meeting students where they are and providing them with a quality education that enables them to be highly competitive in the global economy.

References

Alexander, L. (2008). Pathway to leadership. The presidency. Retrieved from HighBeam Research: www.highbeam.com/doc/1P3-1567875261.html

Allen, W.R. (1992). The color of success: African-American college student outcomes at predominantly White and historically Black public colleges and universities. *Harvard Educational Review*, 62(1), 26–44.

Allen, W.R., Epps, E.G., & Haniff, N.Z. (1991). *College in Black and White: African American students in predominantly White and in historically Black public universities.* New York: SUNY Press.

Allen, W.R., Jewell, J.O., Griffin, K.A., & Wolf, D.S. (2007). Historically Black colleges and universities: Honoring the past, engaging the present, touching the future. *The Journal of Negro Education*, 76, 263–280.

America, R.F. (2012). Can HBCUs compete? *Journal of Blacks in Higher Education.* Retrieved from www.jbhe.com/2012/10/can-hbcus-compete/

American Association of University Professors (AAUP) (2006). *Historically black colleges and universities: Recent trends.* Washington, D.C.: AAUP.

Anderson, J.D. (1988). *The education of Blacks in the south, 1860–1935.* Chapel Hill: The University of North Carolina Press.

Banks, J.A. (1993). Multicultural education: Historical development, dimensions, and practice. *Review of Research in Education*, 19, 3–49.

Bethune, M.M. (1963). My last will and testament. *Ebony*, 18(11), 150.

Blyden, W.E. (1971). Study and race. In H.R. Lynch (Ed.), *Black spokesman: Selected published writings of Edward Wilmot Blyden* (pp. 200–201). London: Frank Cass and Co.

Carruthers, J.C. (1994). Black intellectuals and the crisis in black education. In M.J. Shujaa (Ed.), *Too much schooling, too little education: A paradox of Black life in white society* (pp. 37–55). Trenton, NJ: Africa World Press.

Carter, C. (2016). Winning the wars to save HBCUs starts with honest look at leadership. *HBCU Digest.* Retrieved from www.hbcudigest.com/wars-on-hbcus-leadership-politics/

Chronicle of Higher Education (2011). Average salaries of full time faculty members, 2011–2012. Retrieved from www.chronicle.com/article/average-salaries-of-full-time/133361

Clement, A.J. & Lidsky, A.J. (2011). The danger of history slipping away: The heritage campus and HBCUs. *Planning for Higher Education*, 39(3), 149–158.

Colon, A. (2000). Black studies and historically Black colleges and universities: Towards a new synthesis. In D. Aldridge and C. Young (Eds.). *Out of the revolution: The development of African Studies* (pp. 287–313). New York: Lexington Books.

Colon, A. (2016). Racism in colleges and universities. In K. Lomotey (Ed.). *Education, K-12 and higher education* (Volume I in the People of Color in the United States: Contemporary Issues in Education, Work, Communities, Health & Immigration Series) (pp. 267–274). Santa Barbara, CA: Praeger Publishers.

Council for Aid to Education (2015). *Colleges and universities raise record $0.30 billion in 2015* [Press release]. Retrieved from http://cae.org/images/uploads/pdf/VSE_2015_Press_Release.pdf

Davis, R.B. (1991). Social support networks and undergraduate student academic–success-related outcomes: A comparison of Black students on Black and White campuses. In W. Allen, E. Epps, & N. Haniff (Eds.) *College in Black and White: African American students in predominantly White and in historically Black public universities* (pp. 143–157). New York: SUNY.

Dee, T. and Penner, E. (2016). The causal effects of cultural relevance: Evidence from an ethnic studies curriculum (CEPA Working Paper No. 16-01). Retrieved from Stanford Center for Education Policy Analysis: http://cepa.stanford.edu/wp16-01

DuBois, W.E.B. (1930). Commencement Address, June 6, Howard University. Washington, DC: Howard University Bulletin.

DuBois, W.E.B. (1935). Does the negro need separate schools? *Journal of Negro Education*, 4(3), 328–335.

DuBois, W.E.B. (1968). *The autobiography of W. E. B. DuBois: A soliloquy on viewing my life from the last decade of its first century*. New York: International Publishers.

DuBois, W.E.B. (1970). The Negro College (1933). In M. Weinberg (Ed.). *W.E.B. DuBois: A reader*. New York: Harper and Row.

DuBois, W.E.B. (1973). *The education of Black people: Ten critiques, 1906–1960*, Herbert Aptheker (Ed.). New York: Monthly Review Press.

Edwards, H. (1970). *Black students*. New York: The Free Press.

Ehrlich, T. (Ed.) (2000). *Civil responsibility and higher education*. Washington, DC: American Council of Education/Oryx Press.

Eligon, J. (November 11, 2015). At University of Missouri, Black students see a campus riven by race. *New York Times*. Retrieved from www.nytimes.com/2015/11/12/us/university-of-missouri-protests.html?_r=0

Fanon, F. (1973). *The wretched of the earth*. New York: Grove Press.

Fleming, J. (1984). *Blacks in college: A comparative study of students' success in Black and in White institutions*. San Francisco, CA: Jossey-Bass.

Flowers, L.A. (2002). The impact of college racial composition on African American students' academic and social gains: Additional evidence. *Journal of College Student Development*, 43(3), 403–410.

Foster, L., Guyden, J.A., & Miller, A.L. (1999). *Affirmed action: Essays on the academic and social lives of white faculty members at historically Black colleges and universities*. Lanham, MD: Rowman & Littlefield Publishers.

Freeman, K. & Cohen, R.T. (2001). Bridging the gap between economic development and cultural empowerment: HBCUs' challenges for the future. *Urban Education*, 36(5), 585–596.

Freeman Jr., S. & Gasman, M. (2014). Characteristics of historically Black colleges and university presidents and their role in grooming the next generation of leaders. *Teachers College Record*, 116(7), 1–34.

Freemark, S. (2012). *The history of HBCUs in America*. Saint Paul, MN: American RadioWorks.

Gallup (2015). *Gallup-USA funds minority college graduates report*. Washington, D.C.: Gallup.

Gasman, M. (2007). *Envisioning Black colleges: A history of the United Negro College Fund*. Baltimore, MD: Johns Hopkins University Press.

Gasman, M. (2013). *The changing face of historically Black colleges and universities*. Philadelphia, PA: Center for Minority Serving Institutions, University of Pennsylvania.

Gasman, M. (2016). HBCUs' self-imposed leadership struggles. *Inside Higher Ed*. Retrieved from www.insidehighered.com/views/2016/09/02/boards-hbcus-should-not-micromanage-their-presidents-essay

Gasman, M. & Bowman, N. (2011). *A guide to fundraising at historically Black colleges and universities: An all campus approach*. New York: Routledge.

Gasman, M. & Commodore, F.E. (2014). The state of research on historically Black colleges and universities. *Journal for Multicultural Education*, 8(2), 89–111.

Ginwright, S.A. (2004). *Black in school: Afrocentric reform, urban youth, and the promise of hip-hop culture.* New York: Teachers College Press.

Gonzales, N.A., Cauce, A.M., Friedman, R.J., & Mason, C.A. (1996). Family, peer, and neighborhood influences on academic achievement among African-American adolescents: One-year prospective effects. *American Journal of Community Psychology,* 24(3), 365–387.

Hall, B. & Closson, R.B. (2005). When the majority is the minority: White graduate students' social adjustment at a historically Black university. *Journal of College Student Development,* 46(1), 28–42.

Jacobs, P. (2015). There's an unprecedented crisis facing America's historically Black colleges. *Business Insider.* Retrieved from http://uk.businessinsider.com/hbcus-may-be-more-in-danger-of-closing-than-other-schools-2015-3?r=US&IR=T

Jett, C.C. (2013). HBCUs propel African American male mathematics majors. *Journal of African American Studies,* 17(2), 189–205.

Jewell, J.O. (2002). To set an example: The tradition of diversity at historically Black colleges and universities. *Urban Education,* 37(1), 7–21.

Johnson, B.J. (2001). Faculty socialization: Lessons learned from urban colleges. *Urban Education,* 36(5), 630–647.

Journal of Blacks in Higher Education (JBHE) (2014). *Tracking Black student graduation rates at HBCUs.* Bartonsville, PA: JBHE.

Kim, M.M. (2002). Historically Black vs. White institutions: Academic development among Black students. *The Review of Higher Education,* 25(4), 385–407.

Kim, M.M. & Conrad, C.F. (2006). The impact of historically Black colleges and universities on the academic success of African American students. *Research in Higher Education,* 47(4), 399–427.

Ladson-Billings, G. (1995). Toward a theory of culturally relevant pedagogy. *American Educational Research Journal,* 32(3), 465–491.

Ladson-Billings, G., & Tate, W. (1995). Toward a critical race theory of education. *Teachers College Record,* 97(1), 47–68.

LeMelle, T.J. (2002). The HBCU: Yesterday, today, and tomorrow. *Education,* 123, 190–196.

Lomotey, K. (1989). Cultural diversity in the urban school: Implications for principals. *NASSP Bulletin,* 73(521), 81–85.

Lomotey, K. & Aboh, S. (2009). Historically Black colleges and universities: Catalysts for liberation? In L.C. Tillman (Ed.) *The SAGE handbook of African American education,* (pp. 31–318). Thousand Oaks, CA: SAGE Publications.

Malveaux, J. (2013). Is there a war on HBCUs? *Essence.* Retrieved from www.essence.com/2013/07/22/there-war-hbcus

National Center for Education Statistics (2011). Fall enrollment, degrees conferred, and expenditures in degree-granting historically Black colleges and universities, by institution: 2010, 2011, and 2010–2011. Retrieved from http://nces.ed.gov/fastfacts/display.asp?id=667

Nobles, W.W. (1978). *African consciousness and liberation struggles: Implications for the development and construction of scientific paradigms* (unpublished).

Orfield, G., Frankenberg, E.D., & Lee, C. (2003). The resurgence of school segregation. *Educational Leadership,* 60(4), 16–20.

Palmer, R.T. (2015). HBCUs are more diverse than you think: A look at the numbers. Retrieved from www.noodle.com/articles/the-racial-and-ethnic-diversity-at-hbcus-may-surprise-you

Palmer, R.T., & Gasman, M. (2008). "It takes a village to raise a child": The role of social capital in promoting academic success for African American men at a Black college. *Journal of College Student Development,* 49(1), 52–70.

Peace Corps (2008). HBCUs recognized as top producers of Peace Corps volunteers [Press Release]. Retrieved from www.peacecorps.gov/media/forpress/press/1305/

Perna, L., Lundy-Wagner, V., Drezner, N.D., Gasman, M., Yoon, S., Bose, E., & Gary, S. (2009). The contribution of HBCUs to the preparation of African American women for STEM careers: A case study. *Research in Higher Education*, 50(1), 1–23.

Redd, K.E. (1998). Historically Black colleges and universities: Making a comeback. *New Directions in Higher Education*, 1998(102), 33–43.

Richardson, J.W., & Harris, J.J. (2004). Brown and historically Black colleges and universities (HBCUs): A paradox of desegregation policy. *Journal of Negro Education*, 73(3), 271–299.

Riley, J. (September 28, 2010). Black colleges need a new mission: Once an essential response to racism, they are now academically inferior. *Wall Street Journal*. Retrieved from https://www.wsj.com/articles/SB10001424052748704654004575517822124077834

Rivard, R. (2014). The struggles of historically Black colleges and universities: What must they do to survive? *Inside Higher Ed / Slate*. Retrieved from www.slate.com/articles/life/inside_higher_ed/2014/06/historically_black_colleges_and_universities_are_struggling_and_must_have.html

Robinson, L. (2012). *How HBCUs can increase alumni donation rates*. Columbus, OH: The HBCU Foundation.

Roebuck, J.B. & Murty, K.S. (1993). *Historically Black colleges and universities: Their place in American higher education*. Westport, CT: Praeger Publishers.

Saffron, J. (2016). *Failing HBCUs: Should they receive life support or the axe?* Raleigh, NC: The John William Pope Center for Higher Education Policy.

Scott, D. & Hines, R. (2014). Rethinking and reframing leadership of historically Black colleges and universities: A distributed perspective. *Creative Education*, 5, 1132–1139.

Snyder, S. (2013). Penn professor issues report on historically Black universities. *The Inquirer*. Retrieved from www.philly.com/philly/blogs/campus_inq/Penn-issues-report-on-historically-black-universities.html

Spring, J. (1991). Knowledge and power in research into the politics of urban education. In J.G. Cibulka, R.J. Reed, & K.K. Wong (Eds.) *The politics of urban education in the United States* (pp. 45–56). Bristol, PA: Taylor and Francis.

Spurgeon, S.L., & Myers, J.E. (2010). African American males: Relationships among racial identity, college type, and wellness. *Journal of Black Studies*, 40(4), 527–543.

Stewart, D., Wright, D., Perry, T., & Rankin, C. (2008). Historically Black colleges and universities: Caretakers of precious treasure. *Journal of College Admission*, 201, 24–29.

Strickland, H. (2009). *Still striving: Trustees and presidents of historically Black colleges and universities' unprecedented dialogue about governance and accreditation*. Atlanta, GA: Southern Education Foundation.

Sydnor, K.D., Hawkins, A.S., & Edwards, L.V. (2010). Expanding research opportunities: Making the argument for the fit between HBCUs and community-based participatory research. *Journal of Negro Education*, 79(1), 79–86.

Toldson, I.A., & Cooper, G. (2014). *Historically Black colleges and universities data dashboard: Using the integrated postsecondary education data system to understand the current state of HBCUs*. Washington, D.C.: US Department of Education. White House Initiative on Historically Black Colleges and Universities.

Townsend, L. (1994). How universities successfully retain and graduate Black students. *The Journal of Blacks in Higher Education*, 4, 85–89.

Watkins, W.H. (2001). *The White architects of Black education: Ideology and power in America, 1865–1954*. New York: Teachers College Press.

3

STUDENT AFFAIRS ADMINISTRATORS

A Catalyst for HBCU Transformation

Edward M. Willis and Andrew T. Arroyo

Minority-serving institutions (MSIs) make an important contribution to American higher education. Numbering approximately 650 in total, the racial composition, environments, and practices of MSIs benefit students of color – and their White peers – in ways known to be demonstrably advantageous compared to many predominantly White institutions (PWIs) (Arroyo, Palmer, & Maramba, 2016; Conrad & Gasman, 2015; Gasman, Baez, & Turner, 2008; Gasman, Nguyen, & Conrad, 2015). One might say MSIs are leaders among colleges and universities.

Although MSIs are leaders because of the service they perform, we know very little about leadership *within* MSIs (Esters et al., 2016; Freeman, Commodore, Gasman, & Carter, 2016; Freeman & Gasman, 2014). Critical questions include: (1) Who is an effective MSI leader; (2) What leadership norms need challenging and changing; and (3) How can leaders within MSIs serve as catalysts for institutional transformation? Observers can be left wondering how a new generation of capable MSI leaders might be cultivated to face evolving challenges and maximize fresh opportunities (Carter, 2016; Gasman, 2011). Examining leadership within MSIs, and advancing theories or models of effective MSI leadership (Esters & Strayhorn, 2013), is one way to ensure this eclectic set of institutions thrives in service to students and society.

The current chapter focuses on effective leadership at one group of MSIs, historically Black colleges and universities (HBCUs). We discuss two areas of HBCU senior leadership: chief student affairs officers (CSAOs), especially those who occupy an executive role in the president's cabinet, and the presidents themselves. The chapter advances a working conceptual model of highly effective CSAO leadership for HBCUs, and makes the argument that current and aspiring HBCU presidents can draw important insights from the model. The notion of student affairs leadership as a pathway to the presidency is not entirely novel

(Dungy & Ellis, 2011; Kimbrough, 2011), although it certainly is not the norm. A small number of reputed HBCU presidents have emerged from student affairs (e.g., Walter Kimbrough, Dwaun J. Warmack, Kevin D. Rome). To our knowledge, however, no prior work has advanced a transferrable framework of ideas that establishes HBCU student affairs leadership as a viable trajectory to, or exemplar for, the HBCU presidency. The current chapter takes an initial step to fill that gap.

The chapter begins with a brief review of the relevant literature regarding senior student affairs and presidential leadership at HBCUs. This review allows us to highlight some key leadership requirements across student affairs and the presidency. At the same time, the literature review demonstrates many gaps in the knowledge base due to the infancy of research on HBCU leadership. Next, we offer a model of highly effective CSAO leadership at HBCUs. We conceived of the model in dialogue with essential aspects of the HBCU presidency. This dialogue allowed us to demonstrate how an HBCU CSAO can inform an HBCU presidency due to some noteworthy ways the roles parallel or even intersect. The chapter concludes with implications for research and practice especially related to becoming a catalyst for HBCU transformation. The model advanced in this chapter is an initial step in what we hope will be many future discussions and revisions.

Finally, it is important that we share our positionalities as the chapter's authors since these shape our perspective and model. One of the authors is a vice president for student affairs at Norfolk State University, a public HBCU. He has senior-level experience at several PWIs and HBCUs ranging from the University of Michigan and Rutgers University, to Florida A&M University, North Carolina A&T State University, and Norfolk State University. The other author is an associate professor at Norfolk State University, a researcher of MSIs, a practitioner with experience working as a learning communities co-director and a career pipeline program director in an HBCU. He has also taught at Hampton University. Each author has a longstanding, vested interest in the health and future of HBCUs. Not only are HBCUs the oldest subset of MSIs, but also they continue to serve a vital purpose in society today.

Relevant Literature

Although literature on HBCUs has grown over recent years (see, for example, Arroyo & Gasman, 2014; Perna et al., 2009), two areas that have lagged behind are studies on the HBCU presidency and HBCU student affairs leadership, specifically CSAOs. In this section we discuss the state of the knowledge in these respective areas.

HBCU Student Affairs Leadership

Long (2012) has referred to student affairs as "a distinct profession in higher education" (p. 2). To frame the requirements of this distinct profession, the

Council for the Advancement of Standards in Higher Education (as cited by Long, 2012) has advanced eight core competencies needed for rising student affairs professionals: effectively working with diverse populations, community building and development, conflict resolution, counseling/helping, advising, *leadership*, citizenship, and assessment (emphasis added). Many student affairs scholars have written about the leadership competency specifically (e.g., Dungy & Ellis, 2011; Long, 2012; Love & Estanek, 2004; Porterfield & Whitt, 2016). Others have written about its complexity, citing challenges such as affordability and funding, student access and success, diversity/inclusion, crisis management, and regulations and compliance, to name only some (e.g., Roper & Whitt, 2016; Treadwell, 2016). Since 2003, NASPA, a national association for student affairs administrators in higher education, has produced *Leadership Exchange Magazine*, designed to prepare student affairs administrators for the complex challenges they face. The consensus of the academic and trade literature is that student affairs leadership is a dynamic enterprise requiring intentional development.

Despite the positive developments in student affairs research and practice generally, there remains an alarming absence of literature pertaining to student affairs leadership at HBCUs. In fact, the total corpus of literature on any aspect of student affairs at HBCUs is miniscule (see Arroyo, Palmer, Maramba, & Louis, 2016; Harper & Kimbrough, 2005; Hirt, Amelink, McFeeters, & Strayhorn, 2008; Hirt, Bennett, Strayhorn, & Amelink, 2006; Palmer, Arroyo, & Maramba, 2016). No extant study on HBCU student affairs divisions deals squarely with leadership *per se*. A close read of the available research does, however, yield some insights and recommendations for HBCU student affairs administrators.

For example, Hirt et al. (2006) and Hirt et al. (2008) drew salient findings from a mixed methods study of 70 student affairs professionals at 25 HBCUs. Forty percent of participants served in a cabinet-level role. The researchers found that HBCU student affairs administrators hold fast to the values of racial uplift for Black Americans and cultural advancement. Many of these administrators "view themselves as guardians of not only HBCU students but also of HBCUs as a distinct institutional type" in American higher education (Hirt et al., 2008, p. 228). Forming relationships with students is a core practice of many HBCU student affairs administrators. Consequently, Hirt et al. (2008) recommended that preparatory programs for aspiring HBCU student affairs administrators incorporate skills development in areas such as counseling, interpersonal communication, and relationship building in the culturally specific HBCU context, and also that preparatory programs arm future administrators with deep knowledge about HBCUs as a distinct institutional type in American higher education. The authors also recommend that current senior leaders ensure persons they hire fully understand the historical and ongoing role of HBCUs, and that they recognize and reward the intensive time and effort their employees put into their work with students.

Of note, Hirt et al. (2006) also reported findings related to the day-to-day nature of HBCU student affairs work. Respondents indicated that their work was fast-paced and highly stressful (74%), but overwhelmingly rewarding (80%). This hints at the complex nature of student affairs work, which requires leaders who are adept at balancing many duties through multitasking. In fact, 93% of participants indicated frequent multitasking with limited resources and being driven by a sense of service or duty to students. Among other noteworthy findings were that a majority of participants found their institution slow to change (64%), and approximately three-quarters described their work as team oriented (76%) or collaborative (73%). Although Hirt et al. (2006) did not distinguish between senior HBCU student affairs administrators and others when reporting their findings, it is reasonable to surmise that successful senior leaders must balance many roles, in complex environments, in coordination with others.

Other existing studies on HBCU student affairs divisions offer fewer relevant insights. Harper and Kimbrough (2005) examined the student affairs staffing practices of 52 HBCUs. Data collected on 270 HBCU student affairs professionals suggested a greater need for appropriate master's and doctoral level education among this population, which tends to lag behind the education levels of PWI student affairs professionals. The authors also recommended that more HBCUs launch master's and doctoral programs in student affairs, with the objective of cultivating a new generation of capable leaders well-versed in the HBCU institutional context.

Finally, Palmer et al. (2016) and Arroyo, Palmer et al. (2016), studied the perceptions and actions of HBCU student affairs professionals toward diversification. Both studies indicated a need for clearer leadership on the part of senior administrators. The authors encouraged senior HBCU administrators to lead their student affairs divisions in defining what diversity means for their units, and to develop concrete strategies for reaching the vision. Palmer et al. (2016) explained that this effort would require key skill sets including acknowledging and tolerating differences of opinion and frustration, and drawing dedicated stakeholders toward consensus in collaboration. Not coincidentally, the authors drew a parallel between the leadership of HBCU senior student affairs administrators and the president in providing an institutional vision for diversity.

In sum, despite the lack of literature related to HBCU student affairs senior leaders, the existing literature offers relevant insights for the present chapter. A reader can see how an HBCU student affairs division can be a proving ground for an HBCU presidency. We discuss this idea further in subsequent sections.

The HBCU Presidency

Academic literature exploring the college presidency has developed largely without attention to MSI presidents. Nehls (2015) reviewed the book *Presidencies Derailed: Why University Leaders Fail and How to Prevent It* (Trachtenberg, Kauvar, & Bogue, 2013), noting the complete absence of case studies related to MSIs. Freeman and Gasman (2014) also pointed out that an important study on the career paths of college presidents (i.e., Birnbaum & Umbach, 2001) excluded HBCU presidents. Although the decision in the latter case was made because adding the HBCUs would have created an imbalance in the sample, the outcome is the same: The knowledge on the presidency in majority contexts grows, while our understanding of the HBCU presidency is stagnant by comparison.

Recent studies have addressed this gap in the literature (e.g., Esters & Strayhorn, 2013; Esters et al., 2016; Freeman & Gasman, 2014; Freeman et al., 2016; Henry, 2009; Herring, 2010; Ricard & Brown, 2008). For example, Freeman and Gasman (2014) researched the characteristics of HBCU presidents and their role in grooming a new generation of leaders. One significant insight raised in their review of the literature is that "sector crossing," or moving between the HBCU and non-HBCU context, is rare among presidents (Freeman & Gasman, 2014). This tendency toward institutional continuity across a president's career suggests that leading HBCUs requires development of different skill sets than leading PWIs. Although sector crossing among senior administrative leaders *can* happen – case in point, the lead author of the current chapter has held roles in PWIs and HBCUs – it is not normative among cabinet-level persons in general, and presidents in particular.

Another salient finding from Freeman and Gasman's (2014) review of the literature on HBCU presidents is how most started their career: as faculty members. This finding also comports with how presidents in general tend to begin their career (Birnbaum & Umbach, 2001). Accordingly, Birnbaum and Umbach (2001) recommended:

> To increase their attractiveness and maximize their opportunities, those seeking the presidency should gain full-time teaching experience early in their career. The data indicate that institutions of higher education still want leaders who have pursued scholarly endeavors prior to entering the administrative ranks.
>
> *(p. 214)*

Firsthand experience as a faculty member can be beneficial as the president interacts with his or her faculty. Freeman et al. (2016) found that supporting, negotiating with, and practicing a form of "shared governance" with faculty is necessary for an effective presidency. One HBCU president with an exclusively student affairs background relayed that academic affairs was "very different" territory for him (Freeman et al., 2016). This president underscored the need to understand issues such as academic freedom, the disciplines, and the overall importance of how the "whole academic process" works. It is easy to see how entering the presidency from a student affairs pathway alone could create barriers.

Of course, the traditional pathway that begins with a faculty role does not negate other pathways (Birnbaum & Umbach, 2001; Dungy & Ellis, 2011; Herring, 2010). As Freeman and Gasman (2014) note, the competencies of an effective HBCU president "are acquired as a leader moves through the academic pipeline but can also be gained outside of academe in similar environments" (p. 13). A number of current HBCU presidents began their career in the K-12 pipeline (Herring, 2010). Therefore, given that student affairs falls *within* academe, it certainly qualifies among the continuum of developmental spaces for the presidency (Kimbrough, 2011). And, as subsequent findings related to the characteristics, skills, and challenges facing HBCU presidents will demonstrate, the parallels with effective senior level student affairs administration are remarkable (Dungy & Ellis, 2011). We see value in highlighting these characteristics, skills, and challenges facing HBCU presidents because meeting them is critical to sustaining HBCUs (Freeman et al., 2016).

HBCU presidents engage in fast-paced work that can challenge work–life balance (Freeman & Gasman, 2014; Herring, 2010). In addition to support from family (e.g., spouse) (Herring, 2010), driving and sustaining many HBCU presidents amidst the pressure is a commitment to future generations. This commitment is sometimes expressed as a desire to promote racial uplift and success among the students they serve (Herring, 2010; Ricard & Brown, 2008). It is also reflected in the tangible work of grooming individuals for a presidential role in an HBCU. Many current HBCU presidents are actively working with two or three mentees (Freeman & Gasman, 2014).

Interestingly, but also predictably, research suggests that HBCU presidents tend to groom future leaders of their gender and in line with the pathway they followed (Freeman & Gasman, 2014). Presidents who emerged from the academic ranks insist on a traditional developmental approach, while those who followed an alternative trajectory espouse the value of transferrable skills as providing ample basis for presidential success (Freeman & Gasman, 2014). Given the relatively large percentage of presidents with traditional credentials, we can infer that few are being intentionally cultivated from student affairs divisions at the present time.

As an aside, the literature related to HBCU presidents and mentoring of future leaders is nearly non-existent (Commodore et al., 2016). Some current presidents are intentionally grooming future presidents (Commodore et al., 2016; Freeman et al., 2016), and there is talk of what succession planning might look like in HBCUs (Carter, 2016). Shadowing is another process that has emerged in the research. According to Commodore et al. (2016), shadowing allows a presidential aspirant to follow an existing leader on a day-to-day basis. Nonetheless, many current presidents report having no formal grooming or shadowing, and no longstanding intentions of becoming a president (Herring, 2010). These presidents evolved into the role, although they do cite general mentoring as having been critical in their overall formation, and they point to presidential role models (e.g., Drs. William Harvey, Johnetta B. Cole, Benjamin Mays, Frederick S. Humphries) as being important figures of inspiration (Herring, 2010).

Also notable, if predictable, is that leadership styles vary among HBCU presidents (Henry, 2009). Some research suggests that leadership styles are often demarcated by age (Freeman & Gasman, 2014). Older presidents might tend to favor a traditional top-down approach, although one must take care not to overgeneralize, practice ageism, or promote negative stereotypes about HBCU leaders that are based more in myth than fact (Freeman et al., 2016). Still, research suggests younger presidents have tended to indicate preferences toward empowerment of people (Freeman & Gasman, 2014). The latter is consistent with the current trend in non-higher education environments toward horizontal, non-autocratic structures in the American knowledge economy and post-industrial age. The trend also aligns with evolving practices in student affairs.

Viewing presidential leadership at HBCUs from another angle, Herring (2010) administered a leadership inventory to 14 sitting HBCU presidents. Six (42.8%) practiced leadership that leveraged "rituals, ceremonies, and symbols instead of guidelines and policies" (p. 68) to create momentum. Examples of such symbols can include homecomings, founder's days, and other significant institutional markers in the life of the college that converge to support a "mystique." Four (28.6%) guided their institution through a frame emphasizing human needs and relationships. Four (28.6%) used a structural approach that focused on goals, roles, and relationships to accomplish goals. Only one participant used a combination. Incidentally, highly effective leaders tend to utilize a combination of approaches depending on the situation (Herring, 2010). Transparency and maintaining campus morale are also valued as leadership traits (Herring, 2010). In another study, Henry (2009) found that HBCU presidents uniformly believe risk-taking is a hallmark of an effective leader.

Challenges facing HBCU presidents have also been identified. Raising funds, interfacing with multiple stakeholders, and crisis management are some such tasks universal to all presidents (Dungy & Ellis, 2011). Differentiating the HBCU presidency from the PWI presidency are two key responsibilities that add qualitatively to the leadership burden. First, they must routinely counter perceptions that HBCUs are unnecessary and obsolete in modern times (Freeman et al., 2016). A measure of political savvy is necessary to navigate and push back on such perceptions without alienating the public. Second, as change agents, HBCU presidents must collaboratively craft an institutional vision that blends a historical mission with the demands of a different contemporary and future milieu (Freeman et al., 2016). Racial diversification, as mentioned earlier in this chapter, is an example where collaborative leadership for institutional vision and change is needed from senior institutional leadership (Arroyo, Palmer et al., 2016).

Amidst the macro challenges cited above, the micro challenge of day-to-day time management has been identified. Herring's (2010) study revealed the tendency of HBCU presidents to find themselves entangled in issues more befitting the vice presidential level. Complaints, disputes, "putting out fires," and the like, consume a great deal of time. Such distractions divert energy from matters that only the president can handle. The frontline nature of student affairs work can provide strong preparation here.

Beyond these challenges – or perhaps intersecting with them – are many other requirements of the HBCU presidency. Freeman et al. (2016) cited four: service, respect for traditions, data-driven decision-making, and accreditation and student engagement. Kimbrough (2011) underscores the need for CSAOs and HBCU presidents to be conversant in collecting and analyzing data for assessment and policy-making purposes. Self-awareness, humility, and the ability to project an executive persona or a "presidential presence" (Commodore et al., 2016) have also been identified as critical attributes. Turning now toward a student affairs model of preparation for the HBCU presidency, we will demonstrate how many of these domains are, or should be, shared by today's senior student affairs administrators, especially at the cabinet level.

Toward a Model of the Highly Effective CSAO Leadership

In this section we advance a model (see Figure 3.1) of the highly effective HBCU student affairs senior leader or CSAO. The model captures critical, high-level roles and competencies associated with operating a modern HBCU in the complex and competitive universe of postsecondary education. A leader who fits this model can be a catalyst for HBCU transformation in a number of ways. First, using this model, a CSAO might transform a division of student affairs and become a more efficacious university-wide leader. Second, the CSAO may utilize the model to aid in preparing for the presidency. Third, a current HBCU president might glean significant insights for defining his or her own role.

We describe the model in the subsequent pages. After issuing a critical caveat regarding the senior leader's need to rely on capable people, we first relate Figure 3.1 exclusively to the CSAO by devoting a section to each component. Focusing first on the CSAO apart from the president is important to create context and ground the model. We then discuss the model's relationship to the HBCU presidency. As noted, this model is a starting point for further discussion regarding senior leadership at HBCUs, rather than the final word.

A Caveat: No Leader Operates Alone

Before describing Figure 3.1 as it relates to the CSAO or president, a caveat is important: No leader, in any organization, operates alone (Dungy & Ellis, 2011). Even the most broadly prepared leader has two limitations, time and capacity. The first limitation, time, is a finite resource and the great equalizer. Every individual has the same 168 hours per week. Every hour expires at the same rate, and no hour can be saved or reclaimed once passed. The second limitation, capacity, can be enlarged through strategic personal and professional development. Nevertheless, capacity remains constrained by the absolute boundaries of one's natural born talent. Some individuals are capable of more, some are capable of less, but no one is capable of all.

Our specific focus on the embedded CSAO and/or the president, therefore, should not be taken as a tacit agreement with any theory that relies on the "Great

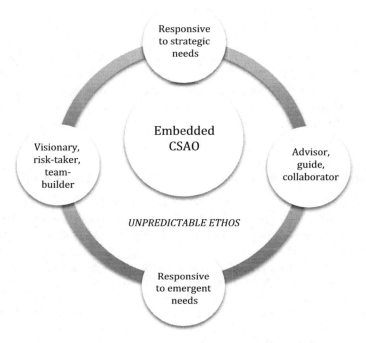

FIGURE 3.1 Model of the Highly Effective HBCU Chief Student Affairs Officer

Man" concept popularized by historian Thomas Carlyle in the nineteenth century. Although we acknowledge the fortuitous emergence of special individuals at key moments in the history of the world, a nation, or an institution, Figure 3.1 espouses a more practical view of everyday organizational leadership. This form of leadership is highly transactional and potentially – hopefully – transformational. It relies on the willingness and ability of the senior leader to acknowledge his or her limitations or weaknesses and to expertly fill in the gaps with competent people. Hetherington (2011) has summarized the situation plainly: "As you assume more responsibility in student affairs, you inevitably are overseeing areas in which you have no expertise" (p. 158).

For example, finance is an area where many senior leaders need more expertise (Barr & McClellan, 2011). Budgetary scrutiny has intensified over recent years. Stakeholders with an interest in monitoring the financial dealings of a university include governmental agencies, accrediting bodies, alumni associations, donors, and many others. Presidential tenures are often cut short by budgetary problems, but CSAOs bear responsibility also. Stewardship of scarce fiscal resources can be pivotal for the CSAO's success. Where acumen is lacking in this important area, the leader would do well to onboard the appropriate expert(s). We revisit this idea later in this chapter.

Student Affairs: An Unpredictable Ethos

We can now turn to Figure 3.1 in relation to the CSAO. At the core of the model is a simple fact: The demands on senior student affairs leaders are qualitatively different compared to other divisional leaders (e.g., vice presidents) in the typical university environment. This difference is due to the unpredictable ethos of the arena to which the CSAO is assigned or "embedded." Acknowledging this backdrop is key for seeing how a CSAO must lead in the student affairs context, and also how the student affairs context can provide a proving ground for the presidency.

To illustrate the unpredictable ethos of student affairs, we can draw a contrast with academic affairs. Divisions of academic affairs are defined by traditions. These traditions tend to be predictable. "There are no emergencies in higher education" is a saying often-heard in academic affairs. Accreditation, curricular planning, committee work, original research projects, and the promotion and tenure process are examples that typify the unhurried pace. Even times during the semester that witness a quickened pace operate on a predictable cycle (e.g., end-of-semester examinations, grading, commencement, registration). Very little happens urgently or off cycle.

Student affairs divisions, too, operate as much as possible by predictable cycles with repetitive activities. However, student affairs divisions exist simultaneously in a very different world – a world where bona fide emergencies *do* exist. Figure 3.1 describes this as an ethos of "24/7" unpredictability. This ethos can devolve from calm to chaos without notice. Preparedness is often tested without warning, and the margin between success and failure can be measured in as little as seconds. An academically struggling student can be identified and brought along by academic affairs over a period of weeks, months, and years. But for a student barricaded in a residence hall room and embroiled in a personal crisis, a day late may be, quite literally, too late. The stakes only grow during a campus-wide catastrophe (e.g., an act of God or a campus shooting). Inclement weather may cancel classes, but residential students still require attention. Days-long weather events can wear on the patience and resources of any institution, and the CSAO is at the center providing active, on-the-ground leadership.

The unpredictable ethos is not exclusive to HBCUs. Student affairs administrators at HBCUs, other MSIs, and PWIs will likely recognize the ethos we have described, as it is common across institutional types. However, what separates institutional types and can add a layer of complexity to the HBCU ethos is thin or stretched resources available to address unpredictable issues. We can take, for example, financial resources. At MSIs generally, annual revenue per full time equivalent student averages approximately $16,648, compared to $29,833 at non-MSIs (Cunningham, Park, & Engle, 2014). Ostensibly, fewer dollars coming into the institution translates into smaller budgets. At HBCUs, finances are consistently identified as among the greatest challenges (Morris, 2016). "Doing more with less" is more than a catchy saying about the yeoman's work of HBCUs; it is a reality with which CSAOs (and presidents) must grapple. This reality provides critical context for the next section of the model on responsiveness to emergent needs.

Responsive to Emergent Needs

According to Figure 3.1, the unpredictable ethos of the student affairs domain – compounded by resource constraints – requires keen responsiveness to emergent needs. An emergent need can arise at any time. It can involve a single student or a whole campus. Consequences of failure to address the need can range from unfortunate to disastrous.

The crisis aspect of student affairs work has no rival on campus save what faces the university president. Although all senior leaders carry an around-the-clock burden to be on-call for the institution during a crisis, the CSAO is often on the front lines. During a crisis, it may be the student affairs leader who briefs the president first and marshals the resources to respond. Even on the average mundane day, student affairs sleeps with one eye open. Between the dismissal of the final evening class – typically in the 9–10pm hour – and the time the campus re-opens to public business in the morning, student affairs personnel remain actively on the job. Compared to the CSAO, no divisional counterpart bears the 24/7 charge for overseeing the thousands of students often left on campus from the close of business to the following morning, including weekends.

It is important to underscore the deliberate verbiage of the model, which is more than rhetorical. Based on the situation we have described thus far, one might define student affairs leadership as fundamentally reactionary. That is to say, event-a transpires, which demands reaction-b, from leader-c, and the cycle repeats. Although this sequence often does describe the chain of events following a crisis, Figure 3.1 frames this aspect of the leader's role more purposefully. True effectiveness in the unpredictable institutional ethos is not reactionary at all. Successful CSAOs are proactive in non-crisis periods, which enables them to respond rather than react during a crisis. A response is a deliberate, grounded approach to addressing and resolving an issue, which is to be distinguished from an off-the-cuff reaction that can produce dissonance or worse. How a leader can respond is discussed next.

Traits and Roles for Emergent Needs

During a crisis, Treadwell (2016) has noted rightly that the individual "most deeply embedded" in the situation is the senior student affairs officer. She writes, "When the worst-case scenario occurs, primary responsibility often falls to student affairs administrators to implement contingency plans, coordinate response efforts, and bring order in the midst of chaos" (Treadwell, 2016, p. 3). Speaking of the senior leader, she writes that his or her "chief role is to guide the campus community through the aftermath," and to "serve as a primary advisor to the university's president, provost, and executive board" (Treadwell, 2016, p. 3).

Given that the highly effective CSAO must be responsive to emergent needs, Figure 3.1 ascribes to this leader three relevant traits and roles. Leaders can and should seek to develop capacity in these areas. First, the leader should be an advisor. Advising is a skill requiring a firm grasp of the facts mixed with the emotional intelligence to know when and how the facts should be delivered. Second, the leader should a guide. As a member of the president's cabinet, this individual should expect to receive the attention of a campus community in need of direction. The leader must be spotlight-ready. Third, the leader should be a collaborator. Whether the CSAO is in the foreground leading the charge, or on the team behind the president, a cooperative posture is indispensible.

The importance of being a collaborator harkens to our introductory caveat. Effective CSAOs depend on others. They welcome 360 degrees of input. When navigating emergent situations, such input minimizes blind spots and the likelihood of error. Ideally, the leader will have had the opportunity to develop a strong team before the crisis. This is a strategic matter, which is addressed next.

Responsive to Strategic Needs

Up to this point, Figure 3.1 has reframed the most universally accepted function of the senior student affairs leader, responsiveness to emergent needs. And yet, responsiveness to emergent needs is a necessary but insufficient condition for true CSAO effectiveness. A complete senior leader must also be responsive to *strategic* needs. Student affairs must be more than an insurance policy that is drawn upon when needed and shelved when not. Successful CSAOs must be proactive in many other areas beyond the crisis, and preferably, before the crisis.

Responsiveness to strategic needs requires a more progressive vision for the CSAO. This vision reimagines the role as it could be in a high-functioning HBCU. Therefore, before we can discuss the CSAO individually, we must consider student affairs divisionally. We should take a step back to think about student affairs divisions as a whole.

We already know an essential institutional role of student affairs divisions is to respond swiftly and deftly in crises. But does student affairs have another role within the institution, a role of complementary and equal significance? We suggest it can. The other role of a student affairs division can be to ask and answer a fundamental but profound question: What does the institution need?

Framed after that question, a division of student affairs can address critical gaps – and, in addressing those gaps, it can build innovative bridges of practice across a university. Notable gaps at many HBCUs center on holistic student engagement and academic success (Arroyo, Ericksen, Walker, & Aregano, 2016; Walker, Arroyo, & Willis, 2016). Needed are responsive divisions of student affairs that are pioneering and adept at building bridges with other divisions, especially academic affairs.

Although the focus of this chapter is conceptual, we can offer a concrete example of a pioneering, bridge-building initiative at Norfolk State University, the public HBCU where we serve at the time of this writing. Together with colleagues, we developed the first non-Eurocentric, HBCU-based model of learning communities (see Arroyo, Ericksen et al., 2016; Ericksen & Walker, 2015; Ericksen, Walker, Laws, Fitzgerald, & Burwell, 2015; Walker et al., 2016). Figure 3.2 displays the model we created and instituted at our HBCU with colleagues. The reader can note in the model the partnership between student and academic affairs. What the reader cannot see is the origination point of the

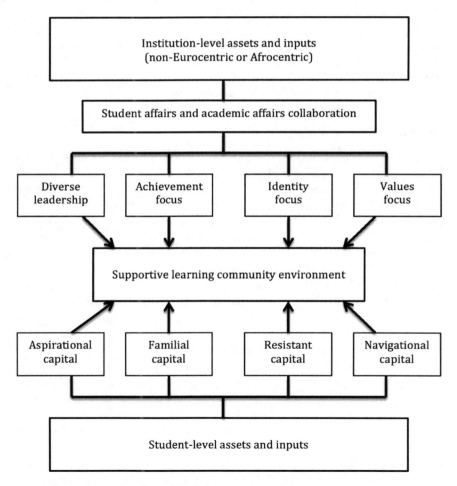

FIGURE 3.2   HBCU–Based Model of Learning Communities

initiative, which began with the division of student affairs looking for gaps, and then focusing significant resources and outreach to academic affairs, over a period of years, to formulate the learning communities partnership. Seeking to be responsive to strategic needs, student affairs demonstrated this concept in action.

Traits and Roles for Strategic Needs

In light of this expanded picture of student affairs as a division capable of meeting strategic institutional needs, Figure 3.1 states that the CSAO must be responsive to strategic needs. This means taking leadership in posing the key question, "What does the institution need?," and then setting out to fill the need.

At least three traits and roles are essential for strategic responsiveness, each of which is specified in the model. First, the leader should be a visionary. Having vision means seeing things as they could be rather than seeing things (only) as they are. Second, the leader should be a risk-taker. Seeing is an important starting point; but action must soon follow. Bold CSAOs are needed who will move carefully but decisively in an uncharted direction. Third, the leader should be a team-builder. This role again ties to the caveat that no leader operates alone. From a strategic standpoint, a CSAO is needed who will know how to identify and place talent in the right places, and then how to facilitate the entire team's productivity. Team building is a skill that takes time to develop, and teams are not constructed overnight. When the crisis strikes, a senior leader must collaborate. The question is whether the leader will collaborate with a random collection of individuals he or she has inherited, or with the team he or she has strategically built.

It is necessary at this point to underscore the difficulty of becoming a strategy-oriented CSAO. As the saying goes, if it were easy, everyone would be doing it. The reality of higher education environments – including HBCUs – is that CSAOs and the divisions they lead are not typically associated with this form of university-wide leadership. More often, the status quo is left unquestioned. Institutional leadership is viewed as the domain of boards, the president, the provost and vice president for academic affairs, and perhaps a vice president for finance. As noted, student affairs vice presidents tend to yield to their colleagues, becoming visible and vocal only when called upon during a crisis. Figure 3.1 offers a distinct alternative that positions the CSAO to be a catalyst for HBCU transformation – and, perhaps, even via the presidency.

From CSAO to the Presidency

A close examination of Figure 3.1 demonstrates that it is easily relatable to the HBCU presidency either as a training ground for the presidency or as a point of reflection and tool of improvement for current presidents. Highly effective HBCU CSAOs possess the knowledge, skills, and abilities foundational for a successful HBCU presidency. Although academics are a university's core enterprise, the president's day-to-day role better approximates the student affairs unpredictable ethos than the traditions-based environment of academic affairs. Such an organization must balance responsiveness to emergent and strategic needs in an unpredictable ethos, which is the milieu described in Figure 3.1.

Despite the relative lack of empirical research on HBCU presidents, the extant research reviewed earlier in this chapter supports several key dynamics housed in the model. The most salient connections garnered from that literature and Figure 3.1 are offered below. For example, the literature supports the notion underlying Figure 3.1 that no effective leader operates alone. HBCU presidents whose backgrounds are exclusively in student affairs may find a steep learning curve in matters of academic affairs. The current chapter has also broached the critical importance of strong fiscal expertise in the modern HBCU – expertise that some presidents might lack. In these and other situations, Figure 3.1 suggests that the CSAO-turned-president can succeed by appropriately relying on cabinet-level experts to oversee those areas. Senior leaders should identify their weaknesses and recruit talented individuals to form a complete team.

The point about team building cannot be over-stressed. There is no one-to-one comparison between the presidency and any prior job a president can hold. Complexities surrounding the presidency are unlike any other office. Problems result when leaders fail to honestly account for their own weaknesses and proceed with an inflated sense of self.

Other lessons from the research literature on HBCU presidents can be related directly to Figure 3.1. One such lesson is the pace of work. The literature describes the presidential workload as incredibly fast paced and defined by "putting out fires." Viewed through the lens of the model, in any given day a president might have to respond both to emergent needs and strategic needs. Best-laid efforts to foster a predictable campus defined by distributed leadership can bolster a campus against many storms, but it cannot insulate the president from the need for 24/7 availability and immediacy in critical scenarios.

Figure 3.1 also speaks to the issue of leadership style. The research literature suggests that presidents tend to differ in leadership styles. Although by no means exclusive to emerging presidents, the empowering leadership style tends to be associated with younger presidents than their elder counterparts. Moreover, the empowering leadership style is also essential to fully operationalize Figure 3.1. One might conceive of ways autocratic leadership styles could interface with the model, but the model is fundamentally dependent on a team-based approach. Thus, while the HBCU president may be a "strong" rather than "weak" president, achieving the ideals of Figure 3.1 will require the president not to be averse to sharing power. Stated differently, Figure 3.1 rests on the assumption that power sharing requires true strength, and leads to true effectiveness, not the inverse. Examples of current HBCU presidents whose leadership styles embody Figure 3.1 include Drs. David Wilson (Morgan State University), Tashni-Ann Dubroy (Shaw University), Harry L. Williams (Delaware State University), and Michael J. Sorrell (Paul Quinn College), to name only four.

Another lesson of Figure 3.1 for the CSAO-turned-president is the challenge of messaging. A core requirement of the model is that the leader understands how to act as a visionary and communicate across multiple constituencies. President Walter M. Kimbrough (Dillard University) is renowned for his powerful and strategic use of social media (@HipHopPrez on Twitter). The research literature on HBCU presidents suggests also that presidents face the challenge of leading their institutions into the future in a manner that respects their histories. They must do this while satisfying diverse sets of stakeholders, requiring a careful balance of risk-taking and collaboration.

These lessons are a sample of many ways Figure 3.1 applies to the HBCU presidency. In sum, if the HBCU president excels in the conceptual ideals conveyed through the model, the result can be an exceptionally strong HBCU that will be positioned to become and remain a model for other institutions, including other MSIs and PWIs.

Implications for Research and Practice

The model introduced in this chapter contains noteworthy implications for research and practice. As the review of the relevant literature established, we know very little about the roles of CSAO and president at HBCUs. Each area offers ample opportunity for empirical investigation. Examinations of the transition from CSAO to president at HBCUs are also needed, in addition to explorations of the experiences of current HBCU presidents whose background was student affairs. Moreover, studies are needed to explore the efficacy of Figure 3.1 for promoting effective CSAO leadership, challenges associated with implementing the model, and the model's transferability to the HBCU presidency. Research of this sort can contribute to new theories of HBCU leadership, which are needed in this emerging area of study (Esters & Strayhorn, 2013).

Practitioners are encouraged to utilize the current chapter in several ways. All practitioners should be familiar with the relevant literature pertaining to senior leadership at HBCUs. Lessons can be gleaned from the literature, which can inform effective practice. Aspiring HBCU leaders can draw from Figure 3.1 as they consider developmental areas on which to focus. Current CSAOs and presidents can use Figure 3.1 as an assessment tool. They can self-assess against the ideals of Figure 3.1, and also they can ask trusted mentors, advisors, and team members to evaluate them on the same basis. Needed are CSAOs and presidents who are willing to lead the way in honest self-assessment for the sake of becoming their very best.

Conclusion

This chapter has addressed the topic of leadership at HBCUs by advancing a model of highly effective CSAO leadership, with implications for the HBCU presidency. MSIs are leaders in American higher education, and HBCUs are leaders among MSIs. Models of senior leadership, such as the one advanced here, can assist with ensuring the perpetual continuation of that critical role.

References

Arroyo, A.T., Ericksen, K.S., Walker, J.M., & Aregano, P.E. (2016). Toward an HBCU-based model of living-learning communities. In C. Prince & R. Ford (Eds.), *Setting a new agenda for student engagement and retention at historically Black colleges and universities* (pp. 80–95). Hershey, PA: IGI Global.

Arroyo, A.T., & Gasman, M. (2014). An HBCU-based approach for Black college student success: With implications for all institutions. *American Journal of Education*, 121(1), 57–85.

Arroyo, A.T., Palmer, R.T., & Maramba, D.C. (2016). Is it a different world? Providing a holistic understanding of the experiences and perceptions of non-Black students of historically Black colleges and universities. *Journal of College Student Retention: Research, Theory, & Practice*, 18(3), 360–382.

Arroyo, A.T., Palmer, R.T., Maramba, D.C., & Louis, D.A. (2016). Exploring the efforts of HBCU student affairs practitioners to support non-Black students. *Journal of Student Affairs Research and Practice*, 54(1). Online.

Barr, M.J., & McClellan, G.S. (2011). *Budgets and financial management in higher education*. San Francisco, CA: Jossey-Bass.

Birnbaum, R., & Umbach, P.D. (2001). Scholar, steward, spanner, stranger: The four career paths of college presidents. *The Review of Higher Education*, 24(3), 203–217.

Carter, J. (2016). What happens when hero presidents leave HBCUs? *HBCUdigest.com*. Retrieved from https://hbcudigest.com/what-happens-when-hero-presidents-leave-hbcus-85c64aa1088d#.83lvw4pgp

Commodore, F., Freeman, S., Gasman, M., & Carter, C.M. (2016). "How it's done": The role of mentoring and advice in preparing the next generation of historically Black college and university presidents. *Education Sciences*, 6(19), 1–14.

Conrad, C.F., & Gasman, M. (2015). *Educating a diverse nation: Lessons from minority-serving institutions*. Cambridge, MA: Harvard University Press.

Cunningham, L., Park, E., & Engle, J. (2014). *Minority-serving institutions: Doing more with less*. Washington, DC: Institution for Higher Education Policy.

Dungy, G.J., & Ellis, S.E. (Eds.) (2011). *Exceptional senior student affairs administrators' leadership: Strategies and competencies for success*. Washington, DC: National Association of Student Personnel Administrators.

Ericksen, K.S., & Walker, J. (2015). The value of academic and student affairs collaboration: Living-learning communities at HBCUs. *Journal of Research Initiatives*, 1(3), article 2.

Ericksen, K.S., Walker, J., Laws, P., Fitzgerald, F., & Burwell, C. (2015). Inventing and implementing LLCs at an HBCU in one year: Lessons learned. *Learning Communities Research and Practice*, 3(2), article 5.

Esters, L.L., & Strayhorn, T.L. (2013). Demystifying the contributions of public land-grant historically Black colleges and universities: Voices of HBCU presidents. *The Negro Educational Review*, 64(1–4), 119–134.

Esters, L.T., Washington, A., Gasman, M., Commodore, F., O'Neal, B., Freeman, S., Carter, C., & Jimenez, C.D. (2016). *Effective leadership: A toolkit for the 21st-century historically Black college and university*. Philadelphia, PA: Penn Center for Minority Serving Institutions.

Freeman, S., Commodore, F., Gasman, M., & Carter, C. (2016). Leaders wanted! The skills expected and needed for a successful 21st century historically Black college and university presidency. *Journal of Black Studies*, 47(6), 570–591.

Freeman, S., & Gasman, M. (2014). The characteristics of historically Black college and university presidents and their role in grooming the next generation of leaders. *Teachers College Record*, 116, 1–34.

Gasman, M. (2011). Perceptions of Black college presidents: Sorting through stereotypes and reality to gain a complex picture. *American Education Research Journal*, 48, 836–870.

Gasman, M., Baez, B., & Turner, C. (Eds.) (2008). *Understanding minority-serving institutions*. New York: SUNY Press.

Gasman, M., Nguyen, T., & Conrad, C.F. (2015). Lives intertwined: A primer on the emergence of minority serving institutions. *Journal of Diversity in Higher Education*, 8(2), 120–138.

Harper, S.R., & Kimbrough, W.M. (2005). Staffing practices, professional preparation trends, and demographics among student affairs administrators at HBCUs: Implications from a national study. *NASPA Journal*, 8(1), 8–25.

Henry, S.M. (2009). *Project demonstrating excellence: A study of the personal and professional characteristics of historically Black college and university (HBCU) presidents* (Unpublished doctoral dissertation). Union Institute & University, Cincinnati, OH.

Herring, P.M. (2010). *Historically Black college and university presidents: Personal and professional challenges, career paths, and leadership characteristics* (Unpublished doctoral dissertation). Fayetteville State University, Fayetteville, NC.

Hetherington, K. (2011). A community college student affairs officer's perspective. In G.J. Dungy & S.E. Ellis (Eds.), *Exceptional senior student affairs administrators' leadership: strategies and competencies for success* (pp. 153–162). Washington, DC: National Association of Student Affairs Personnel.

Hirt, J.B., Bennett, B.R., Strayhorn, T.L., & Amelink, C.T. (2006). "What really matters": The nature of rewards for student affairs administrators at historically Black colleges and universities. *NASPA Journal*, 9(1), 83–99.

Hirt, J.B., Amelink, C.T., McFeeters, B.B., & Strayhorn, T.L. (2008). A system of other-mothering: Relationships between student affairs administrators and students at historically Black colleges and universities. *NASPA Journal*, 45, 210–236.

Kimbrough, W.M. (2011). Just the facts. In G.J. Dungy & S.E. Ellis (Eds.), *Exceptional Senior Student Affairs Administrators' Leadership: Strategies and Competencies for Success* (pp. 183–187). Washington, DC: National Association of Student Personnel Administrators.

Long, D. (2012). The foundations of student affairs: A guide to the profession. In L.J. Hinchliffe & M.A. Wong (Eds.), *Environments for student growth and development: Librarians and student affairs in collaboration* (pp. 1–39). Chicago: Association of College & Research Libraries.

Love, P.G., & Estanek, S.M. (2004). *Rethinking student affairs practice*. San Francisco, CA: Jossey-Bass.

Morris, C. (2016, October 24). Stakeholders cite leadership instability, finances as HBCUs' greatest challenges. *Diverse Issues in Higher Education*. Retrieved from http://diverseeducation.com/article/88473/

Nehls, K. (2015). Presidencies derailed: Why university leaders fail and how to prevent it. [Review of the book *Presidencies derailed: Why university leaders fail and how to prevent it*, by S.J. Trachtenberg, G.B. Kauvar, & E.G. Bogue]. *The Review of Higher Education*, 38(3), 476–478.

Palmer, R.T., Arroyo, A.T., & Maramba, D.C. (2016). Understanding the perceptions of HBCU student affairs practitioners toward non-Black students. *Journal of Diversity in Higher Education*. Online.

Perna, L.W., Lundy-Wagner, V., Drezner, N., Gasman, M., Yoon, S., Bose, E., & Gary, S. (2009). The contribution of HBCUs to the preparation of African American women for STEM careers: A case study. *Research in Higher Education*, 50, 1–23.

Porterfield, K.T., & Whitt, E.J. (2016). Past, present, and future: Contexts for current challenges and opportunities for student affairs leadership. *New Directions for Student Services*, 153, 9–17.

Ricard, R.B., & Brown, M.C. (2008). *Ebony towers in higher education: The evolution, mission, and presidency of historically Black colleges and universities*. Sterling, VA: Stylus Publishing.

Roper, L.D., & Whitt, E.J. (2016). What troubles you? What keeps you up at night? *New Directions for Student Services*, 153, 19–37.

Trachtenberg, S.J., Kauvar, G.B., & Bogue, E.G. (2013). *Presidencies derailed: Why university leaders fail and how to prevent it*. Baltimore, MD: Johns Hopkins University Press.

Treadwell, K.L. (2016). Learning from tragedy: Student affairs leadership following college campus disasters. *Journal of Student Affairs Research and Practice*, 54(1), 52–54.

Walker, J.M., Arroyo, A.T., & Willis, E.M. (2016, March). Living-learning communities: Fostering collaboration to promote holistic student success. Paper presented at the 98th NASPA Annual Conference, Indianapolis, IN.

4

AVOIDING FORCED TURNOVER(S)

Best Practices for HBCU Senior-Level Executive Recruitment

William J. Broussard and Adriel Hilton

Recent announcements of HBCU executive departures and hirings in the first six months of the 2017 academic year leave some campuses and alumni brimming with excitement and others wallowing in regret, confusion, and a profound sense of loss. In the 2016–17 academic year alone, Wilberforce, Arkansas Baptist College, Grambling State University, Southern University-New Orleans, and the Southern University and A&M College Agricultural Research Center will welcome new leadership, support staffs, and renewed vigor around their institutional missions and North Carolina Central University, Bennett College, Johnson C. Smith, Florida A&M University, Allen University, Jackson State University, Alabama State University, and Bowie State University face the prospect of searching for new leadership, direction, and stability. Far from a recent trend, the startlingly high number of HBCU executive departures is a decades-long trend for many institutions, and these come on the heels of a year in which 34 out of the 107 HBCUs announced a chief executive transaction (Broussard, 2016). While this excessive turnover rate often makes for negative press and a debilitating narrative for HBCU institutional progress, a closer look reveals that the problem is much more severe and impactful than the ensuing negative news cycles.

Research on HBCUs often focuses on several themes, including: critical issues facing HBCUs in the current higher education marketplace (Association of Governing Boards of Universities and Colleges, n.d.); revisions to the university mission (Clay, 2012; Minor, 2008); development of enrollment and recruiting strategies (Clay, 2012); strategic initiatives to increase retention (Clay, 2012; Esters and Strayhorn, 2013; Minor, 2008); developing new programs of study (Clay, 2012; Eckel & King, 2004); strategic planning for facility construction and upgrades (Clay, 2012; Brown and Burnette, 2014); enhanced campus life and student development programming (Clay, 2012); using social and traditional media as cost effective marketing (Gasman, 2012; Gasman & Bowman, 2011); increased fundraising, grant-writing, and lobbying of local, state, and federal government (Gasman, 2010, 2013; Gasman & Bowman 2011; Liou, Davis, & Ards, 2007; Minor, 2008; Robinson, 2013), and germane to this commentary, recruiting and developing executive teams (Clay, 2012; Robinson, 2013) as well as HBCU executive leadership crises (Gasman, 2016; Meggett, 1996; Nelms, 2014). Additional studies suggest that an aging pool of current presidents, chiefs of staff, provosts, and executive vice presidents presents an opportunity to appoint diverse leadership talent in the coming decade (American Council on Education, 2008, 2012; Gasman, 2013).

Senior staff recruitment (e.g. Provost/Chief Operating Officers, Chiefs of Staff/ Administration, Chief Advancement Officers, Communications, Intercollegiate Athletics, Human Resources, and Technology/Chief Information Officer executives) remains a challenge because of salary considerations, perceived cultural and political challenges, and public discussion about audit, resource, and student recruitment and retention challenges across the HBCU sector. An additional challenge that often goes unconsidered is how executive turnover impacts the lives and careers of senior-staff administrators at HBCUs *after* the CEOs depart. In particular, the collective experiences of administrators who have decided to accept appointments at HBCUs despite the aforementioned challenges often go unconsidered when the presidential-level transactions garner the headlines. Invariably, those individuals have their lives uprooted and careers derailed, creating a scenario in which they (and perhaps their extended networks of talented and well-credentialed colleagues) may be less likely to pursue career opportunities at HBCUs (Gasman & Commodore, 2014).

At HBCUs, it is customary that the president/CEO starts his or her appointment with senior-level executives in tow, or in mind upon arrival. Therefore, the experience of senior-level executives at HBCUs can be as transient as their presidential executive colleagues. A prevailing perception at most predominantly White institutions (PWIs) is that senior-level executives, if not retained in current positions, are placed in other roles where their talents and expertise can be utilized to aid the university community; however, at HBCUs that is not often the case. This explains an underlying challenge to recruiting a talented and diverse pool of candidates for career opportunities at HBCUs. HBCUs must not only use available data to identify prospects that have previously been prepared or groomed for that institution's success at that given moment, but also recruit against the pernicious typecasting that accepting such positions comes with increased professional and reputational risk.

In past decades, HBCU leadership and those in senior-level executive roles appeared to serve campuses for longer periods. While serving longer periods of time, the leadership established rapport and became friends with close colleagues as well as those outside of the institution. However, the current culture and environment at a significant number of HBCUs precludes personnel from building such important relationships both within and outside the institution, creating tumult for the campus communities and employees while leaving vacuums in leadership. Personnel are not comfortable opening up to others as they may not be present the next week or even the next day, and it can be nearly impossible to determine those individuals' loyalties, ulterior motives, and motivations. Constant turnover at the helm of these institutions has impacted the profile and talent at the institutions significantly, and not just in the Office of the President.

As a result of the increasing occurrence of presidential derailments, HBCU advocates and those that would like to work at HBCUs ask, "What protections are in place for candidates and their families if they become employed at an HBCU?" and "What guarantees are in place that will allow them to perform their job responsibilities without interruption both to serve institutional needs and advance their careers?" Even though a significant number of talented leaders consider it a career goal to work at HBCUs in middle manager and senior-level roles, they opt to be employed at PWIs or higher education associations as a result of this unknown. For those senior-level executives that do elect to assume leadership roles at HBCUs, when presidents are ousted, potential negative experiences may occur. These experiences may include depression, indefinite unemployment and salary interruption, and the potential of harming one's reputation to gain entrée to academe in the future. In addition, aspirant, well-credentialed, and competent individuals building solid curricula vitae and serving student and institutional needs admirably can find their careers derailed for no other reason than the fact that the executive who hired them has been terminated, non-renewed, or has resigned. These negative experiences will continue to keep dynamic persons from leadership roles at HBCUs, despite their cultural importance, historical relevance, and rich traditions.

Excessive executive turnover at HBCUs over prolonged periods significantly hampers the recruitment, hiring, and retention of talented faculty and administrative subordinates who fuel HBCU advancement. This not only results in a challenge for public relations and marketing, but it also represents a persistent existential threat to an already vulnerable sector of higher education, particularly to emerging executives attempting to build careers who are potential heirs and heiresses to HBCU presidencies and chancellorships. A review of scholarship examining the existential and market-driven challenges that HBCUs face in the twenty-first century suggests the overwhelming challenges and inherent risks associated with accepting offers of executive and administrative appointments at HBCUs not just for presidents, but for their most crucial hires – senior staff-level administrators.

Literature Review

The aforementioned risks are particularly pernicious for young administrators being offered non-tenure track/non-contract based administrative and executive positions. Whereas seasoned higher education executives are often protected by tenure (either earned while serving significant terms on the faculty at an institution, or, offered as contract incentive for qualified executives) or long-term contract clauses that guarantee reassignment or negotiated buyouts, executive level administrators without such protections are exposed to the same risks of termination as their hiring benefactors with little to no downside protection, particularly those who work at colleges, universities, or in states that are defined as "at-will" employers.

Even the most uncontroversial executive transitions. resulting from presidents or chancellors who leave without scandal or in a haze of speculation and/or as a result of board or legislative chicanery, present challenges to new leaders who inherit market-based as well as internal crises. New executives recruit support staffs to take on these challenges in often adversarial and political climates and discover almost immediately that the odds against them are stacked high. Clay (2012) points out that HBCU executives must engage in: 1) Clarification, restating, or updating of mission; 2) Changes in enrollment strategy to attract and enroll stronger students; 3) A method to address the needs of less-well-prepared students who might have been admitted in the past but are not admitted now; 4) New majors or programs to address local opportunities; 5) *Strong focus on recruiting a competent and experienced executive team* (emphasis added); 6) Strategic allocation of new faculty hires; 7) Support for and investment in research infrastructure; 8) A campus plan to prioritize opportunities for new construction and major renovation; (and) 9) Enhanced campus life and student development, including facilities and support (pp. 34–35). While some new HBCU presidents will inherit fully staffed cabinets and executive leadership staffs, they will be inevitably tasked with reviewing their performance and in many instances, be forced to make controversial decisions that terminate their employment. Additionally, Gasman (2010) points out that HBCUs in the twenty-first century marketplace:

> must proactively protect and promote their images," "instill a culture of philanthropic giving with their students and alumni," "(encourage) board members to be the lead givers," "invest in more sophisticated databases that more accurately capture their alumni capacity," and "educate their alumni about the make-up of their funding streams," which necessitates the identification of professionals with these skill sets and experience (p. 7).

Particularly when these newly integrated processes promote dramatic culture shifts, led by newly added staff members (who are often placed in charge of staffs without those skill sets and who are unfamiliar with twenty-first century higher education best practices), newly hired executive administrators inherit the controversy and challenges of their presidential leaders often without the protection of long-term contracts or tenure.

Given the precedence of fiduciary concerns at HBCUs, driven by enrollment declines, smaller comparative endowments at private institutions, and dwindling state subsidies to public institutions, new HBCU executives are under the gun to embrace innovative and often controversial solutions that can infuriate alumni, challenge closely held traditions, and take universities in directions that are resisted stiffly by supporters who do not understand the untenable nature of not reviewing and revising the institution's model. Arnett (2015, 2016) suggests that a growing concern among public higher education presidents is continuing reductions in state support, and the possibility that higher education faces a future in which the enterprise may not be publicly funded. Particularly among HBCU presidents, there is a concern that even executives who face these crises head on and grow enrollment, increase private fundraising, and develop new programs face termination when their newly introduced policies upset constituents who criticize their processes or leadership styles. Among private HBCUs, Robinson (2013) notes that executives must be excellent fundraisers, which requires "assertive leadership of the President" in order to overcome "the perception of inferior education" by articulating "a value proposition to internal and external stakeholders" (p. 51). Presidents cannot carry out these new initiatives alone, so the selection of administrators who can is critical. These scenarios require bold and controversial decisions and place inordinate pressure on new executives that are particularly dangerous when those decisions must be made and executed under persistent criticism from internal and external stakeholders by individuals whose continued employment is vulnerable. The perception of extremely high turnover at HBCUs makes this prospect all the more difficult, leading excellent prospects to hesitate to accept positions when offered.

Perceived risks associated with administrators and cabinet-level executives accepting positions at HBCUs also threaten pipelines of HBCU executives, increasing the harm from a current crisis to one that stretches long into the future. As Lewis (1988) points out, "Black college presidents identified their families, role models, professional network, and mentors as being important in their career development" (p. 1). It stands to reason that HBCU presidents will look to their professional networks to continue the process of mentorship. However, given the risk associated with accepting an HBCU presidency, these risks are then extended to those in their networks who become part of their leadership teams, and if administrators early in their careers face terminations or reassignments under controversial circumstances that lead to the terminations of the presidents who hire them, their careers can be derailed and their desire to work at HBCUs reduced. Freeman and Gasman (2014) echo these sentiments, noting that there is a widespread perception that some HBCU presidents over-stay their welcomes while other HBCUs tend to "recycle" presidents, and both of these scenarios are enabled by a lack of qualified executives in the pipeline being mentored to lead HBCUs. This underscores the need for identifying and retaining qualified and talented senior-staffers not only to support presidential efforts to successfully conduct operations, but to strengthen the pipeline for presidential leadership.

Proposed Solutions

While the challenges facing HBCU presidents/chancellors with regard to assembling leadership teams are considerable, their salaries and contracts provide significant protection against the hazards of tempestuous boards, temperamental alumni, and mercurial legislative whims. With administrative tenures growing shorter each year (American Council on Education, 2009), HBCU presidents recruiting senior leadership team members should identify strategies that safeguard, to the best of their and their institutions' abilities, against the turmoil that too often impacts higher education professionals when executive turnover occurs. While substantial scholarship exists regarding approaches to contract negotiations for faculty and athletics professionals in higher education and legal remedies to no-cause related terminations, a dearth of scholarship exists that provides direction to other administrative professionals in the contract negotiation process, particularly administrators proactively negotiating a potential transition to the professoriate, which we will explore in a following section (Sale, 2013). The authors recommend that prospects for these positions should seek first the obvious protections gained by researching the employment history, performance, and results of predecessors at prospective institutions, becoming knowledgeable about political concerns at the state level, diving into institutional history, and contacting industry professionals for feedback. Additionally, anyone considering accepting a cabinet-level administrative appointment should 1) Gain as much protection as possible in the contract negotiation process, including requesting tenure or accelerated tenure-track faculty appointments (for qualified individuals with terminal degrees and extensive teaching experience), and 2) Negotiate multi-year contracts with institutionally appropriate performance standards written into their evaluations. Institutions looking to attract excellently qualified senior staffers should also 3) Embrace administrators versed in and capable of "disruptive" industry practices to accelerate growth and benchmark successes, and 4) Emphasize marketing and branding efforts to counteract and counter-narrate negative elements about HBCUs that permeate the media and higher education literature, while engaging in sourcing and succession planning that allows for the advanced recruitment of potential team members. According to Jarrett L. Carter, HBCU industry expert and founding editor of HBCUDigest.com, these four practices are "paramount to the success of all HBCUs as well as their leaders, be they new to the HBCU presidency/chancellorship or seasoned veterans" (J.L. Carter, personal communication, December 16, 2016).

Identifying Senior Leadership Eligible for Tenure or Accelerated Tenure-Track Faculty Appointments

Considering the relatively small size of most HBCUs with regard to faculty rolls (not to mention the financial challenges that HBCUs are facing writ large, forcing many to supplement full-time faculty rolls with adjunct faculty to maintain the low student to teacher ratios HBCUs are known for), HBCU presidents/chancellors should place a premium on recruiting administrators who are qualified to teach at the assistant/associate professor level in their discipline. Ample research on tenure negotiations for full-time faculty suggests a focus on salary negotiation, teaching loads, research, service, and teaching requirements, sabbaticals, teaching releases, moving expenses and startup money, endowment support for research and teaching/research assistance, supplies, support for conference travel, and various negotiations based on institutional type (Kelly, 2014; Kelsky, 2014; Milgram, 2010; Golde, 1999). Few scholars have addressed tenure negotiation for administrators transitioning into faculty roles (Sale, 2013 is a notable exception), and the authors struggled to identify scholarship that addresses tenure negotiation for qualified administrators accepting full-time administrative positions who wish to continue teaching, producing research, and serving within their disciplines and in their communities in ways commensurate with tenure-track faculty. Based on available research, and the vulnerability of administrators to termination at high-turnover institutions, entering into and proposing tenure-track appointments can be a win–win for institutions and administrators who need the protection of a more permanent employment opportunity. Jarvis Christian College Director of Institutional Research Urban Wiggins, when searching for a new senior-staff level position at an HBCU, was "attracted by a joint faculty appointment" during his search process (U. Wiggins, personal communication, December 17, 2016). Serving additionally as an Assistant Professor and Director of data analytics, Wiggins will also be eligible to perform faculty-related work (teaching, research, and service) and use his background (Ph.D. in computer science) teaching classes and developing student programming. Seasoned and diversely qualified professionals of this sort not only enhance accreditation efforts by adding to the professoriate, but they are a significant value proposition and they can serve to unite the faculty and administration, and put a face on executive administrators for the students. While it adds to the overall workload for full-time administrators who must teach and produce research, the professional and institutional benefits merit the consideration.

While it is not necessarily common that senior-level leaders with extensive experience in areas such as facility management/enhancement, university advancement, intercollegiate athletics, and chief operating officers have backgrounds conducive for dual faculty roles, this is an area for paradigm shifting in the recruiting processes of HBCU executives. HBCUs should not only recognize their rich traditions and history as critical to its recruitment, retention, and revenue-generation efforts, but should also embrace the crises they are facing to take appropriate steps of redeveloping their current business models (Association of Governing Boards of Universities and Colleges, n.d.). While HBCUs must focus on repairing aging infrastructures on their campuses, they would be well-served to embrace best practices and even develop new approaches to leadership that may be prevalent in other sectors of not only higher education, but across the public and private sector. In order to lead in this way, HBCU executives should consider the recruitment of scholar-practitioners whose education *and* experience have prepared them to lead in innovative ways. Recruiting upper-level administrators with advanced degrees not only in higher education leadership, but in organizational and non-profit leadership, business and sport administration/management, as well as established scholars with extensive professional and governmental networks experienced in fundraising, grant-writing, and fund-securing will bring invaluable experience and assets into the fold, and foster innovation in ways critical to the success of HBCUs in the twenty-first century.

The benefits of assembling senior leadership teams with credentials and experience not only in their areas of administrative oversight, but in the classroom, extend beyond the value proposition, innovation, potential revenue generation, and accreditation efforts. The main reason that HBCU presidents should assemble senior leadership teams who can contribute to the faculty is that it is the most crucial contribution that a president can make to an institution. As former University of Arizona president, Ann Weaver Hart noted:

> faculty leadership is so vital. It binds an institution of higher education together, making it into a community of learning where teaching, research, and community engagement work together and respond to the challenges of our world in creating the social, economic, scientific, artistic, and other benefits that we all expect from our nation's great universities.
>
> *(2014, p. 1)*

Additionally, according to industry expert Crystal deGregory, founder of HBCUstory.org:

> No matter what else you offer – fine dining via chain fast food restaurants, dormitories tricked out with cable, homecoming concerts with A-list artists, etc. – education is your product. It is your service. It is why (we) are here, and why (our) students are here, despite the propensity for them, and institutions, to act and recruit otherwise.
>
> *(deGregory, personal communication, December 16, 2016)*

The most pristine facilities, successful fundraising efforts, and state of the art recruitment strategies do not produce the most desired outcomes for institutions of higher education – education, retention, and graduation. Every other factor that universities are measured (and have their funding based) on is either an extension of or is in service to those key elements, and faculty directly impact the aforementioned elements more than administrators or presidents can. Moreover, when it comes to developing the kind of regional and national reputation that impacts recruitment, grants, and corporate partnerships, and state legislature decision-making with regard to subsidies, excellent faculty leadership is crucial.

Administrators who can contribute to the vibrancy of the faculty in the classroom by sharing important professional and networking mentorship to students as well as lending the reputations they've developed in regional and national associations by publishing and presenting at conferences to their new employers are a unique and incredibly important contribution that presidential recruiting efforts can effect.

Negotiating Multi-Year Contracts with Key Performance Indicators

A second protection and recruitment best practice that HBCU presidents/chancellors can offer potential senior leadership team members is a multi-year, performance-based contract. Private HBCUs have much more flexibility to offer such contracts, considering that they only seek board approval, and some public HBCUs may be more limited given their need to comply with larger system-board or state rules and union policies. However, to the extent that HBCU presidents/chancellors can successfully negotiate multi-year, performance-based contracts for new leadership team hires, new hires have the added benefit of both protection against premature contract termination as a result of executive turnover, and, a clear set of directives and "key performance indicators" (KPI) that can be implemented to guarantee growth, production, and contract fulfillment. While many boards and presidents with financial challenges may be tempted to shy away from multi-year contracts for fear that an underperforming staffer's impact on the budget may become protracted, combining a multi-year contract with an annual performance review provides an opportunity for the president/chancellor to provide feedback to the administrator, offer transparency to stakeholders (e.g. via annual reports), and a specific set of metrics for any administrator to demonstrate the value of his/her continued employment. KPIs may also be a last line of defense for HBCU executives dealing with micromanagerial boards by demonstrated accountability and performance that may convince board members to allow university officials to effectively lead while tenured.

Another benefit of institutions beginning to offer multi-year contracts with renewal based on meeting established KPI is that the pool of interested candidates in such administrative positions will be enhanced significantly, both in number and in quality of applicants. According to Jason Horn, Director of Athletics at Xavier University of New Orleans, aside from contracts loaded with financial incentives, which many HBCUs and boards may be leery of offering, "long term agreements help in years when you may not necessarily be able to frontload compensation" (Horn, personal communication, December 16, 2016). Candidates offered the security of a contract may be less likely to be scared off about negative conceptions of high turnover at HBCUs. Additionally, much like non-tenure track/post-doctoral candidates who take contract positions at elite, private, and large research institutions for the opportunity to work with quality colleagues and bright students, qualified, well-credentialed candidates for leadership positions may be more attracted to the challenges of senior-level administrative positions at HBCUs if multi-year contracts are available (Ehrenberg, 2011). As Ehrenberg (2011) notes, "if performance is satisfactory; this provides the faculty member with much more job security than if a decision on renewal is made only when a term contract is about to expire," and the institution is at least nominally protected against effective administrators feeling pressured to test the job market and pursue employment elsewhere if they have the protection of a contract (pp. 14–15).

The implementation of key performance indicators in the annual evaluation of multi-year contracted employees is an industry standard and best practice HBCU presidents/chancellors must employ. As Cave et al. (1996) point out in *The Use of Performance Indicators in Higher Education: The Challenge of the Quality Movement*, the benefits of including them in performance reviews include "strong central direction; accountability for the economic, effective, and efficient use of public money; the measurement of performance against outcome criteria and the substitution of the concepts and methods of management for those of administration or profession-alism" (p. 3). Reilly (2016) offers specific KPI to be implemented in higher education, including graduation rates, awards/grants received, recruitment and enrollment figures (e.g. applications received, processed, and enrollment growth and retention), facility utilization, media engagement, and satisfaction rates acquired via surveys that can be considered as ways to measure growth of areas under specific administrators' purview. These can be tailored to both the short- and long-term needs and strategic plans of each institution. When senior-level administrators are given clear, measurable goals and objectives and expected to produce qualitative and quantitative evidence that those outcomes are being achieved, those individuals are given an opportunity to prove their worth. Addi-tionally, the president/chancellor gains valuable evidence that allows for them to demonstrate success to alumni and legislatively or privately appointed boards and better protect their own interests. Presidents at historically Black colleges and universities (HBCUs) are facing increased pressure to perform in spite of dwindling state and federal support and, at some institutions, increased enrollments. At certain HBCUs there has even been a revolving door amongst top administrative leaders (Meggett, 1996). Introducing and including key performance indicator-based evaluations for key senior-level positions will provide better opportunities and place more pressure on presidents/chancellors to select qualified and experienced leaders to serve institutional rather than personal or political interests that can harm the institution in the short and long term – and perhaps, slow the seemingly ever-revolving doors for HBCU executives and their senior leadership teams.

Embracing "Disruptive" Hires to Promote Diversity and Innovation

A third recommendation for HBCU executives recruiting senior staffers is a philosophical/tactical shift rather than a procedural one. While "disruption" has been both a concept discussed to the point of saturation and near cliché in technology and American industry, traditional higher education as an industry has found itself disrupted – and HBCUs especially, to the point of existential threat – by emerging business models such as for-profit colleges. As winnowing state support for public HBCUs has created conditions that have required perennial tuition and fee increases, and federal revisions to Pell Grant availability and usage and Parent Plus Loan eligibility has priced tens of thousands of potential (and aspiring returning) students out of the market, the convenience of for-profit degrees has become more attractive. While the top 50–100 institutions in America can count on their reputations to avoid enrollment decreases, and large, national and regional research institutions have resources to brand and market their institutions and offer increasingly competitive scholarships to offset external recruiting threats, under-resourced HBCUs where upwards of 90% of students rely on federal financial aid have suffered enrollment declines or flattened enrollment over the past decade. For these reasons, as well as an ever-changing marketplace for higher education, colleges and universities need more than ever to embrace innovation, and particularly, disruption, to continue to carve competitive niches.

Talent, experience, a grasp of historical trends, the contemporary higher education marketplace, and an ability to create and innovate aggressively are needed to create disruption. Defined as both the introduction of services to markets that have not been previously served (new-market disruption) and the introduction of cheaper, more effective, or more convenient services (low-end disruption), disruption is the wave of the present for higher education (Rachleff, 2013). HBCUs are not resourced significantly enough to simply mimic or scale down approaches to recruitment and fundraising employed by high-endowment private institutions or large public research institutions, and further, they will die on the vine if they simply replicate and marry themselves to institutional traditions which, while important, often deliver diminishing returns over time. While a thorough examination of this topic merits a full-length article of its own, in short: 1) Recruitment efforts cannot simply be outsourced to enthusiastic alumni and production can't be doubled simply by doubling the number of recruiters on staff. Institutions are more competitive than ever for prospective students and increasing your institution's exposure simply isn't enough to promote enrollment; 2) Advancement offices can no longer focus solely on stewardship (e.g. throwing parties, tailgates, and galas), but cannot focus all of their efforts on a handful of corporate and private foundation benefactors, either. Philanthropies are engaging and securing donations with lower overheads even in times of recession, and demand for return on investment is higher than ever, even for transactional donors; 3) Athletic departments cannot simply outsource all of their corporate and outbound sales to increase revenues and marketing (as this runs the risk of sacrificing high-touch/high-feel consumer expectations) but cannot rely simply on playing more "guarantee games" or sacrificing home games to play in "classic" games (because this increases revenue but sacrifices the fan base). These shifts, which often garner administrators praise, are neither innovative nor disruptive, and are often untenable. Simply following the traditions and policies familiar to an institution will please alumni and avoid controversy, but they will never carve out the kinds of marketing and branding niches, generate the revenues, or develop the kinds of twenty-first century programs that attract students and inspire alumni.

HBCU presidents and chancellors need to embrace disruptive models for the delivery of higher education to contemporary students, and to do so, they will need to recruit senior-level administrators who understand and are capable of developing disruptive approaches to higher education. Tony Moore, current Vice President of Technology of Administration at Xavier University of New Orleans, notes that "presidents and institutions need to embrace innovation and free-thinking and abandon the status quo to succeed in the current higher education environment" (Moore, personal communication, December 18, 2016). More-over, presidents and chancellors need to support and promote the efforts of senior-staff administrators who engage in and lead these initiatives. The ultimate success of disruptive programs often takes time, and disruptive administrators need the freedom and security to work toward those goals and not have them derailed every time a board member or alumnus phones or emails to complain. Successful disruption also requires, often, initial failures that provide information critical to eventual breakthroughs. Having to litigate each misstep and be micromanaged each step of the way will not allow for successful disruption. Entrepreneurial disruption not only ensures that individual institutions can thrive, but it will create competition in the sector that can improve HBCUs across the board and make them more competitive and attractive options for all students seeking higher education and all stakeholders investing in their institutions' success.

Improving the Hiring Process – Marketing/Branding, Exit Interviews, and Sourcing

HBCUs are competing against other four-year colleges and universities while many deal with dwindling enrollment and a persistent shortfall in funding. In order to attract prospective students, outstanding faculty, incredible executive leaders, donors, and sponsors, HBCUs must develop a good public relations and marketing strategy using traditional and social media – print publications, brochures, paid advertising, websites, and social media platforms. This is the only way HBCUs can establish and control media narratives about their institutions and can also spread the word about what these institutions represent and what they are endeavoring to accomplish, promote faculty research as well as staff and student accomplishments, and attract engagement.

Universities are multi-faceted, so their marketing should have a multi-faceted approach. It should also be the joint effort of the entire campus – from the pre-sident to the faculty to the students to the university staff. With all of the media options available today, the marketing efforts should include a mix of all media, including: paid advertising (both online and print); brochures and view books; the alumni magazine; media relations generated news articles; good use of the university website; and all social media outlets available with which university staff are familiar and competent. Finally, the university's homepage is the "first impression" and should emphasize the institution's accomplishments as the goal is to raise awareness about the university, increase credibility by telling its story, generating buzz and attracting outstanding talent.

HBCUs must engage in aggressive marketing and branding in order to attract top faculty and administrative talent. A study completed in 2012 by the Society for College and University Planning (SCUP), an organization that has a broad interest in higher education and the success of such campuses titled, "Issues Facing Historically Black Colleges and Universities," found that HBCUs are grappling with the following: merging of HBCU institutions, the relevance of HBCUs today; identity (i.e. appeal to a broader audience and the student market); faculty development (i.e. as teachers and researchers); prioritizing academic programs; planning alignment (i.e. academic, facilities, and budget); and a lack of investment in HBCUs (as they are not a priority). This study found that student retention was near the top of the list, but that increasing endowments and marketing HBCUs tied as top priorities. The study participants indicated that HBCUs can attract star talent by: marketing all their strengths – as HBCUs and high quality institutions of learning; gaining adequate funding to meet the challenges HBCUs face; and marketing and branding the institution as well as building alumni donor networks. The survey demonstrates that HBCUs need to work hard at marketing, touting, advertising and the advertisement of career opportunities, publicizing, and promoting all of their positives. Not only are marketing and branding crucial to recruitment and advancement efforts, but they are critical to attracting administrative talent who no doubt read headlines, formulate misperceptions, and make decisions about career options based on all available information. This effort must be led and championed by HBCU executives, through their direct engaged activity and/or delegation to experienced media professionals.

Engagement of prospective administrative talent must not only be reactionary in nature, but proactive. Outstanding talent can be attracted to HBCUs through succession planning and sourcing. Experienced top administrators are often in transient positions at critical times that impact the survival of HBCUs, as leaders come and go so quickly; therefore, succession planning as well as sourcing pools of applicants for critical positions rather than responding each time vacancies occur assists in filling positions more effectively. The processes by which these candidate pools are assembled are rich opportunities to employ an institution's marketing strategy and share its brand. According to the Society for Human Resource Management (SHRM), "Sourcing is the proactive searching for qualified job candidates for current and planned open positions; it is not the reactive function of reviewing resumes and applications sent to the company in response to a job posting or pre-screening candidates" (2016, p. 1). Through networking, conducting research, and relationship building with executives and higher education boards throughout the country and abroad leaders within these institutions can utilize sourcing and succession planning. Both processes ensure smoother transitions when filling critical positions. In addition, on the human resources side, exit interviews also will provide critical feedback to presidents on how to improve the recruitment and retention processes. Information gathered in these interviews can assist with marketing and branding, as well.

Conclusion

HBCU executives must engage in a number of strategies to recruit and retain senior-level administrative talent in order to succeed in their charges to lead their institutions. Regardless what cultural, political, and financial challenges they may encounter, the contemporary higher education marketplace and the diversity of responsibilities necessary to coordinate higher education operations requires a well-trained, talented, and experienced team of administrators in order to succeed. Many presidents and chancellors across America are embracing our aforementioned recommendations, and the authors believe HBCU executives should, as well. Potential senior staff administrators eligible for tenure or accelerated tenure-track faculty appointments are attractive candidates because of what they can contribute to faculty leadership, as well as their potential value proposition. Senior staff-level prospects are also looking for stability in new positions, which can be fulfilled with multi-year contracts with institutionally appropriate performance standards written into their evaluations. Additionally, HBCU chancellors and presidents should embrace administrators versed in and capable of "disruptive" industry practices because of their potential to innovate as they lead. Finally, HBCUs should emphasize marketing and branding efforts to counteract and counter-narrate negative elements about HBCUs that permeate the media and higher education literature, while engaging in sourcing and succession planning to recruit new leaders effectively. These strategies are being embraced by financially stable, highly regarded, and by all measures successful institutions of higher education across the country. The authors believe HBCU executives who do not employ these strategies are not doing everything in their power to ensure these institutions are supported in the most challenging sector of American higher education.

References

American Council on Education (2008). On the pathway to the presidency: Characteristics of higher education's senior leadership. Retrieved from www.cupahr.org/knowledge center/files/PathwayPresidency.pdf

American Council on Education (2009). *Out in front: The college president as the face of the institution.* Lanham, MD: Rowman & Littlefield Education. Published in partnership with American Council on Education.

American Council on Education (2012). *The American college president* (7th ed.). Washington, D.C.: ACE.

Arnett, A. (2015). Tradition of exclusion at PWIs harmful for diversity. Retrieved from http://diverseeducation.com/article/79201/

Arnett, A. (2016). Higher ed business model is being upended by lack of funding. Retrieved from www.educationdive.com/news/higher-ed-business-model-is-being-up ended-by-lack-of-funding/428998/

Association of Governing Boards of Universities and Colleges (n.d.). Top strategic issues facing HBCUs, now and into the future. Retrieved from http://agb.org/sites/default/files/legacy/2014TopStrategicIssuesFacingHBCUs.pdf

Broussard, W. (2016). Hello, new boss: 2015–2016 HBCU executive transactions. *HBCU Digest.* Retrieved from https://hbcudigest.com/hello-new-boss-2015-2016-hbcu-executive-transactions-547e75172b75#.tnepmay9w

Brown, W.A., & Burnette, D. (2014). Public HBCUs' financial resource distribution disparities in capital spending. *The Journal of Negro Education*, 83(2), 173–182.

Cave, M., Hanney, S., Henkel, M., & Kogan, M. (1996). *The use of performance indicators in higher education: The challenge of the quality movement.* London: Jessica Kingsley Publishers.

Clay, P.L. (2012). Historically Black colleges and universities: Facing the future. Retrieved from http://kresge.org/sites/default/files/Uploaded%20Docs/Clay-HBCUs-Facing%20the-Future.pdf

Eckel, P.D., & King, J.E. (2004). An overview of higher education in the United States: Diversity, access, and the role of the marketplace. Retrieved from www.acenet.edu/news-room/Documents/Overview-of-Higher-Education-in-the-United-States-Diversity-Access-and-the-Role-of-the-Marketplace-2004.pdf

Ehrenberg, R. (2011). American higher education in transition. Cornell University, Ithaca, NY. Retrieved from www.ilr.cornell.edu/sites/ilr.cornell.edu/files/WP141.pdf

Esters, L.L., & Strayhorn, T.L. (2013). Demystifying the contributions of public land-grant historically Black colleges and universities: Voices of HBCU presidents. *Negro Educational Review*, 64(1–4), 119–134.

Freeman, S. & Gasman, M. (2014) The characteristics of historically Black college and university presidents and their role in grooming the next generation of leaders. *Teachers College Record*, 116, 1–34.

Gasman, M. (2010). Comprehensive funding approaches for historically Black colleges and universities. Retrieved from www.gse.upenn.edu/pdf/gasman/FundingApproachesHB CUs.pdf

Gasman, M. (2012). HBCU presidents and social media. *Huffington Post.* Retrieved from www.huffingtonpost.com/marybeth-gasman/hbcu-social-media-use-_b_1856214.html

Gasman, M. (2013). The changing face of historically Black colleges and universities. University of Pennsylvania, Graduate School of Education. Retrieved from www.gse.up enn.edu/pdf/cmsi/Changing_Face_HBCUs.pdf

Gasman, M. (2016). HBCUs' self-imposed leadership struggles. *Inside Higher Ed.* Retrieved from www.insidehighered.com/views/2016/09/02/boards-hbcus-should-not-microma nage-their-presidents-essay

Gasman, M., & Bowman, N.I., II (2011). How to paint a better portrait of HBCUs. *Academe*, 97(3), 24–27. Retrieved from www.aaup.org/article/how-paint-better-portrait-hbcus#.Ui2n3DZOOg1

Gasman, M., & Commodore, F. (2014). The state of research on historically Black colleges and universities (HBCUs). *Journal for Multicultural Education*, 8(2), 89–111.

Golde, C. (1999). After the offer, before the deal: Negotiating a first academic job. *Academe*. Retrieved from https://dtm.carnegiescience.edu/sites/dtm/files/AfterTheOffer_0.pdf

Hart, A.W. (2014). The importance of faculty as active leaders and participants in change. Retrieved from: http://president.arizona.edu/communications/blog/importance-faculty-active-leaders-and-participants-change

Kelly, C. (2014). It can hurt to ask. *Inside Higher Ed*. Retrieved from www.insidehighered.com/advice/2014/03/17/essay-how-negotiate-academic-job-offers

Kelsky, K. (2014). Ok, let's talk about negotiating salary. *Vitae*. Retrieved from https://chroniclevitae.com/news/400-the-professor-is-in-ok-let-s-talk-about-negotiating-salary

Lewis, E.F. (1988). The career development of Black college presidents: A case of contest or sponsored mobility (Unpublished doctoral dissertation). The Pennsylvania State University, University Park.

Liou, N., Davis, L., & Ards, S. (2007). Historically black colleges and universities: Three case studies of experiences in community development. Washington D.C.: U.S. Department of Housing and Urban Development. Retrieved from www.huduser.org/publications/pdf/hbcu_vol1.pdf

Meggett, L.L. (1996). The HBCU presidential pressure cooker. *Diverse Issues in Higher Education*, 13(13), 26.

Milgram, S. (2010). Evaluating academic job offers & negotiating positions. National Institutes of Health. Retrieved from www.training.nih.gov/assets/Slides_1_14_10.pdf

Minor, J.T. (2008). Contemporary HBCUs: Considering institutional capacity and state priorities. Retrieved from http://steinhardt.nyu.edu/scmsAdmin/uploads/002/151/MINOR_Contemporary_HBCU_Report_2008.pdf

Nelms, C. (2014). HBCUs: Over-governed and under-led. *The Huffington Post*. Retrieved from www.huffingtonpost.com/charlie-nelms-edd/hbcus-overgoverned-and-un_b_5153102.html

Rachleff, A. (2013). What "disrupt" really means. *Tech Crunch*. Retrieved from https://techcrunch.com/2013/02/16/the-truth-about-disruption/

Reilly, M. (2016). Key performance indicators for schools & education management. *Clear Point Strategy*. Retrieved from: www.clearpointstrategy.com/key-performance-indicators-in-education/

Robinson, P. (2013). The private HBCUs in retrospect and prospect. In Edward B. Fort (Ed.), *Survival of the historically Black colleges and universities: Making it happen* (Chapter 4). Lanham, MD: Lexington Books.

Sale, P. (2013). Leaving the dark side for the light: Twelve strategies for effective transition from academic administrator to faculty member. *Administrative Issues Journal*, 3(2), Article 8. Retrieved from http://dc.swosu.edu/aij/vol3/iss2/8.

Society for College and University Planning (2012). Issues facing historically Black colleges and universities: Results of a focused discussion and survey. Retrieved from www.scup.org/asset/60320/Issues_Facing_HBCUs.pdf

Society for Human Resource Management (2016). Recruiting: Sourcing: What is sourcing? Retrieved from www.shrm.org/resourcesandtools/tools-and-samples/hr-qa/pages/whatis sourcing.aspx

5

PAUL QUINN COLLEGE

Servant Leadership in Action

Marybeth Gasman, Amanda Washington Lockett, and Levon Esters

With the implementation of the institutional ethos, "WE Over Me," President Michael Sorrell has proven that his unique leadership style is helping to revitalize Paul Quinn College while also instituting innovative and strategic developments for the small college's continued progress and evolution (Conrad & Gasman, 2015). Paul Quinn College is a private, faith-based, four-year liberal arts–inspired college that was founded on April 4, 1872 by a group of African Methodist Episcopal Church preachers in Austin, Texas. Today, the college boasts accolades that praise everything from its student leadership style to its institutional motto. Many of Paul Quinn College's accomplishments are the result of its faculty, students, and the dynamic leadership of President Michael Sorrell. Since 2007, under the presidency of Sorrell, Paul Quinn College has grown substantially. His leadership has focused on entrepreneurship, empowerment, and student engagement.

Servant Leadership

President Michael Sorrell's commitment to the art and practice of relationship management has been effective in creating a culture at Paul Quinn where serving and empowering others is a natural way of life (Greenleaf & Spears, 2002). Sorrell's motto of "WE Over Me" is emblematic of the core principles of servant leadership, which emphasize increased service to others, a holistic approach to work, promoting a sense of community and the sharing of power in decision-making (Greenleaf & Spears, 2002; Spears, 2004; Spears & Schmader, 2014). Also contributing to Sorrell's effectiveness as a servant leader is his strong moral compass, disdain for selfishness, and aversion to mediocrity (Spears, 2004).

As is the case for most individuals who engage in servant leadership, Sorrell's approach to leading Paul Quinn has made a positive impact on faculty, staff, and students. For example, Sorrell has made it a priority to serve the community in which Paul Quinn resides. Paul Quinn's approach to community engagement, which will be discussed later in this chapter, allows students to engage in efforts that are larger than themselves. Various community engagement activities allow students to build their servant leadership skills and participate in learning experiences that are transformational in nature. More importantly, exposing students to hands-on servant leadership opportunities helps build their leadership skill tool kit, which can contribute to their becoming more well-rounded individuals. Another by-product of President Sorrell's commitment to servant leadership has been his influence on the level of accountability that students have for themselves and their peers. For example, the notion of accountability is so pervasive at Paul Quinn that students who do not buy-in to the "WE Over Me" mantra typically do not last very long and usually end up leaving the College. Without question retention is important and taken very seriously at Paul Quinn, however, the institution wants to retain students who care about one another and the institution as a whole (Conrad & Gasman, 2015).

President Sorrell has made it a priority for the faculty, staff, and students to engage with the local community through a variety of activities. Interestingly, Paul Quinn's focus on community engagement, which is a by-product of Sorrell's commitment to servant leadership reflects several of Wheeler's (2012) ten principles of servant leadership, with service to others being the highest priority, modeling servant leadership, and the development of more servant leaders. Many of Paul Quinn's community engagement activities involve students' contributing to long-term service learning projects such as the school's recently created organic farm, which provides fresh produce to the local community.

President Sorrell's unwavering commitment to being an innovative servant leader has garnered the attention of individuals across all levels of higher education. His leadership style has empowered faculty, staff, and students, all of which have contributed to Paul Quinn fast becoming recognized as an innovative urban liberal arts institution that serves students from underserved, underprivileged, and low-income backgrounds.

There is much to learn from Sorrell's approach to servant leadership and a good amount of evidence already suggests that his focus of serving others first has been a major factor in helping elevate Paul Quinn into national conversations of HBCUs that are making a comeback (Freemark, 2015).

Branding for the Future

Twenty-first century HBCU presidents who recognize the importance of institutional branding and marketing and who are willing to make it a priority will better enable their institutions to thrive and expand their reach across the higher education landscape (Esters et al., 2016). To this point, there is little doubt that President Sorrell has been highly effective in branding, and in many ways, re-branding Paul Quinn College. President Sorrell has had a significant presence across social and print media and during every public speaking opportunity he makes it a priority to share the "Quinnite" nation story to whoever will listen. Sorrell is exceptional at sharing the successes of current students, alums, faculty, and staff. He is also adept at highlighting various academic programs, curriculum offerings, as well as recruitment and fundraising events. A common thread among Sorrell's branding efforts is his commitment to the "WE Over Me" mantra whereby the successes of others are first and foremost in his messaging (Michael J. Sorrell, personal communication, fall 2015).

President Sorrell has prioritized three distinct areas in his re-branding of Paul Quinn and includes a focus on: 1) Servant leadership, 2) Entrepreneurship, and 3) Academic excellence. Regarding servant leadership, Sorrell highlights the "WE Over Me" mantra, which reflects his commitment and expectation of others to put the needs of others first. Sorrell's actions speak louder than words. He puts the needs of others, namely students, first and expects that faculty and staff do the same. Most impressive is that a culture of peer accountability is pervasive throughout Paul Quinn whereby students hold each other accountable to the "WE Over Me" philosophy (Conrad & Gasman, 2015).

President Sorrell has also made significant progress in taking an innovative approach to using entrepreneurship as a mechanism to create opportunities for the institution. As discussed previously, the "WE Over Me Farm" has been a shining example of Sorrell's vision on how to create a new funding model for Paul Quinn. Sorrell's vision to develop an innovative urban liberal arts institution is being achieved through the farm as it has contributed to Paul Quinn being recognized as a "work college" whereby student debt has been reduced and other costs of attending have been defrayed, resulting in students graduating with less than $10,000 in debt. The farm has also enabled students to gain valuable skills that contribute to them being ready for the workforce.

Perhaps the most important branding effort pursued by President Sorrell is his emphasis on establishing Paul Quinn as a place where academic excellence is integrated within the fabric of the entire institution. On any given day of the week, you will see President Sorrell highlighting the accomplishments of faculty, staff, and students and the growth being achieved by each of these groups. Under President Sorrell's leadership, not only have enrollment, retention, and graduation rates increased; the academic profile of Paul Quinn has been enhanced. For example, the average ACT and SAT scores of incoming students are within one point and 100 points respectively of the national average for African-American students. Other accomplishments include the creation of a Presidential Scholars Program, a robust online degree program, a summer internship program, and a student track record of obtaining employment at highly respected companies (Michael J. Sorrell, personal communication, fall 2015).

Sorrell's commitment to enhancing the academic profile of Paul Quinn has also afforded opportunities for faculty and staff to engage in professional development opportunities that allow them to enhance their course content and learn new and innovative teaching and learning techniques. Paul Quinn's enhanced academic profile has resulted in the development of partnerships with institutions such as Duke, Yale, the University of Pennsylvania, and with business and industry. Study abroad, which was not a part of the Paul Quinn culture prior to Sorrell's tenure, is now embedded within the institution, which provides students with an expanded set of transformational learning experiences. Sorrell's commitment to academic excellence has resulted in numerous opportunities that will continue to raise the profile of Paul Quinn as a premier urban liberal arts institution.

HBCU presidents who are committed to enhancing the public image of their institutions through innovative branding approaches provide opportunities to build stronger support among current students, faculty, staff, alumni, and parents (Esters et al. 2016). What most contributes to President Sorrell's success is his use of consistent, distinctive, and attractive messaging in concert with the strategic use of social media. It should also be noted that President Sorrell's approach to institutional branding and marketing as a serious undertaking has resulted in an uptick in the philanthropic support of Paul Quinn with two of the largest donor gifts being given during his tenure as president. President Sorrell's focusing his branding efforts on servant leadership, entrepreneurship, and academic excellence has done much to elevate Paul Quinn into the national spotlight of institutions that have been able to create a culture of sustained growth and success (Michael J. Sorrell, personal communication, fall 2015).

Community and Civic Engagement

HBCUs have a strong history of community and civic engagement (Gasman, Spencer, & Orphan, 2015) and President Sorrell has been instrumental in elevating Paul Quinn as a national model because of his approach to engaging students in innovative community-based activities. Students attending Paul Quinn have opportunities to participate in a variety of community engagement activities, which focus primarily on service learning and civic participation. It is worth noting that a major outcome of engaging students in community engagement activities is that it provides them with opportunities for transformational learning experiences. In large measure, a driving force behind Paul Quinn's focus on community engagement is President Sorrell's commitment to servant leadership not to mention the institution's location in the middle of a food desert in South Dallas, TX, which provides opportunities for faculty, staff, and students to serve the local residents, many of whom are from surrounding low income and under-resourced communities (Michael J. Sorrell, personal communication, fall 2015).

President Sorrell believes that small urban colleges have a moral and legal responsibility to address the needs of the community in which they reside and in many ways, Paul Quinn has been a shining example of this ideal. Sorrell has worked tirelessly to ensure that Paul Quinn serves as the impetus for economic development for the surrounding community by initiating an innovative community engagement model. Through various community engagement development efforts, Paul Quinn has been able to address the issues and needs important to the community it serves. These efforts have resulted in Paul Quinn serving as an anchor institution for the community. Sorrell's approach to community engagement focuses on serving others, especially those from the inner city, and has helped create a unique institutional niche for Paul Quinn.

President Sorrell's innovative approach to community engagement has resulted in the development of the "WE Over Me" organic farm. Much has been written about the farm and how it came into existence (Conrad & Gasman, 2015; Freemark, 2015). In short, Sorrell eliminated Paul Quinn's football team and decided to turn the football field into an organic farm. The farm serves multiple purposes: 1) as a source of fresh food for students and the local community, 2) as a lab for students to learn about entrepreneurship, nutrition, work, activism, and community politics, and 3) as a source of funding to help reduce student debt and defray the cost of attending Paul Quinn College. A major benefit of having the farm has been that students learn about the role of work, job creation, and most importantly, the role that service to others can play for individuals who are from under-resourced communities. Without question, the "WE Over Me Farm" has been one of Sorrell's most innovative ideas and can serve as a model for other urban, liberal arts colleges that are looking for ways to engage with their local community, expand student learning opportunities, and create new revenue streams for their institution.

President Sorrell's focus on community engagement has resulted in faculty, staff, and most prominently, students participating in student activism efforts. In particular, students from Paul Quinn participated in a protest movement in response to the City of Dallas' decision to expand a landfill in the Highland Hills/Paul Quinn College neighborhood. The movement, which became known as "I Am Not Trash," engaged more than 80 students, many of whom were members of the student government association. Faculty and staff were also involved in several protests. In short, the protests, which included numerous marches, resulted in the landfill expansion project being blocked. Interestingly, the idea of activist leadership, which was shown by the actions of students, permeates the entire campus and students see being civically engaged within the local community as vitally important. Clearly, Sorrell's vision for Paul Quinn's involvement in community engagement activities is very much related to his commitment to servant leadership.

It is clear that President Sorrell has focused much effort on expanding Paul Quinn's footprint within the community engagement movement. The "WE Over Me Farm" has provided students with a variety of quality learning experiences with the major outcome being that they learn the art and practice of being servant leaders. Sorrell's commitment to community engagement also continues to fuel his vision of creating a new urban college model. Other urban-based institutions can replicate many aspects of Paul Quinn's model, such as how the institution engages with the community. Finally, President Sorrell has plans to further expand Paul Quinn's community engagement through the development of a grocery store and "pop-up" restaurant that will further contribute to Paul Quinn's status as a premier urban liberal arts institution (Michael J. Sorrell, personal communication, fall 2015).

Entrepreneurship and Risk Taking

President Michael Sorrell's entrepreneurial spirit is both a driving force in his leadership style and a premiere reason for Paul Quinn College's success. Prior to President Sorrell's appointment, like many HBCUs across the nation, Paul Quinn College faced waning financial support, a limited endowment, and less state support than many of the surrounding larger majority serving institutions (Matthews, 2012). Such limitations can hinder faculty development and stifle new academic programs for students. In fact, in 2007, the Boston Consulting Group predicted that unless drastic measures were taken to address declining student enrollment, low campus morale, and a lack of financial resources, the college would likely be forced to close its doors for good (Watson, 2014). President Sorrell has put entrepreneurship at the crux of his leadership style – a strategy that has proven successful. His entrepreneurial efforts have innovatively garnered additional academic, extracurricular, and financial resources for his students, the institution, and the surrounding Dallas community.

In an interview, President Sorrell noted, "our whole model is built on helping and building the community around us." In the nine years that he has served as President, Sorrell has undertaken several entrepreneurial ventures that have raised Paul Quinn College's visibility and provided additional funding (Michael J. Sorrell, personal communication, fall 2015). Several years ago and as noted earlier in this chapter, recognizing that his college was located in a food desert, he led an initiative to turn the football field into a community farm. Since its 2010 inception, Paul Quinn College's "WE Over Me Farm," has supported not only the College but also community members, restaurants, and grocers with over 30,000 pounds of organic produce. As the mission of the farm is steeped in empowerment and service, 10% of the produce has also been donated to neighborhood charitable organizations.

Continuing to channel his entrepreneurial leadership style, President Sorrell has helped the College and surrounding community access Dallas' vast performing art offerings. Years ago, he convinced the Dallas Symphony to play three concerts on the College's campus every summer. President Sorrell opens the concert to the students, faculty, staff, and general public and builds a stage in one of the student parking lots. He admitted that the first few years were rough as many critics doubted student and community interest in classical music. Despite this opposition, Sorrell boasts that the College's Dallas Symphony concert following has grown from a mere 250 to well over 2,500 audience members from all over the city.

The "WE Over Me Farm" and the Dallas Symphony concerts are just two of the many ways that President Sorrell's innovative and entrepreneurial spirit have profoundly shaped his leadership style. He urges fellow college presidents to lean into the risk of entrepreneurship and nontraditional innovation. His leadership style not only allows him to implement entrepreneurial ventures, but it also inspires him as he continues to uplift Paul Quinn College and the larger higher education community.

Empowerment of Others

A powerful and necessary component of President Sorrell's leadership style is his ability to empower and inspire those around him. He attributes much of his desire to inspire his students to his own upbringing in the rural South. The product of a father who did not go to college and of a mother who was a second-generation college graduate, President Sorrell wholeheartedly believes in creating equally supportive environments for *all* students – those who were raised with "love" and those who were raised with "tough love" (Michael J. Sorrell, personal communication, fall 2015).

As he leads the faculty and staff of Paul Quinn College, he tries to lean into what he jokingly coins as "organized chaos." He empowers his faculty and staff by attempting to hire the smartest and most entrepreneurial people he can find, giving them a goal, and then – after coaching – turning them loose to accomplish the goal. As he leads in this way, he aims to continually push the faculty at Paul Quinn College to adapt to the circumstances that are before them.

His advice for fellow college presidents is embedded in a phrase often used by his grandmother – *"you've gotta give them what the hand calls for."* He hopes to empower college presidents with his personal leadership philosophy of *"giving what the hand calls for"* (Michael J. Sorrell, personal communication, fall 2015).

> In [my personal circumstance at Paul Quinn College], what the hand called for was crises management and in crises management you don't have time to worry about how people's feelings are going to be impacted. We were looking at the extinction of a 135 year old institution. Effectively, the school would have been able to survive post-slavery South but not us. That is a damning statement and it is also an incredibly embarrassing reality. When I looked at all of this and took it into account and tried to rationalize the place that we were in, it was clear that we were in extreme circumstances and in those extreme circumstances we were either going to evolve or perish. There were a lot of people that had bought into the narrative of "we're a struggling HBCU and that's all we've ever been and all we're capable of." They were wrong and I took refuge in the knowledge that there's not permanence in struggle – struggle is merely a state of transition on your way to not struggling. You have to acknowledge your circumstances and also acknowledge that your today will not be your tomorrow.
>
> *(Michael J. Sorrell, personal communication, fall 2015)*

Student Support

Paul Quinn College has soared under the leadership of President Sorrell. Another notable feature of his leadership style is his emphasis on student leadership. Students are at the crux of the Paul Quinn College mission; so much so that the college won the "HBCU Student Government Association of the Year."

As a college athlete who was heavily recruited, Sorrell understands that recruiting is an important key to the success of students at the college. As he recruits students to Paul Quinn College, he messages that students will be a part of accomplishing something bigger than themselves because the college is centered on the mission of "WE Over Me."

He notes that he has successfully attracted students for a few reasons. One of those reasons is that he has created a financial structure that allows students to graduate with less than $10,000 in debt. Additionally, he has worked tirelessly for Paul Quinn College's visibility and opportunities to balloon over the last nine years. Students never know what's coming next and "students like to win ... you come to Paul Quinn if you want to win" (Michael J. Sorrell, personal communication, fall 2015).

As he engages with and produces exceptional student leaders, he suggests that the single best advice is that all leaders have to lead with love. This lesson has taught him that he needs to be more human and that the best way to get through to students is to let them know that they have a support system and, if they choose to come to Paul Quinn College, he will lead in love as he helps them get through the toughest times of their academic and life experiences.

Conclusion

In a time of leadership uncertainty and turmoil at Historically Black Colleges and Universities, Michael Sorrell's example is a crucial one. Presidents inheriting institutions that are teetering on extinction and even those in much better shape would do well to look to his lead and follow his example. With a combination of drive, bravery, integrity, and perseverance in the midst of ridicule and laughter from many inside and outside the HBCU world, Sorrell has transformed Paul Quinn College into a viable player in American higher education.

References

Conrad, C. & Gasman, M. (2015). *Educating a diverse nation: Lessons from Minority Serving Institutions*. Cambridge, MA: Harvard University Press.

Esters, L., Washington, A., Gasman, M., O'Neal, B., Commodore, F., Freeman, S., & Carter, C. (2016). *The 21st century HBCU president*. Philadelphia, PA: Penn Center for Minority Serving Institutions.

Freemark, S. (August 20, 2015). The reinvention of Paul Quinn College. *American Radio Works*. Retrieved from www.americanradioworks.org/segments/reinvention-paul-quinn-college

Gasman, M., Spencer, D., & Orphan, C. (2015). Building bridges, not fences: A history of civic engagement at private Black colleges and universities. *History of Education Quarterly*, 55(3), 346–379.

Greenleaf, R. & Spears, L. (2002). *Servant leadership: A journey into the nature of legitimate power*. New York: Paulis Press.

Matthews, C.M. (2012). *Federal support for academic research*. Washington, DC: Congressional Research Service, Library of Congress.

Spears, L. (2004). *Practicing servant leadership: Succeeding through trust, bravery, and forgiveness*. San Francisco, CA: Jossey-Bass.

Spears, T. & Schmader, W. (2014). *What exceptional leaders know: High impact skills, strategies & ideas for leaders*. New York: Motivational Press.

Watson, J. (2014). Paul Quinn College sharing story of turn around with world. *Diverse Issues in Education*. Retrieved from http://diverseeducation.com/article/67362

Wheeler, D. (2012). *Servant leadership for higher education: Principles and practices*. San Francisco, CA: Jossey-Bass.

PART II

Hispanic-Serving Institutions (HSIs)

6

BEING A CULTURALLY RESPONSIVE LEADER AT A HISPANIC-SERVING INSTITUTION COMMUNITY COLLEGE

Magdalena H. de la Teja

Community colleges are an innovation born of twentieth century American ingenuity and enroll 56% of Latino and 42% of all undergraduates in the United States (College Board, 2016). This chapter reflects on the mission of community colleges and spotlights what it means to be a culturally responsive leader within a Hispanic-Serving Institution (HSI) community college. To understand what attributes are needed by leaders at an HSI community college, it is imperative to briefly review the history of the community college, to explore how and why HSIs came into being, and to consider the characteristics of the students and the challenges related to their success in college.

Most importantly, it is critical to reflect on how to serve as a leader within an HSI community college now and in the future. Three references have been seminal as well as inspirational in the writing of this chapter during my self-reflection as a Latina leader within a community college: *Culturally Responsive Leadership in Higher Education: Promoting Access, Equity, and Improvement* edited by Santamaria and Santamaria (2016); *Salsa, Soul and Spirit: Leadership for a Multicultural Age* by Bordas (2007); and *Identity and Leadership, Informing Our Lives, Informing Our Practice* edited by Chavez and Sanlo (2013).

What is an HSI Community College?

Brief History of Community Colleges and Personal Connection

To better understand the "roots" of the community college, it is important to briefly reflect on its history and mission. The first community college, Joliet Junior College, was founded in 1901 at a time when various local, state, and national leaders (mostly influential White males) were debating about how to expand educational opportunities to more people in the U.S.A. In general, education is recognized today as it has been in the past as a pathway to greater economic prosperity for individuals and communities as well as entire nations. During the early period, the growth of community colleges was relatively slow with 25 junior colleges opening by 1910 (Drury, 2003; Vaughan, 2006). Cohen and Brawer (2008) report that 37 of the 48 states had a junior college by 1922. The junior college was first viewed as a two-year extension of high school and in later years was recognized in its own right as offering the first two years of college and granting the associate's degree. In the early years of the junior college, the curriculum was designed to prepare students in the liberal arts for transfer to a four-year university or college. The students who were primarily attending two-year institutions were from White working-class families. On the other hand, post-World War I and II working-class families of color were using grassroots organizations and litigation (Orozco, 2009; San Miguel, 2013; San Miguel & Donato, 2009) to counter unfair practices and racial discrimination at the workplace and segregation at primary, secondary, and higher education institutions. The two-year colleges were more focused on serving their local communities than were four-year colleges and universities which often followed racially discriminatory practices in admissions during that era (McDonald, 2012/13; Olivas, 2005).

In the 1960s the role of the junior college was expanded, and it was recognized that an open door admissions policy was needed to democratize higher education. There was a transition to more comprehensive community colleges and a surge in growth in their number – 457 new public community colleges opened between 1960 and 1970 (Vaughan, 2006). Community colleges included in their mission a focus on teaching; providing a curriculum preparing students for transfer, including remedial education; offering occupational/vocational-technical education and continuing education; and committing to local community needs (Cohen & Brawer, 2008; Vaughan, 2006).

Not coincidentally, the 1960s were also a period of major social unrest and turmoil as the diversity of the U.S. population grew (more Latinos and Blacks) and increased demands were made for social equality, affirmative action, and access to education. These social and political movements in the 1960s had an impact on higher education in the 1970s through the end of the twentieth century and continue today to pique the conscience of local, state, and national leaders (mostly White males with an increasing number of leaders of color).

My journey in higher education began in 1970 at a public community college in what historically had been a racially segregated central Texas community. The desire to attend college crystallized in the ninth grade after learning of my eligibility for the National Honor Society and fully realizing that grades were important to college admissions. My mother and father were born in Mexico, migrated to the U.S.A. as undocumented, and worked toward gaining their U.S. citizenship after three of the oldest of us eight were born in Mexico. My parents were migrant workers and traveled in the southwestern U.S.A. to pick cotton, vegetables, and fruits until the younger five of us born in the U.S.A., including myself, were ready to attend school. My parents were storytellers and influenced my thinking from an early age. There was a feeling of pride to hear my parents tell stories about the perilous adventures of fording the Rio Grande River several times to cross the border into Texas and start a new life for themselves with few material comforts. While my parents were undocumented, the family was often deported back to Mexico with meager belongings and even less notice.

There was no doubt in my mind from an early age that we were economically disadvantaged (working poor) and that discrimination existed toward us. Since my parents were primarily Spanish-speaking, and the eight offspring had learned English, we often translated for our parents. Navigation skills in a predominantly White de facto segregated community were key to survival, and we learned quickly how to do that (i.e., maintain a low-profile existence). Our parents recognized the importance of education and encouraged us to learn. My father challenged me at solving arithmetic problems, and we laughed together as we raced to see who finished them first. My mother nourished us with her multitude of "*dichos*" – proverbs and sayings in Spanish – and daily home-cooked cuisine of at least "arroz, frijoles, and tortillas" and sometimes homegrown "sandia" for dessert. My father had the equivalence of a high school education in Mexico and my mother had a primary school education.

Familismo, respeto, and allegiance to the Mexican culture (i.e., language and *dichos*, food, spirituality, music), learning, success in school, fortitude (i.e., grit and *ganas* – motivation sufficient to act), and financial survival were early values instilled in me. The local community college I attended felt like home – after all, it was located within 15 miles of my home – albeit it was predominantly White, including students, faculty, and administrators – that was the norm. A decade later it resonated with me that during that period a growing number of first generation, low-income students like myself were finding their way (access) to the local community colleges.

During the twenty-first century, the community college has to be, and often is, pivotal in any serious discussion about higher educational opportunities for first generation, low-income, and underrepresented students. This is the case because we continue to face economic pressures in a technologically complex world to prepare our diverse individuals for the workforce and jobs that do not yet exist (de los Santos & Cuamea, 2010; Smyre & Richardson, 2016). Additionally, access to college remains critical for Hispanics (Santiago, 2009) and other historically underserved populations. Olivas (2005) using a framework of higher education as "place," analyzed university admissions policies and concluded they have resulted in inequalities related to access. In comparison, community colleges have offered open door admissions (Cohen & Brawer, 2008).

According to the American Association of Community Colleges (AACC) formed in 1920 and a national voice for two-year colleges, there are 1,108 community colleges (982 public, 90 independent, and 36 tribal) in the U.S.A.

AACC Fast Facts 2016 describe students enrolled in credit courses at community colleges in fall 2014 as: about 50% White with a growing percentage of diverse students, especially Latinos but also including Black, Asian American, and Native American students; average age of 28; 57% female; about two-thirds attending part-time; and about a third being first generation in college.

Community college students are generally described as being nontraditional, which includes such factors as delaying enrollment, being employed full-time, not having earned a high school diploma, being a single parent, being financially independent, having dependents, and being the first generation to attend college.

HSI Community Colleges

Nunez, Sparks, and Hernández (2011) report in their research of community colleges, that Latino, Black, Asian, other, and multiple race students are much more likely than White students to enroll in an HSI community college than a non-HSI community college. Nunez, Hurtado, and Calderon Galdeano (2015) explain that HSIs first received federal funding in 1994 under Title III of the Higher Education Act (HEA) also known as the Strengthening Institutions Program. Valdez (2015) describes the history, starting in the late 1970s, of the advocacy by a number of Latino and other leaders that led to this landmark legislation. When the HEA was reauthorized in 1998, HSIs were changed from Title III to Title V designation. To be designated as an HSI, an institution's undergraduate full-time equivalent enrollment must be at least 25% Hispanic (i.e. an individual of Mexican, Puerto Rican, Cuban, Central or South American, or other Spanish culture or origin, regardless of race) (National Center for Education Statistics, 2002). The institution must also be accredited, degree-granting, and a public or private nonprofit college or university. Additionally for an HSI to qualify for Title V funding, at least 50% of enrolled students must be low-income (Contreras, Malcolm, & Bensimon, 2008; Mendez, Bonner, Mendez-Negrete, & Palmer, 2015).

HSIs are Minority-Serving Institutions (MSIs) like Historically Black Colleges and Universities (HBCU) and Tribal Colleges and Universities (TCU). However, unlike HBCUs and TCUs that were explicitly created to serve those populations and designated as MSIs in 1992 (Postsecondary National Policy Institute, 2015), most institutions that become HSIs were not founded with a specific mission to serve Hispanic students but rather become HSIs as a result of enrollment shifts over time (Nunez, 2015; Nunez et al., 2015; Gasman, Baez, & Turner, 2008; Mendez et al., 2015).

Gasman et al. (2008) indicate that a significant portion of MSIs are two-year public institutions (40.5%) as are notably about half of HSIs (46.8%). A more recent publication, *From Capacity to Success: HSIs, Title V, and Latino Students* by Santiago, Taylor, and Calderon Galdeano (2016), provides great insights into Hispanic-Serving Institutions as described below. There are 409 HSIs representing 12% of all higher education institutions and about 60% of Latinos enroll in an HSI. Furthermore, HSIs are about evenly split between two-year and four-year institutions – just under half of all HSIs are two-year (203) and just over half are four-year (206) institutions. HSIs are located in 21 states and Puerto Rico, with most located in five states and Puerto Rico: California (139); Texas (75); Puerto Rico (58); Florida (23); New Mexico (23); and New York (19). HSIs are also located in states not known for their high Latino population: Connecticut, Louisiana, Massachusetts, Indiana, Nevada, Ohio, Pennsylvania, Tennessee, Virginia, and Oregon – each have one to four HSIs. Most significantly, on average 46% of students enrolled at HSIs are Latino. Additionally, *Excelencia* in Education has identified that there are 296 Emerging HSIs – institutions with 15–24% Hispanic full-time equivalent enrollment. Emerging HSIs are located in 29 states and the District of Columbia.

The Postsecondary National Policy Institute (2015) notes that many HSI community colleges enroll 2,000 or fewer Hispanic students and that in 2012–2013, nearly 60% of Latino college students attended a Hispanic-Serving Institution, and HSIs were responsible for 40% of all Latino graduates in the U.S.A. Nunez et al. (2015) depict the growth of all HSIs from 189 institutions in 1994 to 370 institutions in 2012–2013 in the table duplicated below.

Table 6.1 shows the heterogeneity of institutional types among HSIs, including both two-year and four-year levels, public and private, not-for-profit sectors. For-profit institutions cannot apply for HSI designation or institutional capacity-building funds. As Table 6.1 shows and as Nunez (2015) explains, when HSIs were first funded in 1994–95 they served fewer than half (46%) of Latino

TABLE 6.1 Number of Hispanic-Serving Institutions

	1994–1995	1999–2000	2004–2005	2009–2010	2012–2013
Total	189	216	242	293	370
% of all Latina/o undergraduates enrolled at HSIs	46%	52%	53%	54%	59%
2-year institutions	103	114	119	150	193
% of all HSIs	54%	53%	49%	51%	52%
4-year institutions	86	102	123	143	177
% of all HSIs	46%	47%	51%	49%	48%
2-year public HSIs	91	101	108	137	178
2-year private not-for-profit HSIs	12	13	11	13	15
4-year public HSIs	30	43	52	62	72
4-year private not-for-profit HSIs	56	59	71	81	105
Emerging HSIs	189	146	183	204	277

Source: National Center for Education Statistics, U.S. Department of Education

TABLE 6.2 Post-secondary enrollment by race/ethnicity and school type (2013)

	Public 2-year schools	*All 4-year schools*
Hispanic	46%	52%
Black	34%	63%
Asian	32%	67%
White	30%	69%

Enrollments include students of all ages. "Asian" includes Pacific Islanders. Whites, Blacks, and Asians/Pacific Islanders do not include Hispanics. Hispanics are of any race. Enrollment in private 2-year schools not shown.

undergraduate students, with this share currently at 60% which represents about a 30% increase. Nunez (2015) projects that based on past and current trends, HSIs will continue to enroll the majority of Latino college students and, therefore, play a crucial role in providing higher education opportunities for the largest and fastest growing population of color in the U.S.A. According to the Pew Research Center's *5 Facts about Latino Education* (2015), Latinos are the largest underrepresented group on college campuses. Furthermore, they cite that Latino student enrollment in a two-year or four-year institution for those aged 18 to 24 has more than tripled from 1993 to 2013. During that same period Latino college enrollment overall increased by 201% compared to Whites at 14% and Blacks at 78%.

Table 6.2, from the Pew Research Center (2015), clearly demonstrates that the trend is indeed for Latinos (46%) to attend two-year public institutions in comparison to White (30%), Black (34%), and Asian (32%) college students.

Gasman, Nguyen, and Conrad (2015) state that the fastest growing demographic are Latinos, who make up 16.3% of the U.S. population. There will also be growing percentages of 15% or more Latinos in Arkansas, Georgia, Maryland, North Carolina, Oregon, South Carolina, and Tennessee. Additionally, what the research shows is that Latinos are enrolling in greater numbers at two-year HSIs than two-year non-HSIs and, hence, there is a high level of interest by researchers in learning more about Latino student success at HSIs in general and specifically at community college HSIs and the leadership at those institutions.

Contreras et al. (2008) reflect that mission statements have cultural relevance for higher education institutions and have historically been a very important way to communicate to the public their primary purposes. These authors studied 10 HSIs eligible for Title V funding, some four-year and some two-year, to determine whether those institutions specifically mentioned the HSI status in their mission statements and websites. Community college boards of trustees and administrative leadership, similar to other colleges and universities, typically take great pride in publically stating their institution's mission statements on their websites and in major publications. Contreras et al. (2008) were interested in learning whether the institutions studied incorporated their HSI identity within their mission statements and how the institutions manifested their HSI identity internally and externally. These authors assert:

> The most surprising and unexpected finding was that none of the 10 institutions explicitly mentioned their designation as a Hispanic-Serving Institution in their mission statement. Based on the website search we were not able to discern a Latino/a agenda across the Hispanic-serving institutions assessed.
>
> *(p. 76)*

Contreras et al. (2008) also examined the status of Latino student access and success measures within these 10 HSI institutions and determined that they did very well attracting and enrolling Latino students. However, on just about all success measures including degree attainment, Latino students were below equity and White students were above equity. Contreras et al. (2008) conclude:

> It is possible that the non-transparency of the Hispanic-Serving identity in the mission statements of the 10 institutions is an indication that not enough attention is being given to student outcomes. Another plausible interpretation for our findings with respect to the institutions' closeted identity is that being an HSI has yet to create a sense of collective responsibility and accountability among institutional leaders and faculty members for producing equitable educational outcomes for Latino/a students.
>
> *(p. 87)*

Garcia and Okhidoi (2015) and other researchers of HSIs often remind us that it is complicated to study to what extent HSIs "serve" Latino students as there are so many variables involved including the fluctuation in Latino student enrollment (e.g., to be designated as an HSI, the institution must have at least 25% Latino student enrollment), heterogeneity of institutional types, geographic location, and the heterogeneity of the Latino students themselves. Garcia and Okhidoi (2015) note that Latino students at HSIs vary in their country of origin, level of college preparedness, socioeconomic background, generational status, immigration status, and language preference.

There is immense need to intentionally work toward transforming HSI community colleges to truly serve Latino students and improve overall outcomes no matter the complexity of doing so (Santiago & Andrade, 2010). It became clear to me in the late 1970s that community colleges were the type of institution at which I wanted to be a leader because I took notice of the projections that low-income people of color would be enrolling in greater numbers at those institutions. Later, it also became apparent to me that working at an HSI community college would be aligned with my professional and personal value of making higher education attainment accessible to Latinos, other people of color, and those from low-income families.

Student Characteristics and Related Challenges

Nunez et al. (2011) offer a review of the literature about the characteristics of community college students and why they enroll in those institutions. These authors and Cohen and Brawer (2008) explain that community colleges are more geographically dispersed and often are in closer proximity to the students who choose to attend them than are four-year colleges and universities. The low-cost tuition is appealing since many Latino students are from low socioeconomic backgrounds and tend to be more averse to taking out loans to pay for college. According to a National Postsecondary Student Aid Study using 2011–12 data (U.S. Department of Education, 2016), the sector that had the lowest percentage of students completing the Free Application for Federal Student Aid (FAFSA) is community colleges. The National Center for Public Policy and Higher Education reports that data from the Education Longitudinal Study (ELS: 2002–06) showed that 44% of low-income students (i.e. those from families with incomes of less than $25,000 per year) attend community colleges as their first college after high school.

Perez and Ceja (2015) present a collection of scholarly articles about the higher education access and choice for Latino students. The researchers in this book explain the challenges Latino parents and students face when deciding about college. Factors related to college choice referred to as negotiation variables including parental influence, financial need, FAFSA and other timelines, academic capabilities, access to resources about college options, and immigration status are explored.

Nunez et al. (2011) indicate that community colleges are viewed as welcoming environments in the college choice process due to the open door admissions, flexible scheduling, and part-time attendance option, which is convenient since most of the students who attend must work. Additionally, two-year institutions offer a variety of academic and student support programs that address the needs of students from underrepresented and nontraditional backgrounds, especially students who are not college ready at entry. These researchers also point out that HSI community colleges are more attractive to Latino students than non-HSI because they tend to have more Latino faculty who can serve as role models and mentors. They studied various factors affecting Latino student enrollment in a community college, especially an HSI vs. a non-HSI. These researchers found that as the number of nontraditional factors increased for Latino students, the more likely it was that those students enrolled in an HSI community college.

Nunez et al. (2011) indicate:

> Our research confirms the critical role that 2-year HSIs play in offering Latino community college students access to higher education. … Our research also suggests that, although females significantly outnumber males among Latino community college students by nearly 2 to 1, being a Latino

(male) is actually *positively* related to enrolling in a 2-year HSI versus 2-year non–HSI.

(pp. 32 and 33)

Laden, Hagedorn, and Perrakis (2008) explored the success of Latino males at one community college HSI and noted that Latino student performance was lower than that of Whites but Latinos were more transfer-prepared. Unfortunately, despite preparedness, Latinos, especially Latino males, did not transfer at the expected higher rates given their transfer readiness. Like other researchers, these authors ponder whether HSIs have a greater responsibility than non–HSIs to actively promote the success of Latino and Latina students.

Saenz, Bukoski, Lu, and Rodriguez (2013) conducted a qualitative study of Latino male students who attended community colleges. These authors recommend:

It is critical that institutions make an effort to directly connect with their Latino male student population. Latino male students tend not to return for additional support services or to the institution. Thus, administrators, faculty, and staff must be prepared to successfully engage and be responsive to Latino male students ... *early* and *often*, in particular early in the semester.

(p. 94)

Saenz, Ponjean, and Figueroa (2016) indicate that Latino males have some of the lowest college enrollment and completion rates of any subgroup. These authors also point out that in 2012, 60% of all associate's degrees conferred upon Hispanic graduates were awarded to females.

Santiago, Taylor, and Calderon Galdeano (2016) documented the success with Latino students of Title V designated HSI funded institutions since their inception. Some of the major points they make include: 1) More Latinos are accessing higher education today ... Latino student enrollment has tripled in the last 20 years from 1 to 3.2 million from 1994–95 to 2013–14; 2) In the last 20 years, Latinos have also doubled their representation in college from 8% to 17%; 3) Latinos' increased access to higher education is consistent with the growth of HSIs during the same period; 4) Latinos have increased their educational attainment, nearly doubling in the last 20 years: from 1995 to 2014, the percentage of Latino adults who had earned an associate's degree or higher rose from 12% to 23%, and during the same period, the percentage of Latino adults who earned a Bachelor's degree or higher rose from 9 to 15%; 5) Latino graduation rates at community colleges have remained about the same over 10 years – 17% for the 2000 and 16% for the 2010 cohort; and 6) Many students at HSIs are post-traditional and less likely to be enrolled full-time and/or continuously enrolled.

These authors (2016) emphasized that by researching the persistence and completion of those students still enrolled beyond the 150% time of initial enrollment, they were able to capture the pathway of part-time and returning students that would have been excluded in graduation rates. Completion rate includes those students who may have transferred and graduated from another institution; these students would not have been included in the graduation rates of either the original or final institution. Among two-year HSIs the combined completion and persistence rates were 58% – the completion rate was 34% and the persistence rate was 24%.

Gasman et al. (2008) advise:

> The importance and strengths of MSIs derive primarily from their collective missions to educate and graduate students from underrepresented groups, the culturally sensitive programs they provide those students, and the public service they perform for their racial and ethnic communities.
>
> *(p. 3)*

HSI community colleges as MSIs fit that description and not only serve Latino students but also other underserved groups.

What Does it Mean to Be a Culturally Responsive Leader Within an HSI Community College?

Santamaria and Santamaria (2016) write about the urgent call for culturally responsive leadership in higher education. Based on their earlier empirical research they identified Applied Critical Leadership (ACL) attributes manifested in the practice of culturally responsive leaders who are from marginalized or oppressed backgrounds. Santamaria and Santamaria (2016) include their definition from an earlier publication:

> Applied Critical Leadership is – a strengths-based model of leadership practice where educational leaders consider the social context of their educational communities and empower individual members of these communities based on the educational leaders' identities (i.e., subjectivity, biases, assumptions, race, class, gender, and traditions) as perceived through a critical race theory (CRT).
>
> *(pp. 4 and 5)*

What these authors documented is that multiple intersecting self-identities and characteristics of the diverse leaders researched impacted their leadership practice.

Further, Santamaria and Santamaria (2016) emphasize that culturally responsive leaders "led in ways that were transformative, counter status quo, and pro social justice, including the promotion of educational equity" (p. 6). Also significant about the research of Santamaria and Santamaria (2016) on ACL is their observation that culturally responsive leaders who are leading transformational change within higher education:

are in the process of pushing their professional *thinking about leadership* for social justice toward *thinking about changing leadership practice* resulting in social justice and educational equity. This way of thinking, leading, and acting moves the leader from participating in an intellectual exercise to applying concrete and possibly measurable action.

(p. 6)

Santamaria and Santamaria (2016) offer their ideology based on empirical research about Critical Race Theory and Applied Critical Leadership that encourages self–exploration and reflection by leaders – the work of these authors is very affirming and inspirational for leaders from marginalized, underrepresented backgrounds, like myself. *Pedagogy of the Oppressed* by Freire (1968) influenced my thinking about learning early on in graduate school because his ideology made me feel empowered as a learner and later as an educator. That is how Santamaria and Santamaria inspired me with their scholarly work – it validated my experiences (past and present) as a Latina leader within higher education.

After completing my freshman year at the local community college, I trans–ferred to a research university in Texas. In fact, my financial aid award letter was my "ticket" to the university because my academic grades were more than enough for admissions. Upon completing the Bachelor's and Master's degrees, it was evident to me that aiming for a doctoral degree and career in higher education administration within a community college was my "calling" and the dream to make true for myself. While a student, my co-curricular service included recruiting underrepresented students to the university and advocating for greater access to higher education. Through my studies I also became keenly aware of the history of discrimination and marginalization of people of color as well as the civil rights legal struggles of "minorities." After earning a doctorate, working at a research university, completing a law degree, and practicing law for three years, my dream came true and my journey as a community college leader began in 1989. My work in the community college and advocacy locally and nationally has included leading toward change to improve access, equity, and success for underserved people of color and those from low-income families.

Martinez (2014) writes about the history and origins (around 1989) of Critical Race Theory based on the earlier 1960s through 1980s critical legal studies movement. Particularly, she explains:

CRT first circulated in U.S. law schools, bringing together issues of law, power, and racism to address power imbalances particularly as these are racialized. ... As a theoretical framework, Critical Race Theory made way for the emergence of critical race counterstory, a methodology utilized in scholarly publications.

(p. 17)

Martinez (2014) also describes LatCrit Theory that emphasizes issues of language, immigration, ethnicity, culture, and sexuality. LatCrit Theory includes a commitment to intersectionality and the use of counterstories to recognize the legitimacy of the experiences and knowledge of people of color which is critical in understanding racism and its effects on individuals and institutions. Martinez (2014) explains:

> A critical race methodology includes a range of methods such as storytelling, family histories, biographies, cuentos, testimonios, and counterstory. Counterstory functions as a method to empower the marginalized through the formation of stories with which to intervene in the erasures accomplished in the "majoritarian" stories or "master narratives".
>
> *(p. 24)*

As a Latina leader, it has been very important to read scholarly publications to expand my knowledge about leadership models, history, privilege, racial discrimination, systemic thinking, organizational theory, and so on – see Nevarez, Wood, and Penrose (2013), McIntosh (1988), and de la Teja (2010) in addition to others cited in this chapter. It has also been critical to participate in and provide leadership and support for professional associations, institutes, and conferences to bring to the forefront the counterstories of people of color. Espino (2015) acknowledges the use of Critical Race Theory and LatCrit in education in understanding racial microaggressions (unconscious or subtle forms of racism) and the need to focus on institutional structure where racism is often engrained. Espino (2015) challenges leaders, "How can we move past incremental reforms in higher education and push for radical transformation, especially at HSIs, an institutional context that has the potential to remedy educational inequities for Hispanic students?" (p. 123).

Bordas (2001) writes about how storytelling is an emancipatory force that Latino/a leaders can use to harness their cultural strengths to understand their agency and challenge institutional norms (organizational culture) that result in inequality and structural forms of marginalization and oppression. Bordas identifies three dynamics of Latino leadership: Preparing Oneself (*Personalismo*), Weaving Connections (*Tejiendo Lazos*), and Developing Skills (*Desarrollando Habilidades*). Bordas' (2001, 2007) work is highly motivating because it describes a humanistic and holistic leadership model that incorporates culture and encourages leadership development using a culturally responsive lens. As leaders in HSI community colleges, we are being affirmed by these scholars that we matter and our cultural experiences are social capital. Furthermore, we are challenged to develop skills (*desallorar habilidades*) to support the success of our Latino and other underserved students and in turn honor and integrate their diverse cultures, experiences, and knowledge (Freire, 1968) into our leadership practice. And mentoring others is critical as a form of Weaving Connections.

Chavez and Sanlo (2013) provide a compilation of essays by current leaders in higher education and Chavez states, "the leaders featured in this book provide insights into the intersections of identity, leadership, and social justice ... transformative efforts to promote equity and social justice are exceptionally complex and profoundly influenced by who we are, how we lead, and how we are perceived" (p. 9). These authors instill hope for the future of higher education and Chavez asserts that the diverse leaders featured:

> put themselves through a process of self-awareness. They are characterized by hope, strength, courage, determination, ingenuity, perseverance, and a willingness to stand forth and take on responsibility for transforming higher education toward greater equity and social justice. These qualities can be cultivated in *any leader* through introspection, observation, ongoing growth, learning, and a willingness to face discomfort and develop empathy in service to others.
>
> *(p. 11)*

Santamaria and Santamaria (2016) also believe that we are capable of change as leaders, and are able to close the achievement gap of underserved students and create more equitable and socially just higher education institutions. Santamaria and Santamaria (2016) reference their earlier research and recommend leaders reflect and ask:

> In what ways does my identity (e.g. race, gender, ethnicity) or biases enhance and/or inhibit my ability and willingness to see alternative perspectives in my leadership practice? What privilege or unearned advantage do I have that might create blind spots in my leadership lens? How can I use my privilege to enact equity and access for systemically underserved groups in my practice of ACL?
>
> *(p. 25)*

Santamaria and Santamaria (2016) also assert that it is critical for us as leaders to further challenge ourselves by asking questions about our educational context:

> What is the theory-in-use and the theory in practice in my organization around assigning or recruiting for leadership roles? Are our words and actions aligned so that they match and we have integrity? Where are the "spaces" in which words and actions are "misaligned"? We suggest that in the gap caused by the misalignment between word and action, educational leaders who are willing to take an honest look often find the "hidden culture or curriculum" ... as well as the organizational inequities that need your attention at your institution of higher learning.
>
> *(p. 26)*

Malcom, Bensimon, and Davila (2010) also acknowledge the value of leaders at HSI institutions examining their own identity and culture and reflecting on ways in which their campus and culture support Latino student, faculty, and staff success. Perrakis and Hagedorn (2010) indicate that representation of Latino faculty members on campus has been shown to be positively associated with student success related to grades and course completions. These authors cite other researchers who have shown that Hispanic and other faculty of color are more likely than other faculty "to offer emotional support and encouragement, raise Hispanic student aspirations, and serve as formal mentors, advisors, and sponsors" (p. 799). Perrakis and Hagedorn (2010), for their study of an HSI community college, interviewed Latino faculty and staff, and a Latino faculty member stated, "I also believe that working at an HSI means that you must be sensitive to student demographics and the potential cultural implications that these demographics may have on their work" (p. 805). And a Latino administrator said:

> The faculty and staff are also reflective of the community and serve as role models for ... students. There has been an increased tie in with faculty, staff, and administrators and the creation of ... a program that focuses on Latinos transferring.
>
> *(p. 806)*

Malcom et al. (2010) indicate that providing access to Latino students is not enough for HSI institutions and recommend that leaders enact policies and practices that support Latino student success. These authors encourage HSI leaders to raise awareness among faculty and staff so they better understand the significance of the HSI status to their institution and their responsibilities related to being more responsive to Latino students. Malcom et al. (2010) suggest that leaders of HSI community colleges or universities can consciously integrate the "Hispanic-serving" designation into their institution's identity, establish related priorities for faculty and staff, and direct resources to achieve them. Malcom et al. (2010) indicate that:

> Leaders of HSIs can set the tone for transformation by engaging institutional members in a serious and long-term dialogue framed by questions such as How is the Hispanic-serving designation reflected in the institution's mission, curriculum, outcomes, resource allocation, hiring, reward system, and priorities? In what ways do leaders embed "Hispanic-serving" into structures, policies, and practices? How is this shared understanding communicated to students, faculty, staff, other constituents, etc.? Does the Hispanic-serving identity drive institutional plans and priorities? What qualifications, experience and knowledge contribute to the effectiveness of HSI leaders and practitioners? Can faculty members articulate how the HSI identity influences course content?
>
> *(p. 5)*

Garcia (2016) advises in her blog on the *Excelencia* in Education website that faculty at HSIs be encouraged to provide culturally relevant curriculum and be trained in validating students in the classroom. Contreras et al. (2008) recommend that for institutional assessment, leaders relate the meaning of Hispanic-Serving to:

> (1) mission and values that guide academic decision making and resource allocation; (2) roles and responsibilities of faculty members, administrators, staff, and trustees; (3) knowledge and competencies that are expected of academic leaders, faculty members, staff, and trustees; (4) criteria for appointing and evaluating the performance of institutional leaders, faculty members, and staff; (5) assessment of institutional performance and effectiveness and student outcomes.
>
> *(p. 87)*

Contreras et al. (2008) go further and recommend that leaders of HSI institutions that receive a grant under the Title V Strengthening Institutions Program be required to:

> report student outcomes disaggregated by gender within racial-ethnic categories on specific measures of success such as year-to-year persistence, six-year BA degree attainment and three-year AA attainment, transfer rates from community colleges to four-year colleges, majors and degree recipients in STEM fields, [and] GPA for graduating students.
>
> *(pp. 87 and 88)*

Malcom et al. (2010) indicate:

> Leaders of HSIs can help institutions meet their Hispanic-serving mission by 1) requiring that all institutional data be disaggregated by race and ethnicity; 2) encouraging faculty, administrators, and staff to engage in collaborative and critical data examination; 3) committing to measurable goals in basic indicators of success (e.g. degree completion, retention, transfer for Latino students); and 4) monitoring progress towards these goals using benchmarking.
>
> *(p. 6)*

By doing the work these authors recommend, HSI leaders can examine the identity and culture of their institutions and develop specific strategies to integrate their Hispanic-serving identity into their core processes and policies.

Disaggregating data by ethnicity, gender, and other factors has been an area of advocacy for me in community colleges, and it was an uphill battle in the 1990s. The struggle now is to go beyond disaggregated data and to have courageous dialogue with faculty and administrators about what institutional changes in policy and practice need to be made to address any achievement gaps.

Felix, Bensimon, Hanson, Gray, and Klingsmith (2015) offer specific strategies that can be used by HSI leaders to understand equity in community college practice and to develop agency for equity-minded change using the Equity Scorecard. The Equity Scorecard was developed by the Center for Urban Education, is theory-based, and includes tools, activities, and processes that can be used by college leaders to embed equity into their structures, policies, and practices.

These authors (2015) explain:

> The Equity Scorecard bridges the gap between data and action by engaging practitioners in a structured process of action research that involves two kinds of inquiry. First, quantitative analysis of data disaggregated by race and ethnicity is used to identify equity gaps in basic metrics of student progress toward degree attainment. Second, qualitative analysis such as observations, interviews, and document review is conducted to investigate practices, structures, and policies through the lens of equity.
>
> *(pp. 26–27)*

Bensimon (2006) states, "While deficit-minded individuals construe unequal outcomes as originating from students' characteristics, equity-minded individuals will reflect on institution-based dysfunctions and consider their own roles and responsibilities as well as those of their colleagues in the production of equitable educational outcomes" (p. 5). Bensimon and her colleagues use an Equity Scorecard process of facilitated dialogue to help faculty and staff develop equity-mindedness that has led to changes in institutional practice and organizational culture. These changes include routinely disaggregating data by race and ethnicity, focusing on equitable outcomes, engaging in and appreciating reflective dialogue, identifying new areas of concern, and making changes to practice only after meaningful and intentional inquiry.

Bensimon (2006) reflects, "The process of inquiry into the problem as well as the understanding that one acquires from it can be a source of expertise, motivation, and empowerment, all of which contribute to transforming an individual into an agent of change" (p. 20). Felix et al. (2015) assert, "Equity-mindedness requires that practitioners accept that higher education as an institution is racialized and that structural racism is produced by everyday practices that are grounded ... on norms and rules that privilege Whites" (p. 38). Use of the Equity Scorecard is a rigorous process and requires commitment and *"ganas"* from HSI leaders, faculty, and staff, but it has led to transformational change and improved outcomes for Latino and other students.

Conclusion

We can gain inspiration from the story of the math teacher Jaime Escalante, who in the early 1980s, led others within his high school in East Los Angeles to transform it into a place better prepared to help students from the barrio to excel in math. As in that situation, it will take *"muchas ganas,"* vision, reflection, collaboration, *"desarrollo,"* commitment, and intentionality to lead toward change within HSI community colleges. This is the case because like educator Escalante, HSI community college leaders will have to sculpt organizations that are more "college-ready" to support Latino students in overcoming the many learning, financial, and other obstacles confronting them and other underserved students in their higher education journeys. *¡Pero, si se puede!* We must reflect on our cultural strengths and our intersectional identities to build alliances and achieve transformational change by together intentionally designing more responsive HSI community colleges.

References

American Association of Community Colleges (2016). Fast facts. Retrieved from www.aacc.nche.edu/AboutCC/Pages/fastfactsfactsheet.aspx

Bensimon, E.M. (2006). Learning equity-mindedness: Equality in educational outcomes. *The Academic Workplace*, 1(17), 2–21.

Bordas, J. (2001). Latino leadership: Building a humanistic and diverse society. *The Journal of Leadership Studies*, 8(2), 112–134.

Bordas, J. (2007). *Salsa, soul and spirit, leadership for a multicultural age.* San Francisco, CA: Berrett-Koehler Publishers.

Chavez, A.F. & Sanlo, R. (Eds.), (2013). *Identity and leadership: Informing our lives, informing our practice.* Washington, D.C.: NASPA.

Cohen, A.M. & Brawer, F.B. (2008). *The American community college* (5th Ed.). San Francisco, CA: Jossey-Bass.

College Board (2016). Trends in community colleges. Retrieved from https://trends.collegeboard.org/sites/default/files/trends-in-community-colleges-research-brief.pdf

Contreras, F.E., Malcom, L.E., & Bensimon, E.M. (2008). Hispanic-Serving Institutions: Closeted identity and the production of equitable outcomes for Latino/a students. In M. Gasman, B. Baez, and C.S.V. Turner (Eds.), *Understanding Minority-Serving Institutions* (pp. 71–90). Albany: State University of New York Press.

De la Teja, J. (Ed.) (2010). *Tejano leadership in Mexican and revolutionary Texas.* College Station: Texas A&M University Press.

De los Santos, A., & Cuamea, K.M. (2010). Challenges facing Hispanic-Serving Institutions in the first decade of the 21st century. *Journal of Latinos and Education*, 9(2), 90–107.

Drury, R.L. (2003, spring). Community colleges in America: A historical perspective. *Inquiry*, 8(1), 1–6. Retrieved from http://files.eric.ed.gov/fulltext/EJ876835.pdf

Espino, M.M. (2015). Researching White student experiences at Hispanic-Serving Institutions. In J.P. Mendez, F.A. Bonner II, J. Mendez-Negrete, and R.T. Palmer (Eds.), *Hispanic-Serving Institutions in American higher education: Their origin, and present and future challenges* (pp. 119–132). Sterling, VA: Stylus Publishing.

Felix, E.R., Bensimon, E.M., Hanson, D., Gray, J., & Klingsmith, L. (2015, winter). Developing agency for equity-minded change. *New Directions for Community Colleges*, 172, 25–41.

Freire, P. (1968). *Pedagogy of the oppressed.* New York: Seabury Press.

Garcia, G.A. (2016). Developing an institutional culture that is relevant and enhancing to Latina/o students (Blog post). Retrieved from www.edexcelencia.org/hsi-cp2/your-voice/developing-institutional-culture

Garcia, G.A. & Okhidoi, O. (2015, February). *Culturally relevant practices that serve students at a Hispanic Serving Institution*. Published online. New York: Springer Science+Business Media.

Gasman, M., Baez, B., & Turner, C.S.V. (2008). *Understanding Minority Serving Institutions*. Albany: State University of New York Press.

Gasman, M., Nguyen, T-H., & Conrad, C.F. (2015). Lives intertwined: A primer on the history and emergence of Hispanic-Serving Institutions. *Journal of Diversity in Higher Education*, 8(2), 120–138.

Laden, B.V., Hagedorn, L.S., & Perrakis, A. (2008). ¿Dónde Están Los Hombres?: Examining success of Latino male students at Hispanic-serving community colleges. In M. Gasman, B. Baez, and C.S.V. Turner (Eds.), *Understanding Minority-Serving Institutions* (pp. 127–140). Albany: State University of New York Press.

Malcom, L.E., Bensimon, E.M., & Davila, B. (2010). Numbers to student success. Retrieved from https://cue.usc.edu/files/2016/01/CUE-policy brief_Malcom_Bensimon_Davila_Reconstructing-HSIs.pdf

Martinez, A.Y. (2014). Critical race theory: Its origins, history, and importance to discourses and rhetorics of race. Retrieved from www.academia.edu/9264464/Critical_Race_Theory_Its_Origins_History_and_Importance_to_the_Discourses_and_Rhetorics_of_Race

McDonald, V.M. (2012/13). Demanding their rights: The Latino struggle for educational access and equity. Invited chapter for: *American Latinos and the making of the United States: A theme study*. Washington, D.C.: U.S. Department of the Interior, National Park Service. Retrieved from www.nps.gov/heritageinitiatives/latino/latinothemestudy/education.htm

McIntosh, P. (1988). White privilege: Unpacking the invisible knapsack. Retrieved from www.cirtl.net/files/PartI_CreatingAwareness_WhitePrivilegeUnpackingtheInvisibleKnapsack.pdf

Mendez, J.P., Bonner II, F.A., Mendez-Negrete, J., & Palmer, R.T. (Eds.), (2015). *Hispanic-Serving Institutions in American higher education: Their origin, and present and future challenges*. Sterling, VA: Stylus Publishing.

National Center for Education Statistics. (2002). *Hispanic Serving Institutions, statistical trends from 1990 to 1999*. Retrieved from http://nces.ed.gov/pubs2002/2002051.pdf

Nevarez, C., Wood, J.L., & Penrose, R. (2013). *Leadership theory and the community college. Applying theory to practice*. Sterling, VA: Stylus Publishing.

Nunez, A-M. (2015), Hispanic Serving Institutions: Where are they now? A discussion paper prepared for: *Hispanic-Serving Institutions in the 21st century: A convening at the university of Texas at El Paso*. Retrieved from www.edexcelencia.org/sites/default/files/Current-HSIs-Nunez_April2015.pdf

Nunez, A-M., Hurtado, S., & Calderon Galdeano, E. (Eds.), 2015. *Hispanic-Serving Institutions: Advancing research and transformative practice*. New York: Routledge.

Nunez, A-M., Sparks, J.P. & Hernández, E.A. (2011). Latino access to community colleges and Hispanic-Serving Institutions: A national study. *Journal of Hispanic Higher Education*, 10(1), 18–40.

Olivas, M.A. (2005, winter). Higher education as place: Location, race, and college attendance policies. *The Review of Higher Education*, 28(2), 169–189.

Orozco, C. (2009). *No Mexican, women, or dogs allowed: The rise of the Mexican American civil rights movement*. Austin: The University of Texas Press.

Perez, P.A. & Ceja, M. (Eds.) (2015). *Higher education access and choice for Latino students. Critical findings and theoretical perspectives.* New York: Routledge.

Perrakis, A. & Hagedorn, L.S. (2010). Latino/a student success in community colleges and Hispanic-Serving Institution status. *Community College Journal of Research and Practice,* 34(10), 797–813.

Pew Research Center (May 26, 2015). 5 facts about Latino education. Retrieved from www.pewresearch.org/fact-tank/2015/05/26/5-facts-about-latinos-and-education/

Postsecondary National Policy Institute (January 1, 2015). Retrieved from www.newam erica.org/postsecondary-national-policy-institute/hispanic-serving-institutions-hsis/

Saenz, V.B., Bukoski, B.E., Lu, C., & Rodriguez, S. (2013, fall). Latino males in Texas community colleges: A phenomenological study of masculinity constructs and their effect on college experiences. *Journal of African American Males in Education,* 4(2). Retrieved from https://interwork.sdsu.edu/sp/m2c3/files/2012/10/latino-males.pdf

Saenz, V.B., Ponjean, L., & Figueroa, J.L. (2016). *Ensuring the success of Latino males in higher education. A national imperative.* Sterling, VA: Stylus Publishing.

San Miguel, G. (2013). *Chicana/o Struggles for Education: Activism in the Community.* College Station, Texas: Texas A&M University Press.

San Miguel, G. & Donato, R. (2009). Latino education in twentieth-century America. A brief history. In E.G. Murillo, S.A. Villenas, R.T. Galvan, J.S. Munoz, C. Martinez, and M. Machado-Casas (Eds.), *Handbook of Latinos and education: Theory, research, and practice.* Routledge Handbooks Online. Retrieved from www.routledgehandbooks.com/doi/10.4324/9780203866078.ch3

Santamaria, L.J., & Santamaria, A.P. (Eds.) (2016). *Culturally responsive leadership in higher education: Promoting access, equity, and improvement.* New York: Routledge.

Santiago, D.A. (2009). *Leading in a changing America: Presidential perspectives from Hispanic-Serving Institutions (HSI).* Washington, D.C.: Excelencia in Education Publications. Retrieved from www.edexcelencia.org/hsi-cp2/research/leading-changing-america-presidential-perspectives-hispanic-serving-institutions

Santiago, D.A. & Andrade, S.J. (2010). *Emerging Hispanic-Serving Institutions (HSI): Serving Latino students.* Washington, D.C.: Excelencia in Education Publications. Retrieved from http://files.eric.ed.gov/fulltext/ED508202.pdf

Santiago, D., Taylor, M., & Calderon Galdeano, E. (2016, May). *From capacity to success: HSIs, Title V, and Latino students.* Washington, D.C.: Excelencia in Education Publications. Retrieved from www.edexcelencia.org/research/capacity

Smyre, R. & Richardson, N. (2016). *Preparing for a world that doesn't exist – yet: Creating a framework for communities of the future.* Alresford, U.K.: Changemakers Books.

The National Center for Public Policy and Higher Education. Retrieved from www.highereducation.org/reports/pa_at/index.shtml

U.S. Department of Education (August 2016). Undergraduates who do not apply for financial aid. Retrieved from http://nces.ed.gov/pubs2016/2016406.pdf

Valdez, P. (2015). An overview of Hispanic-Serving Institutions' legislation. Legislation policy formation between 1979 and 1992. In J.P. Mendez, F.A. Bonner II, J. Mendez-Negrete, and R.T. Palmer (Eds.), *Hispanic-Serving Institutions in American higher education: Their origin, and present and future challenges* (pp. 5–29). Sterling, VA: Stylus Publishing.

Vaughan, G.B. (2006). *The community college story.* Washington, D.C.: American Association of Community Colleges.

7

ACCELERATING STUDENT SUCCESS THROUGH BOLD LEADERSHIP

Joseph I. Castro and Isaac M.J. Castro

Summary

California State University, Fresno (Fresno State) is one of a few universities in the nation that is a Hispanic-Serving Institution and an Asian American Native American Pacific Islander–Serving Institution. Over 70% of the university's 24,400 students are first generation to college and over 60% receive federal Pell Grants.

Through an unwavering focus on serving the unique needs of students, Fresno State's leadership team has implemented several bold new strategies that have accelerated student success to historic levels. Between 2013 and 2015, Fresno State's six-year graduation rate increased from 48% to over 58% and the achievement gap between underrepresented and other students decreased from 10% to 5%. The campus' six-year graduation rate goal is 70% by 2023.

This chapter focuses on the bold leadership strategies employed by one of the authors, as a new President, to create the positive conditions necessary for students, faculty, staff, alumni, and friends to embrace the goal of accelerating student success.

Context

Fresno State was established in 1911 as a teacher's college that primarily served women. Over the first decades of its existence, it evolved to include a strong programmatic focus on agriculture and then in recent decades became a comprehensive regional university. In 2016, Fresno State was classified by the Carnegie Commission – for the first time – as a doctoral university because of its doctoral programs in education, nursing practice, and physical therapy. A fourth doctoral program in audiology is on the horizon.

Throughout its 105-year history, Fresno State has primarily focused on serving students from its region – California's Central Valley. About 80% of Fresno State's students come from high schools or community colleges in the region and 80% of our 220,000 alumni reside in the Central Valley. This region is considered to be one of the most important in the nation and world because of its agricultural productivity. Fresno State graduates have played a leading role in the successful development of this vitally important sector of the national and world economy.

The racial and ethnic composition of students served by Fresno State has changed dramatically over the last 20 years. The number and percentage of students who are Latino, Asian American, African American, and Native American have increased dramatically. Fresno State has emerged as one of a relatively small number of universities that are classified as both a Hispanic-serving and an Asian American Native American Pacific Islander-Serving Institution. The number of Latino students at Fresno State has doubled from about 6,000 in 2009 to almost 12,000 in 2016 and the number of Asian American students has held steady at about 3,400 since 2012.

Minority-Serving Institutions in the United States, including Fresno State, derive strength from their mission to educate and graduate underrepresented students through "in-touch" community efforts and culturally appropriate programming (Gasman, Baez, & Turner, 2008). The challenge – and opportunity – for this generation of university leaders is to boldly embrace an emphasis on access *and* success.

As the first Latino and first Central Valley native to serve as President of Fresno State, one of the co-authors has envisioned a bolder and brighter future for the university and the students that it serves. As a graduate student in higher education administration and leadership at Fresno State, the other co-author has a valuable perspective of lived experience and a research focus on how university leaders of color work to transform their institutions to focus on student success.

New Strategic Focus

Dr. Joseph Castro began serving as President of Fresno State on August 1, 2013. He followed Dr. John Welty, who retired after 22 years, which is the longest tenure of any president in the history of the university. As this leadership transition occurred, Fresno State was amidst a slow and lengthy recovery from a traumatic period of budget reductions during the Great Recession when one-third of its state funds were eliminated within two years. Students were generally frustrated by what they perceived as an uneven commitment to their success, especially as it related to support services and access to classes needed to graduate in a timely way. The faculty and staff were generally frustrated by the experience of having to assume more duties while going six years without any salary increases. Alumni and the community, while remaining steadfast in their loyalty to the university, were concerned about the quality of education and relatively low graduation rates. And all were concerned about the deteriorating physical infrastructure on the university's almost 70-year-old site.

It was clear to the new President that a period of listening to as many voices as possible on campus and in the community was needed before articulating a new vision for the University. Through formal and informal meetings with students, faculty, staff, alumni, and friends – in community centers, backyards, schools, community colleges, art museums, churches, farms, factories, and many other locations – the new President developed an authentic understanding of how those being served by the University were experiencing it at the time.

This broad-based approach to engaging the community led to the development of a renewed vision for Fresno State that prioritized our focus on student success. A new Strategic Plan was developed with a modified mission for the university. The mission adopted in early 2016 is "*to boldly educate and empower students for success.*" The Plan's overriding strategic statement is:

> *Fresno State will implement bold, focused, strategies designed to maximize success for our diverse student body. In collaboration with our community partners, we will provide a transformative educational experience that prepares students to serve and to lead in the Central Valley, the state, and beyond while improving the overall graduation rate.*

Many Fresno State faculty members advocated for the inclusion of the word "empower" in the mission because of the unique student body that the university serves.

The new Strategic Plan for 2016–20 has four strategic priorities:

- Enhancing teaching and learning through high-impact practices leading to student success
- Investing in a dynamic environment to attract, develop, and retain talented and diverse faculty and staff
- Aligning our physical and technological infrastructure to support a sustainable and welcoming campus environment
- Grow and develop collaborative and engaged community partnerships to increase support for students and the University.

The President's Cabinet leads the implementation of the Strategic Plan with a strong and unwavering focus on the success of all students. The Plan embraced the President's graduation rate goal of 70% by 2023.

Embracing High-Impact Programs

Fresno State has prioritized the allocation of resources to effectively implement an array of proven high-impact programs that support student success. The allocation

of resources in a strategic way is more important than ever due to funding constraints faced by public universities (Kuh, 2001). The most prominent high-
impact programs are:

- **Service Learning**

  For many years, Fresno State has had a strong service-learning program.
  Students have an opportunity to gain experience working on real-world
  challenges in the community and around the world. One powerful recent
  example is a service-learning program that has trained students to be
  advocates for low-income families residing in nearby apartment complexes
  that have deteriorated because of neglect by landlords. Over the last ten
  years, Fresno State students, faculty, and staff have engaged in over ten
  million hours of community service. Students receive course credit or
  work-study funds for their exemplary service.

- **Advising**

  Due to funding limitations, the advising structure at Fresno State was uneven
  prior to 2015. Some schools and colleges at Fresno State had professional
  advisors and others did not. Students and families viewed this situation as a
  major weakness of Fresno State because they were often making decisions
  without the benefit of a professional who clearly understood individual
  major or graduation requirements. In 2015, the University invested over
  $1 million in new permanent funding to hire professional advisors in each
  school and college. These advisors are responsible for assisting Fresno State
  students in successfully navigating course, major, and graduation requirements. They also serve as liaisons with other campus services (e.g. financial
  aid, counseling, etc.) to ensure that students receive the support they need
  to graduate in a timely way.

- **Cross-Cultural Center**

  Fresno State serves one of the most diverse student populations in the nation.
  About 80% of the campus' students live in the Central Valley, while over
  70% are first generation to college students and over 60% receive Pell
  Grants. Approximately 1,000 students are undocumented and thousands
  come from small, rural communities that have been historically underserved. Fresno State also serves an array of smaller but equally important
  groups of students who are Lesbian, Gay, Bisexual, Transgender (LGBT),
  African American, American Indian, Armenian American, Hmong American, Indian American, and Portuguese American.

  In 2015, Fresno State established the Cross-Cultural Center to provide space
  and support for its diverse students. Students visit the Center to participate

in programming, to study, and to meet with other students and staff. The Center provides shared spaces for all groups and individual spaces for several student groups, including breast feeding rooms for students who are mothers.

- **Technology-Based Teaching and Learning**

California is widely viewed as one of the world's leaders in technological innovation. Fresno State has seized on this state asset to transform teaching and learning for its faculty and students. In 2014, the university launched the DISCOVERe Program, which has now inspired over 200 faculty members to re-design their courses using digital tablets as a substitute for traditional textbooks. The Fresno State Foundation and other donors have provided over $2 million in scholarship support to offset the cost of tablets for students.

DISCOVERe has grown from 1,000 students in 2014–15 to a projected enrollment of up to 10,000 in 2016–17. Assessments of the program have found satisfaction levels that exceed 90%, higher levels of engagement between faculty and students, stronger academic performance, and significantly reduced costs. Students in DISCOVERe have saved, on average, over 70% on textbook costs. Most importantly, the program has positioned Fresno State graduates to compete more effectively for employment opportunities in an increasingly technology-based global economy. Fresno State has partnered with Apple on this bold initiative, which has emerged as one of the largest of its kind in the nation.

- **Study Abroad**

Study abroad programs have been shown to increase student engagement relative to other students through their senior year (Gonyea, 2008). Despite this convincing evidence, Minority-Serving Institutions like Fresno State have historically had relatively few students participate in study abroad programs. This has been the case because the cost to participate has been prohibitive for virtually all students.

Beginning in 2014, Fresno State embraced this high-impact practice in a more aggressive way. Using a portion of revenue from continuing and global education programs and private funds from donors, Fresno State has expanded its scholarship support for students who desire to study abroad. An unexpected significant bequest was used to create a new endowment fund for study abroad scholarships. These new strategies have resulted in a 34% increase in the number of Fresno State students who studied abroad between 2013 and 2015.

In 2015, Fresno State was invited to join a new international partnership with the Center for Minority-Serving Institutions at the University of

Pennsylvania and the Council on International Educational Exchange. This promising new initiative will enable Fresno State students to participate in international study experiences that are customized to meet their unique needs. The program will offer shorter, in-depth experiences for students who cannot be away from home for a summer, semester, or academic year.

Early Progress

The implementation of several high-impact practices led by faculty, staff, and administrators has led to promising results for Fresno State students.

- **Graduation Rate**

  The six-year graduation rate increased from 48% in 2013 to 58% in 2015. The graduation rate was below the California State University (CSU) system average in 2013 but now exceeds the system average. The graduation rate goal for the campus is 70% by 2023.

- **Graduation Gap**

  The graduation gap, which is the difference in the graduation rate between underrepresented students and other students, decreased from 10% in 2014 to 4% in 2016. The CSU system graduation gap goal is 0% by 2025.

- **Student Borrowing**

  The average student loan indebtedness for Fresno State graduates was $18,000 in 2016. This is substantially less than the $30,000 average student loan debt for graduates of U.S. universities.

- **National Recognition**

  In 2016, *Washington Monthly* magazine ranked Fresno State Number 25 in the nation. The University was ranked Number 1 in the nation in community service, which was defined by the large proportion of work-study students who serve in the community. A significant number of Fresno State's work-study students serve students and families in Downtown Fresno, which has the poorest zip code in California and among the poorest in the nation. The same magazine ranked Fresno State Number 2 in the nation for value, which included metrics for graduation rate performance and cost of attendance.

  Also in 2016, *U.S. News and World Report* ranked Fresno State Number 1 among public universities in the nation for graduation rate performance. Graduation rate performance was measured by assessing the difference between projected and actual graduation rates. The magazine's model predicted Fresno State's graduation rate to be just 40%. Actual performance was almost 20 percentage points higher.

This national recognition led the Fresno Bee Editorial Board to state that Fresno State "is rewriting expectations for first-generation college students, many of whom are poor and come from immigrant families … this is … a defining accomplishment, with the potential to elevate the Valley for many years to come" (Fresno Bee, 2016).

Bold and Inclusive Leadership

Presidents of universities and other institutions possess a range of leadership styles and characteristics (Cohen & March, 1986). The search committee for the eighth President of Fresno State sought an academic leader who could strengthen engagement with the broad range of diverse communities who support the university. There was a perception among some members of diverse communities that Fresno State was not adequately responsive to their desires and needs.

The CSU Board of Trustees appointed Joseph Castro as President of Fresno State effective August 2013. Dr. Castro is the first native of the Central Valley and first Latino to serve as President. Prior to his appointment as President, he had served for 23 years as a professor and administrator in the University of California (UC) system.

President Castro, as a first generation college graduate who grew up in the Central Valley, has a deep personal understanding of the region's unique assets and challenges. This experience provided him with tremendous credibility with the full range of university stakeholders.

The leadership style embodied by President Castro is based upon the development of authentic personal relationships, collaboration with individuals and organizations whose values align with the university's mission, and bold and innovative ideas that serve the unique needs of students. This leadership style is influenced significantly by the experiences of Tomas Rivera, the former Chancellor of the University of California, Riverside, who was one of the first Latinos in the nation to serve as leader of a major university in 1979–84 (Castro, Glasman & Runkle, 2004).

Inclusiveness has been a major theme of Fresno State's leadership since 2013. In addition to traditional campus and alumni events, President Castro and the senior leadership have initiated several new programs to demonstrate authentic inclusion. Some examples follow:

- **Feedback Page**

    The President's Feedback Page allows students, faculty, staff, alumni, and friends to share comments on what they love about Fresno State and where improvements can be made. Submissions can be confidential or signed. President Castro and the senior leadership review and respond to each submission. The comments and responses are posted on the web site for anyone to read. This mechanism for feedback has enabled President Castro to be better informed about challenges that need to be addressed.

- **Campus Forums**

  President Castro hosts several campus forums each year. Forums are held twice annually for students and for faculty and staff. The forums are open to all and provide attendees with the opportunity to ask a question on any topic. At each forum, President Castro is joined by senior campus leaders who assist him in answering specific questions. These forums enable President Castro to hear directly from students, faculty, and staff about the issues concerning them. Topics have included campus safety, transportation and parking, and diversity and inclusion issues.

- **Social Media**

  Fresno State utilizes social media to disseminate information about the campus and to better understand in real time the issues and concerns of students, faculty, staff, alumni, and friends. President Castro is active on Facebook, Twitter, and Instagram and uses these social media platforms to provide brief updates on major events and to communicate with individual students, faculty, staff, and alumni on non-controversial issues. Urgent concerns shared with President Castro on social media are referred to the appropriate campus leader to respond by phone or email on his behalf. Social media provides an alternative way for President Castro and the campus leadership team to stay engaged with the campus and community. Fresno State students and alumni make up the largest proportion of social media users who interact with the President.

  Fresno State's social media connections increased dramatically between 2014 and 2016. During this period, Twitter followers increased from 13,000 to 40,000 (a 300% increase) and Instagram followers increased from 1,600 to 17,000 (a 1,000% increase). Fresno State has a full-time social media coordinator who supports this effort.

- **Conversations on Inclusion, Respect, and Equity**

  In 2015, the Fresno State President's Commission on Human Relations and Equity initiated Conversations on Inclusion, Respect, and Equity. This initiative was developed to provide a safe environment where students, faculty, and staff can come together to discuss issues and concerns related to inclusion, respect, and equity. Facilitated by senior staff and administrators, the discussion is summarized without attribution and shared with

President Castro and the Cabinet. The conversations provide the campus' senior leadership with insightful qualitative data about issues or concerns that need to be addressed.

• **Community Conversations**

Beginning in 2015, Fresno State initiated Community Conversations throughout the Central Valley. These conversations are held quarterly in a different community within the region. President Castro invites all Fresno State alumni and other community and business leaders to attend. Generally, the events have been held at community colleges or K-12 schools in collaboration with other local educational leaders. Community college Presidents and K-12 County Superintendents have hosted these events with President Castro.

The conversations, which generally take place during the evening, include an opportunity for informal networking followed by brief updates from President Castro and one or two other senior campus leaders. After the updates, attendees are invited to ask questions or share feedback about Fresno State. Many hundreds of alumni and community and business leaders have participated in these conversations. The Community Conversations have strengthened connections between Fresno State and alumni and other community and business leaders throughout the region.

The array of challenges faced by universities such as Fresno State require bold leaders who can address complex, dynamic challenges in an ever-changing world (Portney, 2011). The definition of bold is "showing a fearless daring spirit" (Merriam Webster, 2016).

Fresno State, as experienced by President Castro in 2013, was still traumatized by the effects of the Great Recession. It was a community that was proud and strong, but focused more on *surviving* than on *thriving*. There was an environment filled with frustration about what was perceived to not be possible instead of an optimism about what could occur at a great public university that was highly valued by its region. The leadership team in place was highly experienced (as defined by years of service) with many prior successes. However, there was a perception by the campus and community that the leadership team was not fully engaged with those it served and was not maximizing opportunities to learn and improve through its experience. Through retirements and other transitions, the Cabinet has been completely transformed in the past three years and includes talented and diverse mission-oriented professionals. An overwhelming majority of Cabinet members are Fresno State alumni or Central Valley natives. The President's wife is also a Central Valley native who has played a valuable role in representing the campus in the community as a full-time volunteer. The right leadership is now "on the bus" (Collins, 2001).

It was under these unique conditions that President Castro began to urge all at Fresno State and in the community to "*Be Bold.*" Initially, there was no specific definition of what bold meant. Instead, he urged students, faculty, staff, alumni, and friends to share their thoughts, ideas, and dreams for Fresno State with each other and with campus leadership. This lack of specificity was necessary to give everyone the freedom to end individual frustrations with what was not possible and instead begin to dream about what was possible.

President Castro has consistently urged the community to Be Bold. He uses the word "*bold*" in every major speech and the slogan #BeBold is included in almost every significant social media message from Fresno State and himself. The term has gained significant momentum since 2013 and is now the centerpiece of the campus' new regional and national marketing campaign.

Fresno State has emerged as a university that is thinking and acting boldly. This boldness is exemplified in the new campus strategic plan mission ("To boldly educate and empower students for success") and the four priorities that are focused on supporting student success.

Bright Future

Fresno State's trajectory portends a bright future for the university and the talented and diverse students it serves. The current five-year Strategic Plan (2016–20) outlines bold plans. Examples of these plans include:

- **Expanding Innovative Teaching and Learning Programs**

    With a continued focus on scaling up high-impact practices for all students, Fresno State's six-year graduation rate is projected to increase to 70% by 2023. When these graduation rate levels are reached, Fresno State will be a national leader among public universities.

    Fresno State will continue to scale up the successful DISCOVERe Program to serve as many of its 24,400 students as is feasible. With tablets becoming almost ubiquitous, it will become easier to inspire students and faculty to participate in the program. Most importantly, Fresno State students will have a competitive edge when they graduate and enter the global job market.

- **Recruiting, Supporting, and Retaining Talented and Diverse Faculty and Staff**

    As a Hispanic-Serving Institution, Fresno State must continue to aggressively recruit, support, and retain a more diverse faculty and staff. In Fall 2015, about 11% of Fresno State's tenured or tenure-track faculty was Latino. The two most recent cohorts of new tenure-track faculty were more diverse, with about 14% being Latino. This is a much larger proportion than the 2014 U.S. Survey of Earned Doctorates, which had just 5.8% represented by Latinos.

    Fresno State will also invest more funds in professional and leadership development and programs to enhance the diversity of campus administrators, many of whom are promoted from staff and faculty positions.

On a global level, Fresno State has prioritized the allocation of new state funds since 2013 to increase compensation and benefits for faculty and staff. In 2016–17, Fresno State used all of its new state permanent funds for faculty and staff compensation.

- **Enhancing Physical and Technological Infrastructure**

The most significant non–academic challenge faced by Fresno State is its aging physical infrastructure. The main campus site is nearly 70 years old and most of the original buildings and utility infrastructure must be updated as soon as possible.

Over the next five years, Fresno State will invest more state funding and secure additional private funds to enhance the campus' physical infrastructure. A new student union and faculty center, a new mixed use residential housing facility, a new central utilities plant, and an updated football stadium are the highest priority projects. A new performing arts facility is also under active consideration.

With the campus' first Chief Information Officer appointed in 2015, there are bold plans to upgrade and strengthen the university's technological infrastructure. The highest immediate priority has been to improve service levels for faculty and staff.

- **Growing and Developing Collaborative and Engaged Community Partnerships**

Fresno State will continue its comprehensive community engagement program over the next five years. The groundwork is being developed for a new Comprehensive Fundraising Campaign that will help Fresno State to strengthen its academic and athletic programs. The fundraising results based upon increased community engagement are promising. The President's Circle of Excellence, which includes major donors to Fresno State, increased gift revenue by almost 40% between 2014–15 and 2015–16. The number of donors during this period increased by 13%.

The Central Valley Promise will also launch in Fall 2016 to provide clearer academic pathways to Fresno State and increased scholarship support for talented and diverse students in nearby high schools and community colleges.

Conclusion

Bold leadership focuses on actions that serve the greater good of the community. This unique style of leadership calls on everyone, especially the President, to set aside personal agendas and preferences and focus on how to strengthen the university so that it can better serve the needs of its students and the community. Bold leadership that serves the greater good is easier to say than to do because of the significant temptations faced by leaders to make decisions that benefit the most active or influential stakeholders. While serving the greater good may not always lead the President to be more popular, decisions about highly contested issues provide a unique opportunity for the President to re-affirm the core values of the University. If a President is listening to the voices of stakeholders before making major decisions, even stakeholders who disagree with the final decision will respect the President's view because they trust the decision making process.

The path to greater success by Fresno State and other public universities is to have a consistent and robust strategy that deepens authentic engagement with students, faculty, staff, alumni, and friends. It is authentic engagement and careful listening and learning by the President and key campus leaders that leads to sustainable student success. Because of the critically important role that universities play in educating the next generation of leaders for our nation, this generation of leaders matters more than ever. While significant progress at Fresno State has occurred, there should be no illusion that the challenges of high poverty and unemployment can be addressed in the short term. As David Brooks states in his recent book, *The Road to Character*, these are challenges that will take more than one leader's lifetime to fully address (Brooks, 2015). For this reason, there is no better time than now for bold leadership.

On a campus with the rich diversity and great potential possessed by Fresno State, there is a need for bold and collaborative leadership. The academic potential and pride that students have in their region is ripe to be harnessed and transformed into a strong community that works effectively for everyone. A bold leadership approach gives the campus community a clear and strategic direction to head in, but the added element of collaboration and approachability gives an authentic feel that encourages optimism and collegiality among students, faculty, and staff. With many Fresno State students working significant hours or commuting from home to attend classes, that strength of community enables the university to overcome some of the challenges that non-traditional students face by making their campus experience an integral part of their lives on and off campus. By creating multiple potential touch points with high-impact practices, combined with creating consistent avenues for feedback and collaboration with the University, Fresno State is pushing the boundaries of expectation and success for Hispanic-Serving Institutions that elevate the regions they serve.

References

Brooks, D. (2015). *The road to character*. New York: Random House.

Castro, J.I., Glasman, N., & Runkle, K. (2004). The leadership style and interactions of Tomas Rivera, former Chancellor of the University of California, Riverside. Paper presented at the 2004 Conference of the American Educational Research Association.

Cohen, M.D. & March, J.G. (1986). *Leadership and ambiguity*. Cambridge, MA: Harvard Business School Press.

Collins, J. (2001). *Good to great: Why some companies make the leap and others don't*. New York: HarperCollins Publishers.

The Fresno Bee (2016). It's full STEAM ahead for No. 1 Fresno State. September 14. Retrieved from www.fresnobee.com/opinion/editorials/article101842542.html

Gasman, M., Baez, B., & Turner, C.S.V. (Eds.) (2008). *Understanding Minority-Serving Institutions*. New York: SUNY Press.

Gonyea, R.M. (2008). The impact of study abroad on senior year engagement. In the annual meeting of the Association for the Study of Higher Education, Jacksonville, FL.

Kuh, G.D. (2001). Assessing what really matters to student learning inside the national survey of student engagement. *Change: The Magazine of Higher Learning*, 33(3), 10–17.

Merriam Webster Dictionary (2016).

Portney, P. (2011). The leadership vacuum in higher education. *The Washington Post*, October 31. Retrieved from www.washingtonpost.com/national/on-leadership/the-leadership-vacuum-in-higher-education/2011/10/31/gIQA1X0lZM_story.html?utm_term=.5e2987459da2

8

THE EVOLUTION OF HISPANIC-SERVING INSTITUTIONS: PAST, PRESENT, AND FUTURE

Laura J. Cortez

Throughout the history of American higher education congressional mandates have impacted the course of university policies and missions (Altbach, Berdahl, & Gumport, 2005; Cohen, 1998; Lucas, 1994). From the Morrill Land Grant Acts of the nineteenth century to the Serviceman's Readjustment Act (G.I. Bill) of 1944, federal legislation has been used as a way to ameliorate education opportunities across the country and between socioeconomic class and racial divides. Over the past fifty years, one of the most important pieces of federal legislation has been the Higher Education Act (HEA) of 1965. This legislation had several priorities, but its main intention was "to open the halls of higher education to a diverse set of students that had been historically underrepresented at the postsecondary level" (LBJ Library, n.d.).

After the passage of HEA 1965, many proponents of Hispanic higher education felt there was a lack of focus towards strengthening developing institutions that served Hispanics. Between 1965 and 1979, Latino advocacy groups in Washington D.C. began organizing to establish federal recognition and funding for Institutions of Higher Education (IHEs) that enrolled a large number of Hispanic students (Valdez, 2013). After twenty-seven years of congressional testimony and several attempts to include these institutions in the Reauthorization of the HEA 1965, the passage of Hispanic-Serving Institution (HSI) legislation occurred. In 1992, the 102nd United States Congress passed Public Law 102–325 (P.L. 102–325) adding Section 316 and the first definition of a Hispanic-Serving Institution was born.

Hispanic-Serving Institutions are defined in federal law as two- or four-year, accredited, degree-granting public and private nonprofit institutions that have at least 25% undergraduate Hispanic full-time enrollment (Santiago, 2006). Given the historical definition of HSIs, the institutional identity of these organizations is based on enrollment. Unlike other Minority-Serving Institutions (MSIs), such as

Historically Black Colleges and Universities (HBCUs), whose size and mission are likely to remain constant, the number of HSIs and their missions are ever-changing (Núñez, Crisp, & Elizondo, 2016). Hubbard and Stage (2009) argue that HSIs lack the cultural artifacts, institutional missions, or historical rationales of serving Hispanics, which makes the research on HSIs so unique. Furthermore, HSIs vary with regard to Carnegie type, enrollment size, percentage of Hispanic students, and region (Núñez & Elizondo, 2012). Consequently, scholars are faced with studying a complex phenomenon that is in constant stage of metamorphosis.

Over the years, the demand to learn more about HSIs has grown and new research has emerged to define the distinct typology of HSIs and provide a basis on which these organizations can be compared, understood, and categorized (Núñez et al., 2016). In addition, scholars are beginning to expand research on the economic impact of attending HSIs and its effects on labor market earnings for Latina/os, particularly as the value of a postsecondary degree is becoming more scrutinized (Park, Flores, & Ryan, 2015). Researchers are also studying the stages of growth institutions experience on their way towards acquiring the HSI designation (i.e. Emerging HSIs) and they continue to call into question whether institutions are truly of "service" to Hispanic students (Cuellar, 2014; Garcia & Okhidoi, 2015). More recent studies also examine HSIs as racialized spaces and exploring how they impact students' racial/ethnic identity development (Garcia, Patrón, Ramirez, & Hudson, 2016). As for the broader policy impact, educational advocacy groups such as *Excelencia* in Education have been at the forefront of HSI work since 2004, and they continue to analyze how federal investments in these institutions improve Latina/o students' educational achievements (Santiago, Taylor, & Calderón Galdeano, 2016). However, missing from this conversation is a historical roadmap that documents the story of HSIs. Therefore, the goal of this chapter is to provide an analysis of Hispanic-Serving Institutions by journaling their past, present, and future impact. The chapter will also offer specific recommendations for institutional leaders at the helm of these complex entities.

The Past: Understanding the Evolution of HSIs

Hispanic-Serving Institutions are part of a larger group of institutions known as MSIs. MSIs were created to provide higher education opportunities to students that have been historically underserved by predominantly white institutions (Gasman, 2008). These institutions date back to the mid-nineteenth century with the creation of Historically Black Colleges and Universities (Bridges, Kinzie, Nelson Laird, & Kuh, 2008). HBCUs mark the first institutions to serve populations that have been historically excluded from higher education (Kaplan, 2009). The development of HBCUs occurred during the second Morrill Act of 1890, which required states with dual systems of higher education to provide land-grant institutions for both systems (Lucas, 1994; Hoffman, Snyder, & Sonnenberg, 1996). These land-grant institutions were intended to democratize access (Vincent, 2004); and the Morrill Act ultimately set a precedent that paved the way for several designations given to institutions of higher education that serve a large number of minority students that include: Tribal Colleges and Universities (TCUs), Alaska Native and Native Hawaiian-Serving Institutions (ANNHs), Asian American and Native American Pacific Islander-Serving Institutions (AANAPISIs) and HSIs.

Critical to the history of MSIs is the demographic makeup of the students they educate. MSIs serve over 20% of students enrolled in U.S. colleges and universities and they have a legacy of educating low-income, first-generation students while trying to empower and prepare students to succeed in the workforce and beyond (Harmon, 2012; Gasman, Castro Samayoa, Boland, Washington, Jimenez, & Esmieu, 2016). Gasman et al. (2016) found that MSIs typically "boast diverse faculties and staffs, provide learning environments that promote/cultivate leadership, and address students' academic deficiencies due to inadequate preparations" (p. 5). More specifically, it can be argued that MSIs are doing the work predominantly white institutions are not; and they are serving a significant number of historically underrepresented populations while creating a climate that is conducive to these students' lived and learned experiences.

Albeit among the similarities of MSIs, there are also some distinct differences. Compared to other MSIs, Hispanic-Serving Institutions enroll over half (62%) of all Latina/o undergraduate students (Excelencia in Education, 2016). HSIs also perform better in terms of full-time student retention rates (78%), yet their six-year graduation rates (29%) remain relatively low compared to the national average (57.4%) (NCES, 2011b). Unlike their HBCU counterparts, the relevance of HSIs is also more often challenged particularly due to the "arbitrary" 25% designation threshold. Another difference is that HSIs look different all across the nation and they represent an array of institutional types. This variation makes it difficult for scholars to find commonality beyond their enrollment (Núñez et al., 2016). Yet, despite these challenges, HSIs continue to educate a significant proportion of non-traditional students – or as has been more recently coined, "post-traditional students" (Santiago et al., 2016).

Post-traditional students make college choices based on cost of attendance, location, as well as accessibility. On the other hand, traditional students exhibit college-ready characteristics upon graduating from high school and make college choices based on programs and institutional prestige (Hurtado & Guillermo-Wann, 2013; Santiago et al., 2016). The majority of HSIs tend to serve as an entry and transition point for post-traditional students. In fact, nearly 40% of Hispanic community college students are enrolled in Hispanic-serving community colleges (Núñez, Sparks, & Hernandez, 2011). Academically, these students often require additional preparation or remediation to adjust to the rigors of college. They also complete their degrees well beyond the four-year timeframe (Santiago et al., 2016). These student characteristics are of importance because as the number of HSIs increases, institutional leaders across the nation are faced with the challenge of creating programs that can best serve the distinct population of post-traditional students. For instance, descriptive statistics suggest that at four-year HSIs, Latina/o students tend to struggle among their peers and have less access to various forms of social, cultural, and financial capital (Núñez & Bowers, 2011; Núñez & Elizondo, 2012). Therefore, with the new focus on college completion, institutions will need to adjust their educational and social environments to ensure these students succeed.

On the other hand, there is promising data that suggests that with the growth of HSIs more Latina/os will gain access to higher education and improve their academic achievement. Research suggests that the level of Latina/o student critical mass, as found at HSIs, can have a positive influence on academic adjustment (Hurtado, Carter, & Spuler, 1996). In fact, research that analyzed Latina/os' experiences and outcomes across non-HSIs, HSIs, and Emerging HSIs showed positive correlations in students' college experiences, academic self-concept, and campus racial climate at HSIs and Emerging HSIs (Cuellar, 2014). Furthermore, the number of Latina/o adults who earned an associates degree or higher increased from 12 to 23% from 1995 to 2014 (Santiago et al., 2016). Among four-year HSIs, the combined student persistence and completion rates was 74% compared to all other institutions of higher education which was 71% (Shapiro, Dundar, Yuan, Harrell & Wakhungu, 2014). Needless to say, there is evidence to suggest that HSIs are playing a critical role in educating the growing Latina/o population.

The Present: The Growth of HSIs

Nationally, HSIs are growing rapidly. In 2016, data revealed there were a total of 435 HSIs (Excelencia in Education, 2016). This is a significant increase from 265 as recorded in 2006, and over triple the 132 institutions identified in 1990 (Santiago, 2012). The majority of HSIs are geographically concentrated in Southwest region of the United States: California, Texas, New Mexico, and Puerto Rico; and of the 435 HSIs, almost half (219) are two-year colleges and the remaining 216 are four-year institutions (Excelencia in Education, 2016). A closer look at the characteristics of these campuses reflects that the majority of HSIs have a high concentration (40–100%) of Latina/o full-time equivalent enrollment. More importantly, there are another 310 Emerging HSIs (Excelencia in Education, 2016). Emerging HSIs (eHSIs) are institutions at the brink of reaching 25% Hispanic FTE and have a Hispanic population between 15 and 24% (Santiago, 2008). Emerging HSIs are critical to this conversation because they are changing the future educational landscape of the nation and data reflects that almost every state in the U.S.A. has at least one emerging HSI. Therefore, if the 310 Emerging HSIs in the U.S.A became officially designated as HSIs, the nation would have a total of 745 HSIs.

Despite the growth of HSIs, one of the challenges for scholars today is delineating students' experiences and outcomes at HSIs beyond the two existing categories

(HSIs and eHSIs). While these terms have gained traction, most research does not disaggregate HSIs by institutional type, control, or geographic location, making it difficult to make comparisons about these institutions (Núñez et al., 2016). However, there are new attempts to describe the typology of HSIs and a small number of other studies that have delineated HSIs by geographic location. For instance, along the Mexico and U.S. border there are institutions that have long served Latina/os and have an exceedingly high number of these students enrolled. For example, in Texas the racial and ethnic composition of individuals aged 18–35 has changed remarkably from 2009 to 2015 (THECB, 2009). State population projections suggest that the Hispanic population will increase by nearly 2.3 times its size in 2010, to 21.5 million by 2050 (Potter & Hoque, 2014). The regions in Texas that are expected to experience this expanded growth are Central Texas, the Gulf Coast, Dallas Metroplex, and the Rio Grande Valley. With the exception of the Dallas Metroplex and Central Texas, all other regions are located along or within 100 miles of the Texas–Mexico border. The Texas Higher Education Coordinating Board reports these five regions will account for 85% of the 18–35 age group and 86% of the population will be Latina/o.

Given the location of these HSIs, some scholars have begun to categorize these institutions as Border HSIs (Santiago, 2010; Cortez, 2011). There are nine Border HSIs in Texas and they enroll 5% of all Hispanic undergraduates in the United States (Santiago, 2010). They not only have high enrollments but they also rank among the top institutions awarding degrees to Hispanics. The student population at these Border HSIs largely consists of students who are first-generation, low-income, older than traditional college-age, and work while in school (Cortez, 2011). Many of these institutions have served Hispanics prior to the official HSI designation and have Hispanic populations well over 75% (Santiago, 2010). These institutions are also faced with the responsibility of providing a quality education in some of the poorest regions of the United States (U.S. Census Bureau, 2010). These institutions also share a history of limited state financial support to help improve access to and quality of education. From 2005 to 2015, Border HSIs have increased both their enrollment and degrees awarded to Latina/os compared to the national growth. In 2015, Texas public institutions were projected to increase their degrees awarded to Latina/os by 40%, but Texas Border HSIs will increase their degrees awarded by 90% (Santiago, 2010). While the term Border HSIs begins to provide some nuanced distinction, more research is needed to determine whether geographic location can describe HSIs along the border in Texas and states like Arizona, New Mexico, and California.

Along with the challenge of defining HSIs, another strain is the limited funding available to support these institutions in strengthening their capacity to serve Latina/os. In 1998, the Developing Hispanic-Serving Institutions Program, which is commonly known as Title V, was created. The program was designed to provide federal funds for HSIs and allocate dedicated monies to support these institutions (Benítez, 1998). Unfortunately, the growth of HSIs has outpaced the level of funding available. HSIs apply for Title V funds through a competitive application process and funds are not awarded to institutions based on a set criterion such as institutional type, that is, four-year, two-year, public, or private (Cortez, 2011). Instead, funds are distributed to HSIs with the most competitive applications or in other words, best design of programs. This process can give an unfair advantage to institutions that have the most experience in preparing these rigorous applications. It also does not award funds based on the number of Latina/os served, therefore HSIs with a student population of 85% compete with institutions of 26%. Thus, regardless of institutional type any IHE classified as an HSI can compete for Title V funds.

Title V funds are significant because they provide a substantial amount of new money for HSIs. Institutions can apply for two different funding categories: Individual Developing and Cooperative Agreement grants. The Cooperative grant application allows two-year and four-year HSIs to partner for funds, allowing one institution to serve as the fiscal agent. HSIs can also apply for Individual grants of which all the funds are awarded to support one institution. These funds are distributed over a five-year period and can comprise upwards of one to two million dollars. Ultimately, Title V funds are intended to provide start-up monies that are to be institutionalized by the awarded college or university. Hispanic-Serving Institutions are expected to utilize these funds to help raise different areas of institutional capacity (Benítez & DeAro, 2004). The funds can be used for a variety of activities such as: scientific or laboratory equipment for teaching; construction or renovation of instructional facilities; faculty development; purchase of educational materials; academic tutoring or counseling programs; funds and administrative management; joint use of facilities; endowment funds; distance learning academic instruction; teacher education; and student support services (U.S. Department of Education, "Developing Hispanic-Serving Institutions Program," n.d.).

In 2015, a total of 96 HSIs were awarded Title V funds averaging a yearly award of $544,941 and a total of $51.0 million dollars (U.S. Department of Education, "Title V Program," n.d.). This is a decrease from 1995, when more funds were available for a smaller pool of institutions. Since 2004, the total amount of funds appropriated to HSIs was $93.9 million, allowing the Title V program to serve over 223 HSIs with a yearly average award of $421,000. Today, the Title V program funds less than 100 awards per year and the majority of institutions use these funds to support student services and curriculum development.

The Future: Endless Possibilities

Despite the historical importance of HSIs and the role they play in educating Latina/o students, there is a complexity that surrounds their institutional identity. Institutional leaders must be aware that there is an on-going debate on "what it means to be Hispanic-serving." More importantly, students, faculty, and staff perceive the term differently and not all embrace or understand the importance of this designation (Calderón Galdeano, Flores, & Moder, 2012; Cortez, 2011). Therefore, the future for HSIs holds great potential for scrutiny especially at a time when the political climate is less tolerant of providing specific opportunities for one ethnic or racial group.

In a study that surveyed 19,213 faculty at 819 institutions across the United States, institutional type was an important factor to faculty (Hubbard & Stage, 2009). This study focused on faculty's attitudes and satisfaction with their academic career. The overall results indicated that faculty believe there are differences between predominantly white institutions and MSIs. Faculty from institutions with a higher Latino enrollment, 25% or more, revealed they spent a greater percentage of their time teaching compared to faculty at institutions with a lower Latina/o enrollment, less than 10%. However, faculty at these same institutions also indicated they would choose their academic career again, reflecting that they were satisfied with their institution.

Administrators at HSIs have also reported some difficulty in embracing a Hispanic-serving identity. A study that assessed administrators' perceptions of the campus climate at a Border HSI, showed a difficulty in recruiting faculty (Cortez, 2011, 2015). At this particular institution, faculty positions remain open for an extended period of time and there are a limited number of applicants. Administrators blamed the lack of interest in the region, but also discussed the possibility that being a Hispanic-Serving Institution may deter applicants. Overall, institutional leaders shared the struggle in determining how to define their HSI identity and what role this identity should play in the mission, vision, and strategic plan of the university. While further research is needed on faculty and administrators' perceptions, one study that interviewed presidents from top HSIs enrolling and graduating Latinos, suggests that embracing such identity is the best avenue for creating pathways for student success (Santiago, 2009).

Thoughts for Institutional Leaders

By 2050, the majority of the U.S. workforce will consist primarily of Latinos and the nation will forever be changed by the shift in demographics (U.S. Census Bureau, 2010). This growth has also propelled the interest in HSIs, and MSIs in general. Furthermore, these designations have added a complex layer to the world of higher education, framing the narrative beyond the two-dimensional institutional descriptions (two/four year, public/private). With that said, the role of institutional leaders is of great importance.

Personally, I believe administrators can be more intentional about educating their campuses on the HSI designation. One way this can be accomplished is by creating a campus-wide campaign, similar to efforts made during the accreditation process, and to require all units to integrate measurable goals that will improve the capacity of Latina/o students. These efforts should be inclusive of faculty to combat any misperceptions or stereotypes about the academic prestige of HSIs. After all, future projections indicate that the majority of Emerging HSIs will include top-tier research institutions.

Despite the debate over the value of a college degree, the overwhelming belief is that a postsecondary education is both a private and public good. Unfortunately,Latinos don't often share in this personal and economic prosperity when only 13% have obtained at least a bachelor's degree (NCES, 2011a). That being said, it is hard to argue that it is only the responsibility of HSIs to educate Latina/o students. Institutional leaders must be advocates for both underserved Latina/o students attending well-resourced institutions and under-resourced institutions that have historically served Latina/o students. The educational attainment of Latinos is a national imperative and all leaders must be on board.

Along with the role of institutional leaders, there are policy recommendations at the national level that may combat some of the struggles HSIs face. For instance, if institutions apply for an HSI designation and receive approval, a federal policy should require institutions to publically inform constituents of their HSI status and the benefits of being an HSI. Furthermore, it is not enough to state they are "Hispanic-serving," they must also make an intentional effort to change their mission to explicitly serve Hispanics. Such federal policies would deter institutions from applying for an HSI designation but not being intentional on how it serves students. It will also prevent institutions that become HSIs from perpetuating a closeted identity.

While this chapter discusses the on-going struggle to distinguish between the varying types of HSIs, I do believe it is warranted to offer a historical designation to institutions that have served Latinos prior to the creation of the term. Similar to HBCUs, reverence must be given to institutions that have been historically providing access and graduating Latina/o students. Along with creating a historical designation, a federal policy must be created to distribute Title V funds equitably. To accomplish this, a tier system based on the percentage of Latina/os enrolled should be used to guide the distribution of Title V funds. This tier system will allow for Title V funding to be distributed equitably among the various types of HSIs. For instance, HSIs with 85–50% Latino enrollment should complete for Title V funds among all other HSIs with this same enrollment. The same would be true for HSIs between 49 and 35% and those who are serving 34–25%. I believe that if HSIs compete for Title V funds with other HSIs that have comparable Latino enrollment, it will provide an equal playing field.

With regard to research, there is a dire need to expand the literature on HSIs. From campus climate to degree completion, there is an urgency to increase the number of qualitative and quantitative studies on HSIs. It is critical to also examine MSIs that are now acquiring multiple institutional identities such as HBCUs that are also HSIs. Studies should be conducted with all stakeholders and be published in scholarly journals, but also available as policy briefs and handbooks that can be applicable for practitioners. I also support the old saying, "to understand our future, we must understand our past." Scholars should focus on conducting retrospective analysis at individual HSI campuses to assess how Latina/o students have performed over time. For instance, rather than applying certain programs and services that exist at other institutions (although this can be helpful), HSIs should look at how Latina/o students have fared at their own institutions. Such internal analysis will provide a critical view of how Latina/o student have persisted, engaged, and performed unique to their institution. Furthermore, I would caution scholars who utilize the term HSI freely in their studies. Given the popularity of this topic, new studies have emerged using the term Hispanic-Serving Institution but they dismiss the important work needed to examine how such institutional identities impact, improve, or alter the experiences of Latina/os. For these reasons, I encourage scholars to think critically when conducting studies on HSIcampuses, particularly on how such work can contribute to the profound need to expand our understanding of how institutions honor their HSI identity.

In closing, the goal of this chapter was to fill a gap in literature that tells the story of HSIs. In scholarly publications we often want to learn of the outcomes and never the journey of how things begin. This historical journey of the past, present, and future of HSIs serves this purpose. The intention was to inform researchers, policy makers, and practitioners of the rapid, yet complex, identities institutions are facing as the Latina/o population continues to grow. There is no doubt that HSIs have played and will continue to play a significant role. After all, the educational attainment of Latina/os is a national imperative and at one point or another we must acknowledge that the institutional landscape of higher education will consist of more HSIs.

References

Altbach, P.G., Berdahl, R.O., & Gumport, P.J. (2005). The context of American higher education. In P. Altbach, R. Berdahl, & P. Gumport (Eds.), *American higher education in the twenty-first century: Social, political, and economic challenges* (pp. 1–14). Baltimore, MD: Johns Hopkins University.

Benítez, M. (1998). Hispanic-Serving Institutions: Challenges and opportunities. In J.P. Merisotis & E.M. O'Brien (Eds.), *Minority-Serving Institutions: Distinctions, purposes, common goals* (pp. 57–68). San Francisco, CA: Jossey-Bass.

Benítez, M., & DeAro, J.C. (2004). Realizing student success at Hispanic-Serving Institutions. *New Directions for Community Colleges*, Fall (127), 35–48.

Bridges, B.K., Kinzie, J., Nelson Laird, T.F., & Kuh, G.D. (2008). Student engagement and student success at historically Black and Hispanic Serving Institutions. In M. Gasman, B. Baez, & C.S. Viernes Turner (Eds.), *Understanding Minority-Serving Institutions* (pp. 217–236). Albany: State University of New York Press.

Calderón Galdeano, E., Flores, A.R., & Moder, J. (2012). The Hispanic Association of Colleges and Universities and Hispanic-Serving Institutions: Partners in the advancement of Hispanic higher education. *Journal of Latinos and Education*, 11: 157–162.

Cohen, A.M. (1998). *The shaping of American higher education: Emergence and growth of the contemporary system*. San Francisco, CA: Jossey-Bass.

Contreras, F.E., Malcom, L.E., & Bensimon, E.M. (2008). Hispanic Serving Institutions: Closeted identity and the production of equitable outcomes for Latino/a students. In M. Gasman, B. Baez & C. Turner (Eds.), *Interdisciplinary approaches to understanding Minority Serving Institutions* (pp. 71–90). New York: SUNY Press.

Cortez, L.J. (2011). *The campus climate of a Border HSI: Redefining Latino student success*. Ph. D. dissertation, University of Texas at Austin, United States – Texas. Retrieved June 18, 2016, from Dissertations & Theses: Full Text.

Cortez, L.J. (2015). Enacting leadership at Hispanic-Serving Institutions. In A.M. Núñez, S. Hurtado. and E. Calderón Galdeano (Eds.). *Hispanic-Serving Institutions: Advancing research and transformative practice* (Chapter 8). New York: Routledge.

Cuellar, M. (2014). The impact of Hispanic-Serving Institutions (HSIs), emerging HSIs, and non-HSIs on Latina/o academic self-concept. *Review of Higher Education*, 37(4), 499–530.

Excelencia in Education (2016). *Hispanic-Serving Institutions (HSIs): 2014–2015 at a glance*. Washington, D.C.: Excelencia in Education.

Fry, R. & Hugo Lopez, M. (2012). Hispanic student enrollment reaches new highs in 2011. *Pew Hispanic Center*. Retrieved from www.pewhispanic.org

Garcia, G. & Okhidoi, O. (2015). Culturally relevant practices that "serve" students at a Hispanic Serving Institution. *Innovative Higher Education*, 40(4). doi:10.1007/s10755–10015–9318–9317

Garcia, G., Patrón, O.E., Ramirez, J.J., & Hudson, L.T. (2016). Identity salience for Latino male collegians at Hispanic-Serving Institutions (HSIs), Emerging HSIs, and Non-HSIs. *Journal of Hispanic Higher Education*, August 2, 1–16.

Gasman, M. (2008). On Minority-Serving Institutions: A historical backdrop. In M. Gasman, B. Baez, & C. Viernes Turner (Eds.). *Understanding Minority-Serving Institutions* (pp. 19–27). Albany: SUNY Press.

Gasman, M., Castro Samayoa, A., Boland, W.C., Washington, A., Jimenez, C., & Esmieu, P. (2016). *Investing in student success: The return on investment of Minority-Serving Institutions*. Philadelphia, PA: Penn Center for Minority Serving Institutions.

Harmon, N. (2012). *The role of Minority-Serving Institutions in national college completion goals*. Washington, D.C.: Institute for Higher Education Policy.

Hoffman, M., Snyder, T.D., & Sonnenberg, B. (1996). *Historically Black colleges and universities: 1976–1994*. National Center of Education Statistics Publication no. 96–902. Washington, D.C.

Hubbard, S.M., & Stage, F.K. (2009). Attitudes, perceptions, and preferences of faculty at Hispanic serving and predominantly Black institutions. *The Journal of Higher Education*, 80(3), 270–289.

Hurtado, S., Carter, D.F., & Spuler, A. (1996). Latino student transition to college: Assessing difficulties and factors in successful college adjustment. *Research in Higher Education*, 37(2), 135–157.

Hurtado, S., & Guillermo-Wann, C. (2013). *Diverse learning environments: Assessing and creating conditions for student success – final report to the Ford Foundation*. Los Angeles: University of California, Los Angeles, Higher Education Research Institute.

Kaplan, M.A. (2009). Hispanic Serving Institutions – opening the door to higher education. *The Hispanic Outlook in Higher Education*, 19(11), 21–24.

LBJ Library (n.d.). *Media gallery on education*. Retrieved from www.lbjlib.utexas.edu/johnson/lbjforkids/edu_whca370-text.shtm

Lucas, C.J. (1994). *American higher education: A history*. New York: St. Martin's Groffin.

National Center for Educational Statistics (NCES) (2011a). Integrated Postsecondary Education Data System (IPEDS), 2011, glossary.

National Center for Education Statistics (NCES) (2011b). Integrated Postsecondary Education Data System (IPEDS), Fall 2001 and Spring 2002 through Spring 2011, Graduate Rate Component.

Núñez, A.-M. & Bowers, A.J. (2011). Exploring what leads high school students to enroll in Hispanic-Serving Institutions: A multilevel analysis. *American Educational Research Journal*, 48(6), 1286–1313.

Núñez, A.-M., Crisp, G., & Elizondo, D. (2016). Mapping Hispanic-Serving Institutions: A typology of institutional diversity. *The Journal of Higher Education*, 87(1), 56–77.

Núñez, A.-M., & Elizondo, D. (2012). *Hispanic-Serving Institutions in the U.S. mainland and Puerto Rico: Organizational characteristics, institutional financial context, and graduation outcomes*. San Antonio, TX: Hispanic Association of Colleges and Universities.

Núñez, A.-M., Sparks, J., & Hernandez, E. (2011). Latino access to community colleges and Hispanic-Serving Institutions. *Journal of Hispanic Higher Education*, 10(1), 18–40.

Park, T.J., Flores, S.M., & Ryan, C.J. (2015). *Labor market returns for graduates of Hispanic Serving Institutions*. Philadelphia, PA: Penn Center for Minority Serving Institutions.

Potter, L.B. & Hoque, N. (2014, November). *Texas population projections, 2010 to 2015*. Retrieved from http://osd.state.tx.us

Sáenz, R. (2010, December). *Population bulletin update: Latinos in the United States 2010*. Washington, D.C.: Population Reference Bureau.

Santiago, D. (2006). *Inventing Hispanic-Serving Institutions: The basics*. Washington, D.C.: Excelencia in Education.

Santiago, D. (2008). *Accelerating Latino student success at Texas border institutions: Possibilities and challenges*. Washington, D.C.: Excelencia in Education.

Santiago, D. (2009). *Leading in a changing American: Presidential perspectives from Hispanic-Serving Institutions*. Washington, DC: Excelencia in Education.

Santiago, D. (2010). *Reality check. Hispanic-Serving Institutions on the Texas border strategizing financial aid*. Washington, D.C.: Excelencia in Education.

Santiago, D. (2012). *Changes in Hispanic-Serving Institutions: List 2009–10 and 2010–11*. Washington, D.C.: Excelencia in Education.

Santiago, D., Taylor, M., & Calderón Galdeano, E. (2016). *From capacity to success: HSIs, Title V, and Latino students*. Washington, D.C.: Excelencia in Education.

Shapiro, D., Dundar, A., Yuan, X., Harrell, A. & Wakhungu, P.K. (2014, November). *Completing college: A national view of student attainment rates – fall 2008 cohort* (Signature Report No. 8). Herndon, VA: National Student Clearinghouse Research Center.

Texas Higher Education Coordinating Board (THECB) (2009). *Participation forecast 2009–2020*. Retrieved from www.thecb.state.tx.us

U.S. Census Bureau (2010). *Hispanic or Latino origin data 2003-2013, American Community survey*. Retrieved from www.census.gov/population/hispanic/data/index.html

U.S. Department of Education (n.d.). Title V Program. Retrieved from www.ed.gov.hsi

U.S. Department of Education (n.d.). Developing Hispanic-Serving Institutions Program. Retrieved from www2.ed.gov/programs/idueshsi/index.html

Valdez, P.L. (2013). *Hispanic-serving institution legislation: An analysis of policy formation between 1979 and 1992*. Ph.D. dissertation, University of Texas at Austin. Retrieved March 25, 2017, from Dissertations & Theses: Full Text.

Vincent, G.J. (2004). *Community university partnerships in action: A case study of the Louisiana State University–Old South Baton Rouge partnership*. Ed.D. dissertation, University of Pennsylvania, United States. Retrieved June 18, 2016, from Dissertations & Theses: Full Text (Publication No. AAT 3124701).

PART III

Tribal Colleges and Universities (TCUs)

9

TRIBAL COLLEGE AND UNIVERSITY LEADERSHIP

Overcoming Challenges through Service and Collective Leadership

Ginger C. Stull and Marybeth Gasman

Tribal Colleges and Universities (TCUs) are generally small, rural campuses located on or near Native American reservations. They are usually tribally controlled, but serve both Native and non-Native students. The history of TCUs began with the founding of Diné College by the Navajo Nation in 1968. Today there are 37 TCUs, in 14 states, 34 of these are accredited by mainstream accrediting bodies, and have a total enrollment of approximately 28,000 students (Stull et al., 2015). TCUs are unique compared to other higher education institutions in their mission to serve tribal priorities while maintaining and growing tribal culture.

Any discussion on American Indian education in the United States must mention the shameful history of forced education and assimilation at the hands of both European colonists and later the U.S. government. Millions of Indigenous people perished and with them Indigenous languages and traditions as the United States took foot as a nation. Missionary-led boarding schools aimed at forcing a Eurocentric lifestyle on Native American youth were also common (Stull et al., 2015). In the early twentieth century, the federal government controlled tribal education, with schools focused on assimilation practices. Recognizing the importance of preserving and growing the Nation's Indigenous heritage, tribal leaders called for an end to curricula driven by an unnecessary need to indoctrinate Native Americans into White middle class values, and began a political movement of self-determination (Oppelt, 1990). Tribally controlled colleges and universities first emerged in the 1960s as part of this "self-determination" era of Native American education (Carney, 1999; Oppelt, 1990), and from the onset were established to serve a unique mission of sustaining tribal culture and nations (Stull et al., 2015).

Historians and scholars have often portrayed Native Americans as receptors of one-way assimilation, being overtaken by the Eurocentric culture. But assimilation happened both ways, with Native Americans contributing much to the culture and leadership practices of the United States. Many U.S. citizens do not realize that our interstate freeway system was built on pre-existing Native American roads (Dunbar-Ortiz, 2015). Or that Native American agriculture and irrigation technology built our agrarian system (Dunbar-Ortiz, 2015). The same can be said of Native American leadership practices, practices that centered on democracy and federalism long before the arrival of colonists. The influence of Native American leadership practices on the United States likely began as soon as European colonists landed. It is well documented that the Iroquois Confederacy's Great Law of Peace was influential to the founding fathers as they developed the Constitution (Dunbar-Ortiz, 2015). Throughout the country's history, Native American leadership has influenced Eurocentric leadership practices in seen and unseen ways (Dunbar-Ortiz, 2015).

This chapter focuses on Native American leadership practices as they relate to TCUs, with the hope that Native American leaders can continue to influence other leaders and improve higher education leadership. In this chapter, we discuss how Indigenous Ways of Knowing and historic leadership approaches to Native American schooling provide a backdrop to contemporary TCU leadership. We discuss the unique and not-so-unique leadership challenges that TCU leaders face, and finally we discuss leadership strategies that tribal and TCU leaders employ to effectively serve their students and communities. While Native American approaches to leadership may be useful to all higher education institutions, these concepts may be especially useful to institutions that serve populations that have endured years of systemic social and economic inequality.

Indigenous Ways of Knowing

To fully understand TCU leadership, we must take a step back and explore how Native perspectives on knowledge construction influence leadership strategies and education. Indigenous knowledge is said to come from three sources – historical knowledge passed down from generation to generation, empirical knowledge or knowledge gained through experience, and revealed knowledge from spiritual sources. TCUs honor Indigenous Ways of Knowing and center curriculum and pedagogy design around this way of viewing the world (Crazy Bull, 2015b). Predominantly White institutions (PWIs) focus on methodologies that do not honor this way of knowing, and focus curriculum on the promotion of Western culture, capitalism, and individualism (Crazy Bull, 2015a). Indigenous Ways of Knowing differ from traditionally Eurocentric ways of knowing that tend to look to authority figures as sources of knowledge rather than the community and self. Indigenous Ways of Knowing are also different from Eurocentric leadership approaches of hierarchal decision making.

A History of Failed Leadership Attempts

Native Americans have always led the education of their children and communities through passing down knowledge from generation to generation. The following discussion specifically focuses on the failed leadership of European colonists, and later the federal government, in creating and leading formalized educational institutions that eventually gave way to TCUs. In the colonial period, institutionalized education for Native Americans was promoted as a way to spread Christianity and civilize Native people and was heavily financed by British philanthropists and led by elite higher education institutions (Thelin, 2011; Wright, 1988). Philanthropists made significant donations to colleges like Harvard, Dartmouth, and William and Mary with the intention of indoctrinating Native students with Christian values (Thelin, 2011; Wright, 1988). However, only handfuls of Native students were educated with this money; instead institutional leaders diverted these funds to expanding facilities for White students, essentially swindling their philanthropist funders (Wright, 1988).

After the United States won its independence, the federal government led efforts in Native American higher education, beginning what is often referred to as the federal period (Carney, 1999). Turning away from religious conversion, higher education for Native Americans focused on assimilation through vocational and agricultural training; assigning Native American college graduates to the lowest wage-earning capacities in society and teaching basic agricultural skills to people who were relocated from their lands to sub-par reservation lands (Carney, 1999). The federal government led the missions and agendas of these institutions, but day-to-day management was left in the hands of religious organizations, and rarely if ever included Native Americans in curriculum development or decision making (Carney, 1999). Throughout both the colonial period and federal period of Native American education Native leaders led forms of resistance.

The Meriam Report of 1928 recognized the failure of Native American education and criticized the Bureau of Indian Affairs' (BIA) approach, noting that no previous BIA efforts included the input of American Indians in their design or leadership (Gasman, Nguyen, & Conrad, 2014). Over the coming years the federal government grew increasingly aware of their failed leadership in regard to Native American education. Finally, as part of the Native American self-determination movement of the 1960s and 70s, Native peoples demanded that the federal government fulfill its treaty and trust promises by providing educational funding to Native nations to use as they saw fit, in schools governed by their chartering tribes and led by tribal members and tribal governing boards. In 1968, Navajo Community College opened on the Diné Reservation, becoming the first tribally led formal higher education institution (Gasman, Nguyen, & Conrad, 2014). Shortly after that multiple TCUs opened in the Northern Plains region, and in 1973 the first six TCUs formed the American Indian Higher Education Consortium (AIHEC) a membership organization focused on advocacy and development of TCUs through legislative and education policy (Crazy Bull, 2015b). In 1975, President Nixon signed the Indian Self Determination Act, relinquishing some federal authority over tribal education, health, and social services.

For the first time Native students had access to tribally led higher education focused on the mission of strengthening tribal sovereignty (Gasman, Nguyen, & Conrad, 2014). The history of poor leadership and governance of Native American higher education at the hands of predominantly White missionaries and government officials continues to provide an important reminder of the need for tribal sovereignty and self-governance. Today there are 37 members of AIHEC, including one Canadian institution, 31 tribally chartered institutions, and five non-tribally chartered institutions aimed at educating Native American students (Crazy Bull, 2015b). These institutions are led by Native American presidents who bring knowledge of their communities and culture to their presidency (Crazy Bull, 2015b). And they are governed by boards comprised of graduates, tribal members, and Native American leaders who have a deep understanding of the cultural and spiritual characteristics of the community (Crazy Bull, 2015b).

Contemporary TCU Leadership Challenges

Each TCU leader faces their own challenges in their own contexts, but leaders and researchers also identify some common challenges experienced by many TCU leaders. These include: having to balance tribal needs and mainstream expectations; unfulfilled trust obligations; chronic underfunding and budget unpredictability; an overreliance on competitive grants; being located in rural communities that lack infrastructure and services; and serving underresourced students.

Native American leaders and scholars often discuss the challenge of "walking in two worlds" (Bad Wound, 1991; Bordeaux, 2012; Guillory & Ward, 2008; McLeod, 2002; Munson, 2007; Randall, 2015). In a TCU context, that most often means the challenge of maintaining focus on the institutional mission of promoting tribal self-determination and teaching tribal culture, while maintaining focus on mainstream accountability measures needed to maintain accreditation (Bordeaux, 2012; Randall, 2015). Accrediting agencies can potentially have influence over all aspects of institutional life, including curriculum, organizational structure, and leadership decisions (Bad Wound, 1991). But, TCU leaders realize they cannot lose sight of their true mission of promoting tribal sovereignty, a goal rarely reflected in accreditation success (Bad Wound, 1991; Bowman, 2009). To meet accreditation requirements while maintaining the institutional mission tribal leaders feel they must know and understand the needs of their tribe while knowing and understanding how to meet mainstream academic standards (Munson, 2007).

Meeting accreditation standards can be a challenge for TCUs, as they must also focus on their tribal missions (Guillory & Ward, 2008). TCU leaders must also teach their students to live in two worlds, the tribal community and the mainstream United States economic system (Bad Wound, 1991; Bowman, 2009). This can present curricular challenges as TCUs must teach courses that provide students with a deeper understanding of their tribal history and culture, while also ensuring these courses will transfer to a four-year institution to meet mainstream degree requirements (Bad Wound, 1991). This dilemma of dual missions and worlds, while presenting a challenge, also created the opportunity for TCUs to become national leaders in developing curriculum on Native American history and culture.

Tribal leaders consider the federal government's failure to honor its legal and moral trust obligations to American Indian and Alaskan Native peoples as one of the most chronic challenges that tribal leaders face in regard to education (U.S. Department of Education, 2010). Over the centuries, AIAN groups in the United States signed over 350 treaties with the federal government, relinquishing one billion acres of land. These treaties were intended to secure the wellbeing of American Indian people, including access to healthcare and education, in exchange for the use of their land. Unfortunately the U.S.A. has not fully honored these treaties and tribal schools and health systems remain some of the most underfunded in the country.

Similarly, chronic underfunding and budget unpredictability are a major challenge for many TCU leaders (Guillory & Ward, 2008). The Tribally Controlled Community College Assistant Act (1978) is the major legislation that provides federally allocated base operating funding for TCUs. It currently authorizes funding of $8,000 per Native student (citizens of federally recognized tribes). However, this designated amount has never been fully funded. In FY 2013, Congress appropriated $5,665 per Native American student, with no funding for the non-Native students who compose about 20% of all TCU enrollments. Awarding the fully designated amount of $8,000 per student could be the most important first step the federal government could take in stabilizing the operating budgets of TCUs. Providing appropriations for non-Native students would also help stabilize TCU funding. TCUs do not receive state or federal funding for non-Native students, except for in Montana. Both Native and non-Native students pay tuition, which averages $2,500 across TCUs per term, or $5,000 per year. This means that when combining federal appropriations and tuition revenue, TCUs receive about one half the revenue from a non-Native student as they would a Native student, but provide both students with equal services and benefits. This lack of resources can make meeting accreditation standards difficult, as TCUs often lack the sophisticated data and information management systems that can assist with maintaining accreditation (Bowman, 2009).

TCUs also rely on other competitive grants offered from federal agencies such as the Bureau of Indian Affairs, National Endowment for the Humanities, and the National Science Foundation. However, unlike mainstream institutions, TCUs often use competitive grants to fulfill their base operating budget, creating a fiscal environment that does not promote long-term planning and growth (HLC, 2013). Continuously applying for and using grant funding strains human resources (HLC, 2013). Institutions often do not have dedicated grant-writing staff; they depend on staff members in other roles to write proposals (HLC, 2013). Relying on federal grants as part of the core operating budget is problematic for many reasons. Institutions in O'Laughlin's (2003) study reported challenges such as:

- The lag time between incurring expenses and the actual receipt of the funds from the federal government.
- The difference between the authorized amount of funding and the actual appropriations funded.
- The amount of time, staff, and other resources required to apply for, account for, and report for federal grants.
- The low amount of indirect costs that the TCUs collect for administering federal grants.
- Federal grants are discretionary and may or may not be renewable each year.

(p. 214)

TCU leaders also identify the challenges that come with offering higher education in areas with under resourced infrastructure and services (Guillory & Ward, 2008). For example, students have challenges accessing transportation, technology, and sometimes food (Guillory & Ward, 2008). Tribal students live in rural communities that may lack government services, housing, health care, and business services (Crazy Bull, 2015a).

Like many MSI leaders, TCU leaders face the challenge of serving under-resourced students (Bowman, 2009; Guillory & Ward, 2008). In 2012, MSIs enrolled over 20% of all college students, and enroll a far larger share of minority and low-income students than PWIs (Gasman & Conrad, 2014). It is estimated that 98% of African American and Native American students who attend Historically Black Colleges and Universities (HBCUs) or Tribal Colleges and Universities (TCUs), respectively, qualify for Pell (Conrad & Gasman, 2015). In addition to lacking the higher incomes that White students tend to enjoy, tribal students often have little exposure to higher education (Crazy Bull, 2015b). The personal and historical experiences with formalized education that TCU students have had are often filled with trauma (Crazy Bull, 2015b). Many TCU students are juggling family and financial responsibilities as they attend college (Bowman, 2009). And, many Native American students are debt-averse, and have limited financial resources (Brayboy, Fann, Castagno, & Solyom, 2012).

Many of these challenges are unique to TCU leaders, while many may be commonly faced by higher education leaders, especially those who serve students typically underserved by mainstream higher education. Clearly, TCU leaders face many daily and long-term challenges, but they also employ effective leadership strategies to overcome these challenges.

Qualities and Strategies to Meet Leadership Challenges at TCUs

If the history of Native American formalized education tells us anything, it is that Native Americans are the most capable people to lead tribal education efforts. Although there is far less research on tribal leadership practices than White male leadership practices, the research that does exist reveals common themes and illuminates a variety of practices from which non-Native leaders can learn. Although there are common themes across the leadership qualities and practices of TCU leaders, it must also be noted that Native Americans are not a monolithic group, and that across TCUs leadership practices will vary. Through research and writings on tribal and TCU leadership, the following themes emerge: a dedication to serving the community; the importance of knowledge, both of their tribal culture and the people they serve; decentralized leadership and collective decision making; leading and learning by example; and persisting through difficult circumstances.

One of the most important qualities that a TCU leader can possess is a dedication to serving the community (Guillory & Ward, 2008; McLeod, 2002; Munson, 2007). In Munson's (2007) study of leadership theories among Tribal Council members, the most common theme that emerged is "that a Native American leader is there to help the people" (p. 82). Every interview participant discussed the importance of being there for the tribe. Themes of "looking out for the whole of the tribe, protecting the tribe, providing a future for the younger generation, and helping the elders" were all encompassed in ideas of what makes a good tribal leader (p. 82). One participant noted that Native American leaders often do things that are seen as "below their station" by other cultures, and gave an example of a TCU president who would pick up garbage across campus when needed (Munson, 2007). Generally Native American leaders are seen as people that look after the whole of the tribe and its future, and exhibit empathy and compassion for the people they serve and take the good of the people to heart (Munson, 2007). Tribal leaders even define success as "having the ability to take care of people, understanding the people and doing something to help them, or simply as helping others" (Munson, 2007, p. 105). Munson (2007) also found that "looking out for the whole tribe, always trying to make things better, and caring for the less fortunate were also seen as part of being successful" as a Native American leader (p. 105). This leadership quality is reflected in TCU practices. TCUs often use community-based research to identify and address tribal needs, and create and improve upon programs and interventions aimed at meeting community needs (Crazy Bull, 2015b). TCUs reach out to and serve tribal communities in ways that mainstream institutions do not because of the nature of their educational services and the commitment of their leaders to the community (Crazy Bull, 2015a).

A second theme that emerges is that TCU leaders are knowledgeable; knowledgeable from formal education, knowledgeable about the tribal culture of the TCU they serve, and knowledgeable about the community (Bowman, 2009; Munson, 2007). Knowledge of tribal culture and understanding life on the reservation was central to this, as good Native American leaders are expected to represent their people well (Munson, 2007). Fully understanding the community they serve as TCU leaders includes knowing the current political, social, and family elements of the chartering tribe, as well as the ancient cultural and linguistic foundations that inform contemporary tribal life (Bowman, 2009). They must be able to represent their people to non-reservation outsiders, such as the federal and state governments, as well as represent their students, staff, and administrators to each other and other tribal citizens (Munson, 2007).

Collective leadership and decision making is an important quality of Native American leadership (Bryant, 1996; McLeod, 2002). Centralized authority residing in a singular final decision maker is pervasive in mainstream Western leadership practices and organizations; including higher education (Bryant, 1996). This sort of leadership approach is unacceptable in tribal leadership; in fact, top down management is often seen as in conflict with traditional Native American values (Bryant, 1996). Further, ineffective tribal leaders are those who are seen as prone to nepotism or micromanaging rather than empowering people (Munson, 2007). Instead Native American leadership relies on each person making a unique contribution to the organization to meet goals (Bryant, 1996). Leadership roles will often change hands as people oversee their component parts of the greater picture, with no single supervisor overseeing the work in a hierarchal fashion (Bryant, 1996). In a modest way, TCU leaders will often attribute the success of their institution to team effort rather than individual leaders (Bowman, 2009). The collective voice and leadership embodied by AIHEC provides a rich example of this leadership quality. As an organization AIHEC has maintained a collective voice among TCUs to draw attention to legislative funding needs, the unique government-to-government relationship that Native Nations maintain, and the importance of TCUs as an act of tribal sovereignty (Crazy Bull, 2015b). This collective voice and leadership has been an effective strategy for advancing the needs of TCUs. As part of this collective leadership comes collective decision making. In mainstream, Western leadership it is common for a single individual or small group of individuals to make decisions that the rest of the organization are expected to agree to or work towards. In Native American leadership practice, when an important decision must be made, all stakeholders are involved (Bryant, 1996). All participants contribute through speaking, listening, or both, and a decision is reached when all discussion has been exhausted and a course of action has been agreed upon (Bryant, 1996).

Leading and learning by example is also a common theme in TCU leadership (Paetz Sitting Crow, 2013). In her study of eight female TCU leaders, Paetz Sitting Crow (2013) found that all shared childhood experiences of learning leadership skills through observing parents, grandparents, aunts, and uncles as they demonstrated leadership through their examples of hard work, modesty, and generosity. Stories of leaders who led through example are common through research and writings on Native American leadership.

Persisting through difficult circumstances is another quality that TCU leaders have (Paetz Sitting Crow, 2013). When asked what skills they feel are necessary to become a female TCU leader, female TCU leaders often noted resilience (Paetz Sitting Crow, 2013).

Lessons that Majority and other Minority-Serving Institutions Can Learn from TCU Leadership

There are myriad lessons that can be learned from the leadership at TCUs. We offer the following recommendations for consideration. 1) Hierarchal leadership is not necessarily the most effective type of leadership and is not applicable for all contexts. Understanding the most applicable leadership approach for various situations is a valuable tool. 2) It is important to recognize the value in all things and the way that various issues and individuals are connected. This kind of approach leads to less misunderstanding within organizations. 3) Listening to all voices within an organization leads to increased empowerment and the retention of staff and faculty, and people feel that they are collectively creating an organization and jointly making decisions. 4) Valuing students' backgrounds and the knowledge that they bring to campus – seeing their experiences as assets to the institution – leads to stronger retention. 5) It is important to focus on community goals rather than completion and materialism in order to stay focused on student and institutional success; caring for those who seek opportunities. 6) Practicing humility leads to a more inclusive working environment and one that empowers a greater number of individuals. It is essential that one's leadership focuses on others rather than self.

Conclusion

TCUs are environments dedicated to enhancing and enriching tribal colleges and uplifting Native Americans. They have significant human resources. This unique environment creates opportunities for creativity and requires leadership that is humble and open to collective decision making.

References

Bad Wound, E. (1991). Teaching to empower: Tribal colleges must promote leadership and self-determination in their reservations. *Tribal College Journal of American Indian Higher Education*, 3(1), 15.

Bordeaux, L. (2012). The call to lead: Words of wisdom from the longest serving tribal college president. *Tribal College Journal of American Indian Higher Education*, 24(2), 26.

Bowman, N. (2009). Dreamweavers: Tribal college presidents build institutions bridging two worlds. *Tribal College Journal of American Indian Higher Education*, 20(4), 12–18.

Brayboy, B.M.J., Fann, A.J., Castagno, A.E., & Solyom, J.A. (2012). Postsecondary education for American Indian and Alaska Natives: Higher education for nation building and self-determination. *ASHE Higher Education Report*, 37(5), 1–154. San Francisco: Jossey-Bass.

Bryant, M.T. (1996). Contrasting American and Native American views of leadership. A paper presented at the annual meeting of the University Council for Educational Administration, Louisville, KY.

Carney, C.M. (1999). *Native American higher education in the United States*. New Brunswick, NJ: Transaction Publishers.

Conrad, C. & Gasman, M. (2015). *Educating a diverse nation: Lessons from Minority Serving Institutions*. Cambridge, MA: Harvard University Press.

Crazy Bull, C. (2015a). Transferring knowledge of the Tribal College movement. In G.E. Gipp, L.S. Warner, J. Pease, & J. Shanley (Eds.), *American Indian stories of success: New visions of leadership in Indian country* (pp. 293–298). Santa Barbara, CA: ABC-CLIO.

Crazy Bull, C. (2015b). Wōksápe: The identity of Tribal Colleges and Universities. In D. Aguilera–Black Bear & J.W.Tippeconnic III (Eds.), *Voices of resistance and renewal: Indigenous leadership in education* (pp. 35–48). Norman: University of Oklahoma Press.

Dunbar-Ortiz, R. (2015). *An indigenous peoples' history of the United States* (Vol. 3). Boston, MA: Beacon Press.

Executive Office of the President (2014). 2014 Native youth report. Retrieved from www.whitehouse.gov/sites/default/files/docs/20141129nativeyouthreport_final.pdf

Fitzgerald, T. (2003). Changing the deafening silence of indigenous women's voices in educational leadership. *Journal of Educational Administration*, 41(1), 9–23.

Gasman, M., & Conrad, C. (2014). *Minority-Serving Institutions: Educating all students*. Philadelphia, PA: Penn Center for Minority Serving Institutions.

Gasman, M., Nguyen, T.H., & Conrad, C.F. (2014). Lives intertwined: A primer on the history and emergence of Minority Serving Institutions. *Journal of Diversity in Higher Education*, 8(2), 120–138.

Grande, S. (2004). *Red pedagogy: Native American social and political thought*. Oxford: Rowman & Littlefield.

Guillory, J.P., & Ward, K. (2008) Tribal Colleges and Universities: Identity, invisibility, and current issues. In M. Gasman, B. Baez, & C. Sotello Viernes Turner (Eds.), *Understanding Minority-Serving Institutions* (pp. 91–110). Albany, NY: SUNY Press.

Higher Learning Commission (HLC) (2013). Distinctive and connected: Tribal colleges and universities and higher learning commission accreditation – Considerations for HLC peer reviewers. Retrieved from www.aihec.org/our-stories/accreditation.cfm

Institute for Higher Education Policy (2007). The path of many journeys: The benefits of higher education for Native people and communities. Retrieved from www.ihep.org/research/publications/path-many-journeys-benefits-higher-education-native-people-and-communities

Jennings, M. (2004). *Alaska native political leadership and higher education: One university, two universes*. Walnut Creek, CA: AltaMira Press.

McLeod, M. (2002). Keeping the circle strong: Learning about Native American leadership. *Tribal College*, 13(4), 10.

Minthorn, R., & Chavez, A.F. (2015). *Indigenous leadership in higher education*. New York: Routledge.

Munson, T.E. (2007). *Native American leadership theory: A tribal perspective*. Unpublished dissertation.

O'Laughlin, J.M. (2003). *The financing of tribal colleges*. Dissertation Abstracts International, 64(04). (UMI No. 3086755).

Oppelt, N. (1990). *The tribally controlled Indian colleges: The beginnings of self-determination in American Indian education*. Tsaile, AZ: Diné College Press.

Paetz Sitting Crow, K. (2013). *Native American female leadership in tribal HE*. Unpublished dissertation.

Randall, M. (2015, May 2). The challenge of TCU leadership. *Tribal College: Journal of American Indian Higher Education*, 26(4). Retrieved from http://tribalcollegejournal.org/the-challenge-of-tcu-leadership/

Stull, G., Spyridakis, D., Gasman, M., Samayoa, A.C., & Booker, Y. (2015). *Redefining success: How Tribal Colleges and Universities build nations, strengthen sovereignty and persevere through challenges.* Philadelphia, PA: Penn Center for Minority Serving Institutions.

Thelin, J.R. (2011). *A history of American higher education.* Baltimore, MD: The Johns Hopkins University Press.

U.S. Department of Education (2010). Tribal leaders speak: The state of American Indian education. Retrieved from www.ed.gov/edblogs/whiaiane/files/2012/04/Tribal-Leaders-Speak-2010.pdf

Wright, B. (1988). "For the children of the infidels"?: American Indian education in the colonial colleges. *American Indian Culture and Research Journal, 12*(3), 1–14.

10

TRIBAL COLLEGES AND UNIVERSITY LEADERS

Warriors in Spirit and in Action

Cheryl Crazy Bull

That is my commitment. This whole institution – with its full history – has an amazing impact on our graduates, and I am committed to making sure that tradition continues. I am responsible to give it my best and I will do that.

Dr. Vernida Chenault, upon her selection as the president of Haskell Indian Nations University (Native News Online)

Itancan, Lakota for the one who is in charge
Bacheei-tche, Crow for the leader, the good man
Ogimaa, Ojibwa for the one who is held in high esteem

Each American Indian tribe and Alaska Native people has their own way of addressing their leaders. This is true at our tribal colleges and universities (TCU) as well. With those terms of address comes the responsibility and expectations of leadership. The presidency of a tribal college or university is a unique position. While TCU presidents operate higher education institutions with many of the same expectations as other post-secondary institutions – maintaining accreditation, improving student success, assuring financial oversight, and good governance – they do so at institutions that are contextually and physically place-based and culturally rooted. Each of the institutions they oversee operates in a manner that is specific to its geographic location, history, and mission. The establishment of these institutions came from the sacred vision of their founders, creating an ancestral responsibility to lead in a manner that ensures the survival of their people. Their institutions not only educate students through personal self-determination, they build tribal self-determination. Leaders of tribal colleges must possess very diverse skills and act in ways that reflect the qualities and values held in high regard by their tribal people. Operating in environments where there are often extreme social and economic disparities, and forced to comply with externally generated standards and expectations, tribal college leaders must be visionary, effective, and progressive within very complex circumstances. They must be warriors, using all the skills and resources they can access to ensure the survival of their institutions so that their people may prosper and their Tribes can thrive.

Nearly all tribal colleges and universities are chartered by their Tribes. This can be analogized to the ability of states to establish their own higher education systems. Their establishment is rooted in tribal self-determination and in inherent rights of indigenous people. It is also closely entwined with the federal/tribal relationship built upon both inherent rights and treaties. While this chapter does not discuss governance and identity of indigenous communities, it would not be possible to discuss the tribal college presidency without at least some understanding of the fundamentals of indigenous self-governance and identity. These fundamentals include:

- Indigenous people have their own homelands – the knowledge of place where they emerge as human beings is unique to each Tribe.
- Indigenous people have their own Native languages – words and their meaning are given to each people by the Creator.
- Tribal people have their own spiritual ways – traditional practices and prayers belong to each Tribe in the way that Creation has informed them.
- Each Tribe has its own social, economic, and political systems – family and social relationships, the way people provide for themselves, and the way they govern themselves is unique to each indigenous people.

It is also not possible to examine the leadership of TCUs without an understanding of how educational experiences evolved in the lives of tribal citizens. Prior to European contact, Tribes had a variety of approaches to learning, most closely tied to the age and status of each tribal citizen and informed by the circumstances under which each Tribe sought to thrive in whatever environment they lived in. Each Tribe has its expectations of the stages of human development, its own child-rearing and socialization practices, and its own understanding of what it means to be a complete man or woman. Tribal societies thrived in countless ways throughout what is now North America. Upon the arrival of Europeans, a dramatic and oppressive shift in educational systems occurred quite quickly. Up until the mid to late 1960s, assimilationist and often genocidal government and social policies and practices influenced Native education and the social fabric of tribal life in very detrimental ways. These practices included forced attendance in boarding schools, forced conversion to Christianity, relocation to reservations or in the case of many tribes, relocation to the State of Oklahoma, intended to be an "Indian" state, and in the 1940s and 50s relocation from reservation and rural areas to cities and sometimes termination of tribal governments.

In the 1960s with the civil rights movement in the United States came a renaissance in tribal governance and indigenous cultures. This led to establishment of the first tribally controlled higher education institutions with the founding of Navajo Community College (Diné College) in 1968. In June 2016, there are now 35 accredited members of the American Indian Higher Education Consortium, the membership organization of the TCUs. There are also several TCUs operating at various stages of program delivery that are not yet accredited on their own.

Presidency of the TCU

> *During a strategic planning session at the Fall 2011 AIHEC board meeting, President Lionel Bordeaux of Sinte Gleska University discussed the words and vision of one of the founders of SGU, Stanley Red Bird, Sr., that tribal colleges would provide the leadership to redefine and restructure Indian education and that TCUs would create new structures and approaches to education that are based on our spirituality, cultural values and customs. Lionel shared Stanley's words: "we have the land and we are smart, we are people of intellect, strength and courage." He also spoke to the need to use this knowledge to look at the form of our tribal governments and to go back to our traditional leadership practices.*
>
> *(AIHEC website, personal communications)*

In an effort to contextualize the presidency of tribal post-secondary institutions, I am going to discuss the position using the framework of leadership found in most tribal cultures. President Bordeaux's comments are typical of the expectations of tribal colleges and their presidents. Tribal college leaders must be visionary, effective, and progressive within very complex circumstances. They must be warriors, using all the skills and resources they can access to ensure the survival of their institutions so that their people may prosper and their Tribes can thrive. This leadership framework is cultural and contextual:

1.   The president as visionary – understanding our identity and our ways of knowing and seeing what the future holds for us
2.   The president as hunter/gatherer/grower – being able to find the tools and resources needed to fulfill the vision and mission of their institution
3.   The president as translator/interpreter – being able to explain how our traditional knowledge and ways of knowing can be used in today's society
4.   The president as orator/advocate – in our societies, the person who is called upon to speak has listened to everyone and has the role of sharing knowledge and inspiring
5.   The president as warrior – TCU presidents must have moral authority to act in the best interest of the people they serve and they must take action, sometimes very assertively
6.   The president as storyteller – preservation of our knowledge is key to the survival of tribal people

7.   The president as spiritual and physical leader – upholds our values and relationships with the Creator and always present to do the work required to get things done.

Warner (in Shanley, 2015, pp. xi–xii) has a model for American Indian Leadership that frames similar roles. At the center is the "one who speaks for us at all times" surrounded by the roles of wisdom keeper (tradition), role model (experience), researcher/observer, and storyteller/narrator.

Vision and Values

Badwound and Tierney (1988) describe the widely divergent values of tribal colleges from those held within the experiences of the western rational model in its approach to the organization of higher education. The divergence is fundamental in that the rational model promotes competition and meritocracy whereas the tribal college organizational model promotes generosity and wisdom. Bordeaux (personal communications) has often described the vision for Sinte Gleska University (SGU) that was given to him when he was recruited for the presidency in 1972 and when he was inaugurated in early 1973. The vision of the founders of SGU was not only for an institution of higher education that would blend western education with Lakota values and knowledge but also one that would lead the way to better tribal governance. Being charged with the duty of transformation of community and reform of government in an inauguration that combined traditional Lakota practices with western practices created a unique and necessary framework for his leadership.

There is considerable research within various fields about the importance of vision to the success of institutions. In the context of tribal communities, vision is particularly valued because it is often seen as derived from a connection between the vision and the visionary through spiritual guidance or interventions. Hart (2006) found in his study of tribal leadership among the Winnebago Tribe of Nebraska that the people believe "A true leader has vision, knows traditional ways, shares and develops leadership, serves and protects the tribal community, develops trust, and shows respect for all tribal people." Krumm (1995) described how:

> the vision of tribal colleges' leaders puts students first, balancing the needs of the community with the needs of the individual, grounding those needs in the wisdom of the past, the knowledge of the present, and the hope for a better future.

Forkenbrock (2015) shares that leaders of tribal colleges not only had vision but they had identified what they wanted to achieve (objective) and knew the path they wanted to take to do so (workable plan).

This is in line with the understanding of tribal people that having a vision was not enough; presidents must also know what must be done to achieve the vision through progressive movement and perseverance. The late Stanley Red Bird, Sr., founder of Sinte Gleska University and a leader in the tribal college movement, always said, "this is the way it must be," conveying the belief of tribal people that the path of the tribal colleges was pre-destined by the vision of the founders and those called upon to carry out that vision.

Presidents must understand the vision of the founders of their college. This is both a concrete and an interpretative experience. There are often living founders with whom the president can consult or there may be documentation such as written materials or visual media. It may take interpretation to be able to identify the intentions of the founders from the perspective of self-determination because it often looks like tribal colleges are founded for economic purposes – to train people for jobs. In fact, they are founded for much more complex reasons including cultural preservation, family and individual wellness, and the need for a sanctuary for creative approaches to community development.

Hunter/Gatherer/Grower

All traditional societies survived because of their ability to adapt to their environments to produce the goods and resources needed for their well-being. If societies and cultures disappeared, it is fairly safe to assume that some traumatic social or environmental event occurred. In most cases, the adaptability of each society to social and environmental changes was the key to their prosperity and often to their very survival. Tribal college presidents must possess the skills of our ancestors in their ability to find the tools and resources needed for our survival.

TCU presidents face challenges in this area. It is no secret that TCUs are severely underresourced and are heavily reliant on federal government support in order to provide for the needs of their students and institutions. In addition to serious financial limitations presidents must address almost on a daily basis, they must also deal with very limited access to qualified human capital and adequate physical resources. Many times, presidents don't have ready access to individuals with the academic qualifications to teach at their institutions or to administer the numerous programs their institutions offer. They frequently don't have affordable access to qualified contractors and sub-contractors for construction and renovation projects, or even for needs such as new electrical or water systems. This is not only a condition of their rural locations but is also the result of a lack of sufficient investment to build a pool of qualified professional, technical, and skilled workers.

The ability to attract human and financial resources must be balanced by presidents against the demands of their communities for academic, vocational, and community programs. Tribal communities served by TCUs have such myriad needs for educated and skilled workers and for restoration of cultural knowledge and health through outreach that the ability to establish priorities and allocate insufficient resources for the greatest return is critical to the success of the president and his/her institution.

Tribal colleges are often cited as community centers but recently Dr. Nathanial St. Pierre, President of Stone Child College has promoted a different description by calling tribal colleges centers of community (personal communications). This description is important because it acknowledges the incredible challenge that presidents face trying to find sufficient resources to meet all the needs of their communities.

Not only do tribal colleges serve unique Native populations, they are often primary educational and service institutions for rural populations, particularly along the northern tier of the United States and in the Southwest.

Presidents have opportunities that can strengthen their ability to serve diverse and complex needs through partnerships with other higher education institutions regionally and nationally. These partnerships can increase academic and vocational programming, provide technology rich access (distance learning via broadcast, internet, and through independent studies).

Implementation of grow-your-own programs is an already proven resource – in this case, the tribal college commits to educating its own citizens and local residents through whatever advanced degree program or training is necessary for them to fill existing and new positions.

The development of a network of experts who can consult on local issues involving construction and technology especially within the tribal college system would be invaluable.

Presidents can also ensure that their partnerships are high quality by following the guidance provided by Guillory (2013): with a focus on process, ensure the appropriate fit through alignment of mission, capacity, and sustainability; build relationships through open communications, flexibility, and trust that recognize the unique institutional and tribal identity of partners; appoint appropriate personnel to manage the relationship; and keep a focus on service to students and communities.

Translator/Interpreter

Littlebear (2009) speaks to the role of TCUs as institutions that influence the direction of their tribes. Littlebear notes that culture is dynamic and enduring. Warner and Tijerina (2009) note that the influence of cultural values provides the framework for the world view of tribal college leaders. In 2003 the Kellogg MSI Leadership initiative, a collaboration of AIHEC, Hispanic Association of Colleges and Universities (HACU), and National Association for Equal Opportunity in Higher Education (NAFEO) through the Alliance for Equity in Higher Education, collected information from tribal college Fellows participating in training programs for presidential roles, who indicated that certain skills and experiences were necessary:

1.   Budget development and monitoring
2.   Academic/instructional leadership
3.   Fund-raising
4.   Strategic planning
5.   Active participation in accreditation activities
6.   Community leadership
7.   Negotiation skills and experiences.

All of those skills could apply to any college presidency so an exploration of how this is different for tribal college presidents connects the skills to the translator role of TCU presidents. For example, tribal colleges rely on federal funding to provide operational support from their institutions through the Tribally Controlled Community College Assistance Act. This Act supports funding based on a formula whereby institutions are required to demonstrate that they are "counting" only those students who are members of federally recognized tribes or direct descendants of enrolled tribal citizens. This is specific to tribal colleges' federal funding, requires reporting to a federal agency, the Bureau of Indian Education, and necessitates advocacy with Congress and with federal agencies to influence funding levels and requirements.

Another example is the experiences of TCUs with accreditation. One way to explore accreditation experiences of TCUs is the examination of both the systems of public accountability that are driven by data analysis and the teaching and learning environments in which TCUs operate. All of the current TCUs are accredited by either the Higher Learning Commission or the Northwest Commission on Colleges and Universities. All are subject to the same rigorous standards as other higher education institutions. All must provide public accountability through the same processes as other institutions such as IPEDS and the College Scorecard.

As I shared in "Tribal colleges and universities: From where we are to where we might go" (2009, p. 213) on the future of tribal colleges:

> There is a close link between the preservation of our traditional knowledge and with the experiences of accreditation and assessment. In order for tribal nations to survive with intact resources and unique identities, we had to be accountable to each other, to ourselves, and to Creator. Accreditation is a similar experience translated into contemporary terms and using contemporary methods. Native people always had standards of accountability and peer review. What has been most difficult for us has been the translation of our traditional and community-based approaches into the frameworks established to primarily serve western models of educational delivery. Accreditation as a process rooted in shared standards for performance and accountability and in the peer-review experience has a long history in U.S. higher education. For tribal colleges accreditation is a comparatively recent

experience and is often viewed as fundamentally outside of the Native experience and occurring with peers who don't have similar experiences.

Accreditation offers public accountability, recognizes performance and quality, and establishes a shared framework from which to evaluate institutions both from student and public perspectives. Presidents have been longtime advocates for the necessity and value of participating with mainstream accreditation processes while also advocating for appropriate consideration of the differences of TCUs from other higher education institutions. Those differences are based in tribal identity, self-governance, cultural practices, and community expectations. Presidents use their authority and voice to persuade others to consider alternative approaches to accreditation practices to accommodate unique tribal college/education needs.

A good existing example of advocacy within the arena of public accountability is the establishment of the World Indigenous Nations Higher Education Consortium (WINHEC), created in August 2002 at a convening of indigenous educators in Alberta, Canada. WINHEC organizers demonstrated the foresight and leadership of indigenous educators seeking to use their diversity and vision as strengths leading to a broad coalition supporting indigenous knowledge as the basis of public accountability. WINHEC created an accreditation process focused on cultural knowledge and practices as foundational to their success. This opportunity for a culturally appropriate accreditation process can be used by TCU presidents to reinforce cultural missions and allocation of resources.

Tribal colleges through AIHEC have also prioritized the establishment of their own accrediting agency in recognition of their unique missions, place-based priorities, and special populations. Among the first goals of AIHEC when it was established in 1973 was the creation of its own accrediting body. This goal remains and presidents must develop a deep understanding of accreditation because as they navigate regional and specialized accreditation environments, they must not only advocate within their own contextual differences but also serve as advocates for all TCUs as distinctive institutions. The Higher Learning Commission which serves the majority of TCUs has published their own guidance for peer reviewers, *Distinctive and Connected: Tribal Colleges and Universities and Higher Learning Commission Accreditation – Consideration for HLC Peer Reviewers*, guidance that summarizes these unique differences and gives peer reviewers new perspectives on the dynamics under which they review TCUs for accreditation.

Orator/Advocate

Often the role of orator is closely tied to being visionary or being the translator of traditional knowledge into contemporary settings. For presidents, however, being an orator is a particularly important identification because it is closely tied to the ability to persuade, inspire, motivate, and clarify the needs of the people served by the tribal college and the ability of the college to represent itself to the people it serves. This quality is essential in an era of limited resources and high demand for services and support. This skill also serves as a tool that can be used by presidents to help their staff, students, and community focus on the goals that can be accomplished with available resources and relationships.

The style of oratory of presidents is often rooted in Native language, in Native language discourse patterns, or in local dialect. This is invaluable when communicating with people whose first language is their tribal language or whose communication skills are formed by local speech patterns. This can be challenging, however, when a president is called upon to speak to external audiences. Presidents are adept at modifying their speech and their discourse styles to accommodate the audiences they encounter. It is important for presidents to be able to adapt their oratory style to the message and the audience. A president can find him- or herself speaking to a gathering of tribal elders one day and before a Congressional hearing the next.

Presidents should feel comfortable using written speeches or talking points and could have themes or persistent points they want to make in diverse settings. It is helpful to keep a collection of current statistics pertaining to Native populations and TCUs, and updated information regarding the tribal college to use in public presentations.

Warrior

In the early years of the tribal college movement, presidents quickly learned that they were combatting deeply rooted attitudes and beliefs about the capability of tribal people to create and operate their own tribal higher education institutions. Numerous accounts by presidents and their colleagues document both the ignorance and the racism they encountered.

Janine Pease, founding President of Little Big Horn College, studied the funding mechanisms associated with tribal colleges (1994) but also discussed the characteristics of presidents, describing them as representative of the Plains warrior tradition. She noted that among Plain tribes, military or warrior service is highly honored and that the characteristics of the young leaders of tribal colleges included the spiritual strength and courageous dedication required of warriors. She considered them to be acting in defense of their people defying the odds. Pease also noted that the presidents at that time were all enrolled tribal citizens raised in communities where relationships, generosity, commitment, and spirituality were valued and most importantly practiced.

I am reminded of a teaching I learned that Tom Sampson, elder of the Tsartlip Nation, shared during teaching sessions at Northwest Indian College. Tom spoke often about the expectations of his people of their leaders. His teaching focused on the necessity of being the leader that your people expected based on centuries of traditions and experiences. And he often shared the new necessity of being able to navigate the modern world, especially the non-tribal world. Tom characterized this experience with the imagery of being able to cross the bridge over to the white man's world to protect tribal rights and knowledge while coming back to your community to fill your spirit and to be in the appropriate relationships required of us as tribal people. He reminded us of the risks of staying in the white man's world when the work of our people required us to be centered in our tribal identities.

For presidents the tradition of being a warrior can be maintained by continued engagement with tribal values such as generosity, courage, industriousness, and compassion. Living a life that constantly practices those values, especially from childhood is naturally the best road on which to travel as a president. But often, presidents need reminders that their tribal values are there for them to use in their decision making and to cope with the many challenges they face.

There is an important transfer of knowledge from the warrior tradition of early or long-standing tribal college presidents and newer presidents that greatly strengthens the ability of presidents to continue their work. My essay, "Transferring Knowledge of the Tribal College Movement" (2015a) discusses how emerging leaders of the TCU movement experience leadership differently from our ancestors. Leaders today operate in a technologically accessible and global environment and are much more diverse in their identity and experience. To maintain the warrior traditions of our founders, a deliberate transfer of knowledge about our history and vision is necessary. Presidents can accomplish this through formal and informal means such as leadership institutes and mentoring.

Storyteller

While it would seem that the oratory/advocacy role of the president would be a storyteller role, I would argue that the storyteller in tribal culture has a particular role to preserve and share historical information and experiences. The development of tribal colleges was a remarkable grassroots initiative and the context of their creation and implementation requires observation and memory to be preserved and sustained.

Many of the contributors in the 2015 book, *American Indian Stories of Success: New Visions of Leadership in Indian Country* are founders of the tribally controlled education movement. A series of chapters are devoted to the storytelling role, defined by the editors (p. 125) as "combining narration with subjective, intuitive insights to portray beliefs and values of the culture." David Gipp, longtime former President of United Tribes Technical College, founding executive director of the American Indian Higher Education Consortium (AIHEC), and emeritus trustee of the American Indian College Fund, in, "In the Spirit of Life Renewed" (2015), shares the story of his grandparents to illuminate his own path to leadership. He tells of the many experiences he had that led him to leadership, calling upon traditional characteristics attributable to the *itancan* (leaders) and the *akicita* (warriors) of his Hunkpapa people, and how all of those attributes both supported him and created his path. It is a story of a person within a context and a set of circumstances that can only be shared as a story. It is an evolutionary story. And, as intended, the story contains the elements of a movement in the telling of a person's life.

It is noteworthy that many writers who contributed to *Stories of Success* expressed discomfort with talking about themselves. Many come from tribal cultures where the task of sharing someone's accomplishments is undertaken by a "speaker," someone whose role either in family or community is to share about someone else. This affirms the need for specialized training of leaders from tribal communities as it is often difficult to learn from the stories and experiences of others if they are not accustomed to sharing those stories as a way to teach.

Good examples of the value of storytelling exist in the literature about tribal colleges. Stein (1992) shares the experiences of presidents of TCUs who founded the American Indian Higher Education Consortium in his book, *Tribally Controlled Colleges: Making Good Medicine*, experiences that exemplify the challenges the founders faced. One early president was confronted by opposition from other higher education organizations who questioned why tribes needed their own institutions. He responded by sharing that for one thing, tribal colleges don't teach that Columbus discovered America. Another president often shared the story that Congressional leaders felt that Indians were "good with their hands" and should stay in the trades rather than trying to get a professional education to become teachers, doctors, or managers.

Broad Considerations of the TCU Presidency

Political and Public Scrutiny

One of the greatest challenges faced by presidents is the success of their institutions in environments of extreme social and economic distress. This creates an unusual level of scrutiny that requires anticipation and management. Janine Pease, after serving 22 years at Little Big Horn College on the Crow Indian Reservation, 18 of those years as the founding president, underwent an intense revolt within the tribal government system that resulted in her dismissal. Years after this traumatic event, documented in "Helps the People: The Dance of the Seasons" (2015), she noted several circumstances that can exist in many tribal settings:

1. Sudden and dramatic progress, often the result of years of effort, shows advancement but can also bring scrutiny and even suspicion.
2. Tribal nations' leadership succession is very challenging and often lacks the compassion associated with cultural norms.
3. Support can change from a positive to a negative abruptly.
4. Impact of a change in support can be dramatic and far-reaching.

Pease's experience has been replicated in various forms at different tribal colleges over the years, demonstrating an unusual aspect of the presidency of a tribal college – the inherent risk of operating a successful institution in an environment of economic deprivation.

Tribes are in many social aspects large extended families and like all families there are a variety of forms and relationships. This can lead to challenges for presidents when families fall in or out of favor within tribal government. Presidents, especially since many are enrolled members of their tribes, must manage this dynamic.

Navigating tribal political environments requires both skills and values – skills in negotiation, communication, and governance and values such as persistence, patience, wisdom, and generosity. It is important to be able to communicate with tribal government and its programs in myriad ways – usually tribal colleges provide at least an annual report to their tribal councils and often provide regular oral and written reports through formal presentations or in the form of newsletters and press releases. Some colleges are able to participate with local cable television or tribally run radio stations.

Negotiation skills are also valuable – the ability to find areas of compromise is important in any leadership role but is particularly useful when dealing with the scarce resources and personal relationships that are part of tribal governance. Negotiation skills fall back on the traditional characteristics discussed earlier – the president's role as storyteller, advocate, and warrior – being able to reinforce values, offer strategies for solutions, and act within a vision contribute to satisfactory negotiations.

Navigating the national political climate is as challenging as tribal climates. Congressional and federal oversight of higher education applies to TCUs as well as other institutions. State policies and practices influence the experiences of tribal students and their institutions. Presidents must be knowledgeable about their institutions in the context of higher education in the country. This knowledge is gained through participation in national and statewide organizations and associations and through connecting to media sources.

It is also important for presidents to be prepared for media scrutiny. Often mainstream media demonstrates a fairly dramatic lack of understanding about tribal governments and about areas such as education, health, and economic development. This lack of understanding leads to misrepresentation of tribal education and that can cause significant problems for TCUs. Presidents should not only have contingency plans to address media inquiries in the event of a crisis but should have quickly available talking points to respond to media requests.

Socio-economic Conditions

Perhaps the greatest challenge and greatest opportunity faced by presidents is the socio–economic conditions under which they must lead their institutions. The 35 accredited tribal institutions (as of August 2016) serve populations with unemployment ranging from as high as 80%, and people under the age of 25 are often more than one-half of the population. Most jobs are public service positions in tribal or federal governments, in schools, or in social services. While many tribes have businesses including light manufacturing, public utilities, and entertainment operations such as casinos, few individual or family small businesses exist. Poor health conditions are exacerbated by a lack of access to quality care, housing is woefully inadequate, and sufficient transportation rarely exists.

This creates an environment ripe with opportunity. Tribal colleges have historically focused on certificate and degree programs in fields where jobs exist – teachers, social workers, health care providers, and areas such as the construction trades or natural resources. In recent years, increased interest in technology, entrepreneurship, and the environment means that tribal colleges extended their offerings into new fields of study. This means that tribal colleges are generating new development by providing education that drives growth rather than only filling existing jobs.

Although completed in 2000, the report, *Tribal Colleges Contributions to Local Economic Development*, prepared by the Institute on Higher Education Policy, is still relevant today. Its continued relevance affirms the persistent barriers experienced by rural, resource rich tribal communities. These barriers are rooted in cultural and social differences, location, government policies, and business practices. In 2016, the American Indian Higher Education Consortium published an analysis of the economic impact of TCUs (AIHEC, 2016), while the North Dakota Tribal College Association conducted a similar analysis of the impact of their five institutions on the ND economy as part of their advocacy (Coon, Bangsund, & Hodur, 2013). While analysis of the contributions of TCUs to economic prosperity is important, the role of this information in the analysis of TCU presidencies is the focus of this review. Presidents of TCUs, similar to the presidents of community colleges with a focus on local development and to the presidents of institutions with community-based baccalaureate programs, have to be stewards of opportunities to lead to effective management of human and natural resources, create partnerships that transfer knowledge and technology toward economic opportunities, and promote certificate and degree programs that address workforce skills and education.

To foster their social and economic development skills, presidents should regularly survey available resources and research, participate with local and tribal social and economic development efforts including tribal committees and community boards, and should network with regional and national community and economic development groups, especially those that prioritize economic access such as the National Center for American Indian Enterprise Development.

Educational Qualifications and Experience

One of the challenges faced by tribal colleges is dealing with the qualifications and experiences needed to fill vacancies in presidential and other leadership positions. While finding qualified faculty and professional staff can be equally challenging it is particularly difficult to find individuals who have the education, experience, and desire to serve institutions located in extremely rural areas with limited financial resources both for adequate pay and benefits and for managing their institutions. At the time of this writing, 17 of the 35 accredited tribal college presidents (including interim presidents) are women and 26 of them have doctorates or other terminal degrees. Tribal colleges have always been exceptionally good places for women to attain leadership roles but the lack of doctorate or terminal degree holders can safely be assumed to be related to the adequacy of the pool of candidates. Sixteen of the tribal colleges have presidents who have served less than five years (including the three institutions with interim presidents who will serve six months or more), and nine have had at least two presidents in those five years.

Having academic qualifications prepares presidents for accreditation, curriculum development, teacher evaluation, and for the responsibility of interacting with faculty. It is useful to have financial knowledge and to have experience working with diverse constituencies as tribal college consumers, supporters, and advocates all vary in their social and educational backgrounds.

So what can be done when the most desirable candidate – a tribal member with excellent personal qualities and a willingness to serve – doesn't have critical qualifications? The college's board should invest in a good professional development plan that supports the attainment of appropriate educational credentials and mentoring from other college or business leaders with expertise in human capital and financial management. This kind of support also ensures that valuable resources are allocated to two of the most significant attributes required of a president – the development of their wisdom and of their ability to lead. In the dynamic worlds of higher education, tribal society, and society in general, wisdom and leadership skills are essential.

Social Justice and Equity

Finally, tribal college presidents must be prepared to address persistent concerns regarding equitable opportunities and resources that are often rooted in long-standing policies and practices derived from racial and economic oppression. In today's society there is an incredible lack of public knowledge about the existence and status of American Indians and Alaska Natives. We are often considered to be relics of the past, existing on the periphery of society and without access to opportunities because of racial, social, and economic barriers.

Presidents must be keenly aware of the ways that these injustices enact themselves in the allocation of resources, access to participation, and even with opportunities to be heard. We are often invisible, even when we are standing right in front of those who should be supporting us.

In addition to directly confronting injustices, presidents can insist that Native people be at the table as equal participants with any opportunities, can advocate for research and scholarship that promotes indigenous knowledge, and can build students' skills as leaders and change agents.

Being a Warrior is a Way of Life

There are many stories among our tribes of warriors who drive stakes into the ground to stand and fight against the onslaught of an enemy that is driving toward them, of warriors who ride into battle to touch the enemy, counting coup, then returning to the front lines of their own soldiers, and of leaders who made agreements and treaties that settled differences, shared resources, and promoted peace. Those are the stories of our modern day warriors – the presidents of tribal colleges and universities.

References

American Indian College Fund (n.d.). Retrieved from www.collegefund.org

American Indian Higher Education Consortium (AIHEC) (2016). Retrieved from www. aihec.org

Badwound, E., & Tierney, W.G. (1988). Leadership and American Indian values: The tribal college dilemma, *Journal of American Indian Education*, 28(1), 9–15.

Coon, R.C., Bangsund, D.A., & Hodur, N.M. (2013, February). *Economic contribution of North Dakota tribal colleges in 2012*. Agribusiness and Applied Economics Report No. 709. Fargo: North Dakota State University.

Crazy Bull, C. (2009). Tribal colleges and universities: From where we are to where we might go. In G.E. Gipp and L.S. Warner (Eds.), *Tradition and culture in the millennium: Tribal colleges and universities* (pp. 209–217). Charlotte, NC: Information Age Publishing.

Crazy Bull, C. (2015). Transferring knowledge of the tribal college movement. In G.E. Gipp, L.S. Warner, J. Pease, & J. Shanley (Eds.), *American Indian stories of success: New visions of leadership in Indian country* (pp. 293–298). Santa Barbara, CA: Praeger.

Economic Modeling Specialists International (EMSI) (2015). *The economic value of American Indian and Alaska native tribal colleges & universities. An analysis of the economic impact and return on investment of education*. Retrieved from www.aihec.org/our-stories/docs/reports/EconomicValue-AIAN-TCUs.pdf

Forkenbrock, J. (2015). The tribal college movement: My observation of leadership in Indian country. In G.E. Gipp, L.S. Warner, J. Pease, & J. Shanley (Eds.), *American Indian stories of success: New visions of leadership in Indian country* (pp. 201–207). Santa Barbara, CA: Praeger.

Gipp, D. (2015). In the spirit of life renewed. In G.E. Gipp, L.S. Warner, J. Pease, & J. Shanley (Eds.), *American Indian stories of success: New visions of leadership in Indian country* (pp. 127–137). Santa Barbara, CA: Praeger.

Gipp, G., & Warner, L.S. (Eds.) (2009). *Tradition and culture in the millennium: Tribal colleges and universities*. Charlotte, NC: Information Age Publishing.

Gipp, G., Warner, L.S., Pease, J., & Shanley, J. (2015). *American Indian stories of success: New visions of leadership in Indian country*. Santa Barbara, CA: Praeger.

Guillory, J. (2013). *Tribal college collaborations*. In Heather J. Shotton, Shelly C. Lowe, & Stephanie J. Waterman (Eds.), *Beyond the asterisk: Understanding native students in higher education* (pp. 95–107). Sterling, VA: Stylus Publishing.

Hart, J. (2006). Exploring tribal leadership: Understanding and working with tribal people. *Journal of Extension*, 44(4). Retrieved from https://articles.extension.org/sites/default/files/w/9/92/Exploring_Tribal_Leadership_Understanding_and_Working_With_Tribal_People.pdf

Higher Learning Commission (2013). *Distinctive and connected: Tribal colleges and universities and Higher Learning Commission accreditation – consideration for HLC peer reviewers.* Retrieved from www.aihec.org/our-stories/docs/Accreditation/HLC_TCU.pdf

Institute on Higher Education Policy (2000). *Tribal colleges contributions to local economic eevelopment.* Washington, DC: Institute on Higher Education Policy.

Institute on Higher Education Policy (2004). *Leading the way to America's future. A monograph about the launch and implementation of the Kellogg MSI Leadership Fellows Program (2002–2004).* Retrieved from www.ihep.org/sites/default/files/uploads/docs/pubs/leadingtheway.pdf

Krumm, B.L. (1995). *Tribal colleges: A study of development, mission, and leadership.* Dissertation, University of Nebraska – Lincoln. Retrieved from http://files.eric.ed.gov/fulltext/ED404064.pdf

Littlebear, R. (2009). Understanding American Indian cultures. In G.E. Gipp and L.S. Warner (Eds.), *Tradition and culture in the millennium: Tribal colleges and universities* (pp. 89–106). Charlotte, NC: Information Age Publishing.

Pease, J. (1994). *The Tribally Controlled Community College Act of 1978: An expansion of federal trust responsibility.* Retrieved from scholarworks.montana.edu

Pease, J. (2015). Helps the people: The dance of the seasons (Ak bi li kkux shei: Ash he'e lee tass li ssua): A retrospective on leadership. In G.E. Gipp, L.S. Warner, J. Pease, & J. Shanley (Eds.), *American Indian stories of success: New visions of leadership in Indian country* (pp. 153–176). Santa Barbara, CA: Praeger.

Shanley, J. (2015). Introduction. In G.E. Gipp, L.S. Warner, J. Pease, & J. Shanley (Eds.), *American Indian stories of success: New visions of leadership in Indian country.* Santa Barbara, CA: Praeger.

Stein, W. (1992). *Tribally controlled colleges: Making good medicine.* New York: Peter Lang Publishing.

Warner, L.S. & Tijerina, K.H. (2009) Indigenous governance. In G. Gipp and L.S. Warner (Eds.), *Tradition and culture in the millennium: Tribal colleges and universities* (pp. 89–106). Charlotte, NC: Information Age Publishing.

Asian American and Native American Pacific Islander-Serving Institutions (AANAPISIs)

11

LEADERSHIP IS MORE THAN A CHECKLIST!

Exploring Leadership at AANAPISI Community Colleges

Loretta P. Adrian, Kathi Hiyane-Brown, and Naomi Okumura Story

There are distinctively distinguishing qualities that exist between and among the 50+ Asian and Pacific Islander ethnic and subgroups; differences also occur with those who migrated or who were born and reared in the United States. For example, language, religion, and backgrounds are unique to the various Southeast Asian communities. There are generational differences with early Asian Americans and Pacific Islander (AAPI) immigrants such as Filipinos, Chinese, and Japanese and today's Asian and Pacific Islanders.

The purpose of this chapter is to begin to examine the desirable leadership characteristics and leadership requirements to support Asian Americans and Pacific Islanders in the United States. As the most diverse minority population, Jonathan Ong, Paul Ong, and Elena Ong in *The Future of Asian America in 2040* stated that "According to the U.S. Census Bureau, the number of Asian Americans will increase 74 percent, from 20.5 million in 2015 to 35.7 million 2040, making Asian Americans the fastest-growing racial population in the nation" (aapi nexus, 2016, pp. 14–29).

Setting the Context

For many years, perpetuated by literature, Hollywood, and mainstream media, AAPIs as a whole have often been generalized, misperceived, mischaracterized, and/or ignored. Yet, today's AAPIs have complex and contrasting backgrounds, perspectives, and needs based on differences in ethnicities and subgroups (50+), gender, generations, religions, languages and dialects, regions, cultural, political, and historical perspectives, and many other social and economic differences.

Furthermore, as the fastest growing and most diverse minority population in higher education (aapi nexus, 2016), AAPIs are often challenged to succeed and complete their higher education goals because of prevailing assumptions and misperceptions as the *Model Minority*. For example, the total enrollment for Asian Americans in 2013 for 18–24 year olds was 67% (ACS, 2013), which is considered high among all college-going populations. However, when one looks more closely at the Asian subgroups, the rates were much lower with Bhutanese (20%), Burmese (28%), Cambodian (41%), Bangladeshi and Hmong (48%), Laotian (49%), and Filipino (57%). Except for the Vietnamese at 69%, the overall college-going rate for Southeast Asia (60%) was much lower than the overall Asian rate (ACS, 2013).

Aggregated data have painted a superficial view of AAPIs as high achieving and motivated, which may be true among certain subgroups in selective colleges and universities. However, when we look more closely into the data and where most AAPIs matriculate, more are attending community colleges. According to the 2010 CARE report, college enrollment at two-year public institutions in 1985 was 41.7% and in 2005 AAPI enrollment increased to 47.3%, while between those years at public four-year institutions, the percentage decreased from 41.8% in 1985 and 38.4% in 2005 (CARE, 2010, Figure 10, p. 16). With the lower tuition rates, open admissions policy, and closer proximity to home, community colleges have become much more of a choice for AAPIs. Additionally, with 1,655 colleges in the United States (U.S. D.O.E. OTAE website), the community college is becoming the portal to higher education, especially for those who are economically challenged.

Diversity in economic status, background, language and educational preparation, and aspiration among AAPI students makes the community college environment a realistic transition into higher education across the country. However, when delving more deeply into the data, educational attainment among AAPI subgroups differs greatly. According to the 2010 CARE report (Figure 1), over 40% of Asian Indian, Filipino, Japanese, Korean, Pakistani, Chinese, and Thai subgroups attained their bachelor's degrees or more between 2006 and 2008, while Vietnamese, Hmong, Laotian, and Cambodian attainment rates were below 30%. Pacific Islander subgroups (Tongan, Samoan, Guamanian/Chamorro, and Native Hawaiian) were significantly below 20%.

There are also wide gaps between subgroups in workforce participation. The unemployment rate between 2006 and 2008 (CARE, 2010, p. 7, Figure 2) is much higher for Pacific Islanders and Southeast Asian subgroups: Tongan (15.7%),Samoan (10.1%), Hmong (9.4%), Laotian (8.5%), and Cambodian (8.4%), while the lowest unemployment rates were recorded for such Asian subgroups as Japanese (3.5%), Sri Lankan (3.7%), Thai (4.1%), Chinese (4.7%), and Asian Indian (4.8%). Data of those living at or below the poverty line impact AAPI ability to participate, let alone complete degrees or certificates in higher education.

Further, AAPI students in community colleges tend to be less likely to be academically prepared. According to the 2010 CARE report, "in 2003, 55.2

percent of AAPI students entering two-year colleges had never taken a math course beyond Algebra II in high school, compared to only 12.7%" who entered four-year institutions that year.

Factors such as mastery of English language skills, college enrollment, and management combined with other *risk factors* such as delayed enrollment, lack of a high school diploma, part-time enrollment, having dependents other than spouse, single parent status, and working full-time while enrolled plague AAPIs in community colleges and influence their ability to persist or complete their degrees or certificates (CARE, 2010; APIASF, 2016).

The Pacific Islander student population provides an excellent example of how aggregated numbers can be misleading. Based on an extensive study with ACT and the Asian & Pacific Islander American Student Scholarship Fund, findings indicated that 14% of Native Hawaiians and Pacific Islanders have a bachelor's degree or higher, which is less than half of the national average of 27%. More than 1,300 languages are spoken in the Pacific Islands region and Hawaii. And, for those who took the ACT, many identified themselves as first-generation high school graduates. Most fell into the low-income range with a poverty rate of 20.4% with large family households. When examining their ACT College Readiness Benchmarks in English, Math, Reading, and Science, Pacific Islander students have similar scores to Hispanic students and significantly lower than Asian students.

The assumption that AAPIs are highly motivated and successful in higher education is shown to be false when data are disaggregated. Yet, these stereotypes exist and are detrimental to large numbers of students, who are often ignored and misperceived. Nationally, there is a low representation of AAPI faculty and staff, who might debunk or demystify prejudices or discriminatory behaviors AAPI students may experience or conversely create and establish cultural understanding and open dialogues with their peers about AAPI students' unmet needs. Based on data on the most recent IPEDS Human Resources Fall 2009 Employees in Postsecondary study, AAPI faculty and staff numbers still fall below other minority counterparts. Even lower in participation are AAPI college presidents. Currently, among CEOs, only 2% are AAPI leaders across all accredited U.S. colleges and universities, even though AAPIs are the fastest growing student population in higher education (Gee & Yamagata-Noji, 2016).

Why AANAPISIs?

In 2008, through the use of the Higher Education Opportunity Act, the U.S. Department of Education established The Asian American Pacific Islander-Serving Institutions Program. It was designed to provide grant funding to institutions that serve the needs of AAPI students. AANAPISI (Asian American and Native American Pacific Islander-Serving Institution) grants were created to address the significant number of underserved AAPIs with unique and culturally sensitive programs and services. To qualify for program and project funding, the higher education institution must certify that it has an undergraduate enrollment of at least 10% Asian American Native American Pacific Islander students (U.S. Department of Education, n.d.).

AANAPISI funding also allowed for projects that focused on access, curriculum, teaching and learning support, as well as community research on demographic and cultural shifts for the many subgroups and their completion needs. In an October 2016 Minority-Serving Institution (MSI) Convening in Dallas, UCLA Professor Robert Teranishi (2016) reported continuing research and evaluation data on AANAPISI initiatives that illustrate the positive impact of funding on student success and transfer among community colleges. Teranishi cited results from three community colleges: DeAnza College in Cupertino, South Seattle Community College, and City College of San Francisco. Each college differed in addressing different subgroups (Chinese, Vietnamese, Filipino) with culturally relevant pedagogy, comprehensive wraparound services and programs, and institutional partnerships that improved student success.

Professor Teranishi further expressed the need for scalability and institutionalization of programs and services, especially with the increase in the number of colleges that are eligible and facing diminishing funding for college support services.

AAPI Leadership

Transforming and sustaining effective practices to support student learning and achievement of student success and degree completion often requires institutional and organizational change and leadership commitment. So, when funding allows for innovation and change, it now becomes the responsibility of the institution to imbue the transformation. Systems, whether they are policies, networks, procedures, or structures require modification, renewal, and/or transformation. Thus, transformative leadership becomes necessary.

Why Leadership at AANAPISIs?

Nakanishi (2015) acknowledges that recognition and research literature are sparse on Asian American leadership. Limitations are attributed to the underrepresentation or "bamboo ceilings" (p. xvii) in various sectors. However, Asian American leadership has existed historically in the United States in several arenas: business and industry, government and policy, education, arts, music, fashion, and the community at large. Today, slowly but definitively, more AAPIs receive recognition, break through barriers and persist in leadership roles and opportunities in various fields (Nakanishi, 2015).

Henry Gee, Vice President of Student Services at Rio Hondo College, CA and Audrey Yamagata-Noji, Vice President of Student Services at Mt. San

Antonio College, CA have facilitated the Leadership Development Program for Higher Education Summer Institute sponsored by LEAP (Leadership Education for Asian Pacifics, Inc.) since 1997 to increase the number of AAPI administrators in higher education. Between 1997 and 2016, the Institute has had 633 participants. In *MIA: Missing in Administration – Asian Pacific Islanders and the Bamboo Ceiling*, Gee and Yamagata-Noji (2016) also articulate the cultural values and leadership styles that can be seen as positive and negative perceptions, that is, hard working, analytical, smart, quiet, reserved, being humble, don't rock the boat or speak up, persevere, save face, and so forth.

Knowing when and how to apply, balance, and transcend cultural influences is significant for AAPI leaders. AAPI college presidents or CEOs lead institutions with other non-Asian cultural, social, and institutional norms and expectations. Kahneman (2011) posits that knowing how and being able to shift between two systems of thinking and behaving are critical in how and when choices and decisions are made in our work and our lives: "fast, intuitive, and emotional" and/or "slower, more deliberative, and more logical." Using AAPI cultural influences and benefits simultaneously with non-AAPI behaviors and expectations can be an asset. For example, there are times when making decisions or managing different personalities within an organization require quick, firm, bold, and intuitive solutions. These may not be an intrinsic leadership style for an introspective or analytical AAPI leader, yet he/she can develop other tactics such as using participatory and diverse teams, relationships, and networks, and analogies or storytelling to address issues and to foster his/her success as a leader for all.

Adrian (2004) found in her study that, in contrast with primarily negative stereotypical perceptions about Asian American leadership, Asian American college and university presidents construct and exercise leadership in a complex, multidimensional, dynamic, and fluid fashion; based on multiple interpretive frames including ethnicity, multiple identities (bicultural, bilingual, and academic identities), values (cultural, personal, religious, and family), organizational structure and culture, and leadership characteristics and styles. The study suggests a different paradigm for examining Asian American leadership.

Is leadership for AANAPISIs different from leadership of other Minority-Serving Institutions (MSIs)? It is assumed because of the distinct differences with AAPI student groups, that there are unique challenges and issues that need to be addressed. However, because of the limited research in MSI leadership, it is not clear if there may be common or different leadership characteristics and strategies across other MSIs. Does one need to be an AAPI leader to preside over an AANAPISI college? It is common sense that leadership competency – behaviors and values – is critical regardless of her/his race/ethnicity. Basic organizational leadership skills and authentic personal values in leading an institution are critical for all successful community college presidents. However, there are specific and complex needs of AAPI students that are often ignored and if a college president is not sensitive to them or lacks knowledge or understanding about their individual differences and dynamics, then neither the students nor the organization can thrive or succeed. For example, with challenges such as cultural and linguistic diversity, generational and historical nuances and undercurrents, political, economic, and social differences, homeland connections and interplay, the AAPI experience can be very complex and unique *within and among* the AAPI population, and thus difficult for any leader to grasp or understand.

In addition, as Gee and Yamagata-Noji (2016) point out, there are significant institutional issues such as "invisibility, profiling, marginality, the Model Minority Myth, the Glass (Bamboo) Ceiling, and having no *career GPS*" that negatively impact AAPIs and continue to prevail across higher education. So, how does one lead and deal with such a dynamic and multi-faceted population, especially within a community college setting, which is already challenged?

In this chapter, the authors delve deeper into the leadership qualities, perspectives, and vision in the higher education landscape, specifically for community colleges designated or eligible as Asian American Native American and Pacific Islander-Serving Institutions (AANAPISIs) across the country. Based on prior dialogues on leadership competencies and value among community college leaders, the authors query and reflect on factors that form and inform community colleges as they evolve with the significant increase and complexities of diverse student needs. Furthermore, the authors not only focus on AAPI leaders and their competencies, values, and challenges, but also describe those leadership aspects for those non-AAPIs leaders who successfully lead AANAPISIs.

Today, most institutions of higher education are challenged with recruiting, hiring, and retaining visionary and entrepreneurial leaders who are competent, skilled, and experienced, but also represent or understand the values and needs of all students. What, then, are critical factors and qualities in leading an institution, where highly diverse AAPIs can thrive and succeed? Just because one is Asian does not necessarily mean that person is representative or understanding of the needs of all AAPI students. Often, one subgroup is culturally different or historically may have adversarial relationships with each other, for example, Asian Indians and Pakistanis. Even within subgroups differences could exist based on region, such as Asian Americans in urban and rural settings, West Coast versus East Coast, Midwest, South, or Southwest states. Factors such as gender, cultural upbringing, or generational knowledge and experiences often influence the strategies adopted and used in successful leadership, especially within AANAPISIs.

Furthermore, many AANAPISIs are led by non-AAPIs. For non-AAPIs leaders, are there unique or common experiences, values, or specific competencies that support their leadership and organizational success? Based on results from focus group discussions with over 200 presidents and CEOs at the 92nd Annual AACC Convention in 2012, Anna Solley and Naomi Story (2015) elicited and surfaced a series of essential leadership competencies for community college leaders. These lists were categorized based on critical knowledge, abilities, and attitudes or predispositions necessary for community college president to possess as twenty-first century leaders. Solley and Story (2015) suggested that these lists be used as part of search processes as starting points for discussion. For example, under Knowledge, the top two items were 1) Globalism and being part of a global society and 2) Diversity/inclusion/cultural competence. Under Ability, leaders stated 1) Build and sustain partnerships and collaboration; team building and 2) Nurture and cultivate others/mentor/professional development. Using these factors, a search committee can discuss what each competency means and agree to develop a set of rubrics to assess each potential candidate.

With implications for leadership and professional development, authors identify and discuss the critical leadership competencies, qualities, predispositions, and values that significantly influence the success of CEOs and presidents with diverse and growing numbers of AAPIs in their institutions. For example, they describe the knowledge and abilities required such as relationship building, balancing details with "big picture" goals, aligning specific cultural competence and understanding with knowledge of differences and similarities among people, and so forth. Further, are there common and unique leadership traits and attributes necessary for AANAPISI success and sustainability? Are there common leadership qualities shared across race, ethnicity, and gender that allow leaders to lead successfully at AANAPISIs?

To inform and extend critical and courageous dialogues, the authors in their research identify the complex and compelling issues that leaders will need to confront in the near future. For example, with multiple agendas and limited resources, community colleges will further be challenged with reinventing themselves in meeting the needs of a much more diverse and changing economy and society. Dealing with fluctuating student enrollment, meeting the demands and accountability of Federal, state, and local policies and provisions, having a fiscally conservative governing board and vocal community members, competing with private and alternative credentialing organizations, and addressing multiple demands for transfer and workforce needs are just a few of such complexities that community colleges must tackle. What, then, are the specific challenges and directions that concern AANAPISI leaders?

In addition, because of their democratic and changing mission and agendas, community colleges are grappling with complex demands and needs, specifically among AANAPISIs. AANAPISIs, unlike HSIs, HBCUs, or Tribal Colleges, are the most recently acknowledged and least funded of Minority-Serving Institutions. Therefore, what are the critical challenges unique to their leaders, especially with recent Federal grant changes? Are there specific strategies and solutions that AANAPISIs can employ in addressing those challenges and issues? What must leaders and potential candidates do to succeed in such contrasting communities and needs?

National organizations such as the American Council on Education (ACE) and the American Association for Community Colleges (AACC) have studied aspects of leadership over the years. ACE continues to examine factors that influence the success and challenges of leadership with their American College President Study 2012. ACE researchers established a profile of the state and profile of presidents from over 800 colleges and universities. They also identify the lack of diversity and limited pipeline to the presidency.

In 2012, AACC formed a committee of community college leaders, who spent a year studying and defining leadership competencies. They published the *AACC Competencies for Community College Leaders, Second Edition* (AACC, 2013). The five AACC leadership skills and knowledge were: 1) Organizational Strategy, 2) Institutional Finance, Research, Fundraising, & Resource Management, 3) Communication, 4) Collaboration, and 5) Community College Advocacy. They were listed in terms of college leaders based on a time continuum from emerging to new (first three years) to CEO (three plus years). Competencies were stated as a real-life, yet generalized statement of characteristics and behaviors, but not specific to diverse student populations, nor were cultural competence or diversity identified as critical skills and knowledge.

The notion that good leadership in community college AANAPISIs can be determined or assessed with a generic checklist of competencies and experiences is naïve and shortsighted. At the 2016 AACC Pre-convention workshop, *Leading and Sustaining an Inclusive Organization: Be the Bold Community College Leader*, which was facilitated by diverse presidents and chancellors representing the African American, Asian American, and Hispanic affiliated councils of AACC, participants were asked state and discuss their perspectives about what would be essential as leaders of inclusive institutions. The final facilitator, Lori Adrian (2016) summarized key points:

a   Diversifying management and CEO positions
b   Sustaining organizations through intentional and mindful organizational development
c   Developing, practicing, and modeling cultural competence
d   Extending difficult and courageous conversations and best practices in regions not as diverse
e   Acting as change agents and ambassadors of inclusion, equity, and social justice
f   Challenging ourselves to be *bold* and *brave* leaders
g   Working together toward a shared purpose – focus on collaboration and partnership
h   Developing a holistic view of diversity – not just race/ethnicity, but also gender, sexual orientation, socio-economic status, religion, age, abilities, and disabilities, etc.

Summary results identify the need to recognize the diverse undercurrents and changing demographics of institutions and a need for an authentic, courageous, and committed leadership. These were consistent with comments from previous workshops that the three AACC minority council leaders facilitated in the past.

In contrast with AACC Core Competencies, workshop participants were much more fluid or organic in defining the essential factors in leadership. Characteristics and abilities such as technology acumen and skill or budget development were not as compelling as the need to connect with others or to build networks and communities. Deeper examination of barriers to accessing education, culturally responsive learning paradigms, strategic planning for sustainable systems, mentoring, being role models, and creating inclusive climates were also consistently mentioned. How then do we identify and develop leaders who possess and are predisposed to addressing specific conditions and situations unique to AANAPISI community colleges?

How We Shaped Our Inquiry

There were two parts to the investigation on perspectives on leadership competencies, characteristics, and values that support the success of AANAPISIs. The first involved a 15-item survey based on a series of questions that the authors could disseminate to current presidents and CEOs of AANAPISI community colleges. The survey was disseminated electronically to over 100 CEOs of AANAPISI-designated colleges over a two-week span. Of the nine who completed the survey fully, four identified themselves as AAPI and five indicated that they were Caucasian. Three stated their position titles as Chancellor and six were Presidents. Three respondents had been in their positions for less than a year, while six had served for more than five years. Aeron Zentner, DBA, Dean of Institutional Effectiveness from Coastline Community College, CA, compiled results. For the 12 open-response items, Zentner used a simple factor analysis and identified common themes in four areas: Leadership, Actions, Growth, and The Future.

In the second part, the authors conducted in-depth interviews with basic and follow-up questions with four AANAPISI presidents. The questions were tested and edited prior to implementation. The authors interviewed the AANAPISI CEOs (two males and two females) from different regions of the country: Pacific Islands, Northwest, Southwest, and East Coast. Two of the interviewees are AAPIs and two are Non-AAPIs.

What We Discovered from the Survey

From the survey results with Zentner's help, the authors were able to pinpoint common themes and perspectives that support leadership effectiveness.

Leadership

- Competencies: Modeling cultural competence, tracking student attainment gaps, collaboration through evidence-informed planning, and communication.

- Values: Student-centered; listening and communicating, fostering social justice and equity, respect for diversity of thought, having vision, and supporting risk-taking and change.
- Philosophy: Being innovative and a supporter of change, being inclusive and collaborative, and behaving ethically with integrity and respect.

Actions

- Employment Engagement: Engaging employees to foster critical leadership goals through professional development activities was a common practice. Activities built college unity in awareness, motivated employees to change behaviors, and facilitated change to better serve underserved populations.
- Challenges: The collective challenges faced by leaders appeared to be centralized around inertia with resistance to change. Additionally, the lack of local and external resources hinders institutions from effectively serving the total student population. The leaders indicated that little movement had been made to shift away from the stagnancy. However, a few outlying institutions indicated using creative ways to involve all constituent groups and to empower movement at their institutions.

Growth

- Leaders indicated that their leadership capacities have matured in the areas of community engagement through collaboration, listening, and defining measurable outcomes. As leaders of AANAPISIs, they indicated having a greater sense of openness, appreciation for diversity, and dedication to social justice.

The Future

- Leaders felt a successful legacy would encompass the development of effective strategies/programs that promote equity and that close the achievement gap for AAPI students. These efforts would be sustained and become a part of the institutional culture. Additionally, leaders provided recommendations to strengthen leadership effectiveness by promoting professional development activities at their institutions (e.g., retreats, seminars, mentorship, etc.).

Survey results suggest that leaders of AANAPISIs are in agreement and consistent with research about competencies, values, and philosophy that are focused on student success. However, they are cognizant of the immediate and compelling needs of AAPI students and the dynamics and undercurrents of leading organizations with diverse student populations. They translate practices and actions that not only support AAPI students, but also the institution as a whole in addressing change and transformation with such ongoing endeavors as professional development, innovation, and mentorship.

AANAPISI leaders are concerned about operationalizing and perpetuating inclusion and equity in their actions and practices, especially among college employees. There is a strong sense of social justice among those who completed the survey. As a commitment to diversity and inclusion, leaders "worry" about the external factors that may deter or negate their momentum or progress, especially with decrease in funding, growing demands, overall institutional commitments that threaten AANAPISI program goals, resistance to change, and measurable outcomes and accountability. However, they are hopeful about the future of their students and are people who are committed to serve and support their diverse student populations.

Communication and networking appear to be important means for engaging in institutional efficacy, as well as to inform and empower others. Listening, evidence or informed decision-making, and group or collaborative works mentioned in the survey are values that Gee and Yamagata-Noji (2016) stated as "AAPI values and practices." Professional development was consistently mentioned as a means to transformation and innovation. However, based on the survey, AANAPISI CEOs consistently mentioned listening, collaboration, evidence-based or informed planning or decision making as critical leadership practices. To delve more deeply into AANAPISI leadership philosophy and actions, the interviews were essential.

What We Heard from the Interviews

Each author interviewed one to two college presidents for 30–45 minutes to elicit deeper perspectives about their leadership experiences and perspectives in AANAPISIs. Although the authors had eight questions and asked follow up questions, they agreed that as long as the first two questions on background and leadership perspectives stayed consistent, they could direct the interviews based on the flow of conversation with each interviewee.

With different and unique backgrounds, the four interviewees provided deeper meaning and viewpoints about essential leadership competencies, values, and philosophies. Influenced by extensive personal and professional experiences, each president/chancellor shared and described several common aspects of leadership such as the need for cultural knowledge and competence. For example, Interviewee #1 reflected on his motivation, strategies, and actions based on his parents not completing high school and coming from "the Projects," while Interviewee #2, who excelled and graduated from highly selected universities often progressed and viewed leadership from an immigrant perspective. In addition, both Interviewees #2 and #3 discussed that their leadership values and philosophies were not just influenced, but defined by their AAPI cultures. Interviewees #2 and #3 also stated that their changes in venues and career context helped to form their leadership knowledge and skills. Interviewee #1 was most specific about challenges and issues he faced as a leader of AANAPISIs, which included dealing with the NAACP and the internal community, addressing cultural gaps and differences, and taking care of AAPI students among all students. Interviewee #2 also mentioned challenges, yet was more contextual and broad-based about issues and dealing with them. Interviewee #3 was very reflective about leadership and what works well and not well personally. Interviewee #4 stated that as a non-AAPI leader, her personal experiences and professional career journey helped her develop a mindset to embrace diversity and to foster compassion for the human condition. Interviewee #4 spoke often about needing and understanding the disaggregation of data among AAPIs and their subgroups to build essential and meaningful programs and services. She also discussed the attention necessary to the hiring process so that culturally competent teams were formed. Professional development and continuous learning and performance improvement were critical values and priorities for Interviewee #4.

In general, all four leaders were primarily and deeply focused on students and their diverse needs, creating and sustaining deeper awareness, advocacy, and empowerment of individuals, whether students, faculty, staff, or community partners. Each leader pointed to the importance of professional development and ongoing learning, establishing authentic relationships and collaborative partnerships to create and sustain cultural competence, diversity, and inclusion. They were committed to planning, developing, and sustaining a strong infrastructure and organization to sustain successful and innovative elements beyond the grant funding. Each also stated the need to show and report evidence and data that showed change, improvement, and transformation, not just to funders but also the community-at-large. Interviewee #4 mentioned continuous improvement and learning as a constant and shared her learning journey about AAPIs and their diversity.

As leaders, they saw their role and responsibility in constantly communicating the rationale, philosophy, practices, actions, and results for diversity and social justice to various publics: internal and external. They were sensitive to differences among and within minority populations. They also spoke about challenges and concerns in articulating clearly specific and unique needs of AAPIs to diffuse the Model Minority myths and stereotypes. In part, they stressed ongoing communication to address resource development and continuity among external partners and grant sources.

In addition, leaders were clear that it was essential that they "walk their talk" through their actions and decisions in promoting their social justice. Leaders need to be role models and demonstrate their commitment to equity and diversity through their actions, big and small. They used and related stories about their personal journeys in illustrating and valuing their diverse student populations. They had a strong sense of responsibility for students' growth and success not just academically, but also as graduates who would be global citizens and culturally knowledgeable contributors to society and the economy. Leaders also felt that their institutions and employees with community partners had a moral obligation to establish and sustain respect, inclusiveness, access, and equity consistently and with a long view.

What We Learned from AANAPISI Leaders and Essential Actions and Strategies for Institutional Success

Community colleges, like many higher education institutions, continue to be swirling in the undercurrents and dynamic forces of change across the United States. Specifically, as communities impacted by social, political, economic, and demographic issues evolve, community colleges must be nimble and quick to transform themselves to meet new challenges and needs. Having the best president or CEO to lead and guide the community college becomes immensely critical to its success and its future.

This chapter focused on the leadership of AANAPISI-designated colleges across the country because of the complexities and misperceptions of the AAPI population as the fastest growing minority population in higher education with the largest continuing increase in community colleges.

The authors found that AANAPISI leaders possess and apply very similar skills, knowledge, and values as part of their leadership toolkit. Whether they are AAPIs or non-AAPIs, leaders were much more apt to be culturally sensitive about interpersonal dynamics and communication. They consistently mentioned the need to listen, seek, and learn from and with others to address diverse and complex student needs. Especially because of multi-level complexities and dynamics of the various AAPI subgroups, both AAPI and non-AAPI leaders appeared to be much more reflective and sensitive to cultural differences. They used their own stories and experiences to exemplify and perpetuate social justice and diversity agendas. Their personal histories of working with diverse groups and individuals served as an impetus to motivate and influence their AANAPISI teams, as well as to gain support from internal and community members on their AANAPISI grant activities and projects.

In terms of leadership values and philosophies, leaders made statements that focused on personal backgrounds and experiences. For example, the journeys taken to become presidents appeared to influence empathy, understanding, and their willingness to persevere not just as leaders, but also to advocate and promote diverse student needs. It also appeared that they were intrinsically motivated to work hard and to establish and sustain meaningful and worthwhile programs and services.

Team building and valuing good and innovative teaching and effective student learning were important and commonly stated beliefs for both AAPI and non-AAPI leaders. Whether it was about forming culturally competent staff members for student services or instilling culturally significant curricular elements in teaching and learning activities, leaders stressed faculty and staff working together to complement the total college student experience.

Finally, the notion of *being present* was a common attitude. Overall, the values that each mentioned were closely aligned with several listed as AAPI Cultural Values by Gee and Yamagata-Noji (2016). Leaders expressed the need to be vigilant for the success of the AANAPISI college by balancing their focus on the "big stuff" and sharing their care for the "small things." Whether by acknowledging or celebrating successes or sharing lessons learned, it was important for AANAPISI leaders to communicate regularly within and outside the college community, as well as with other AANAPISIs, MSIs, and community college colleagues and leaders.

Leaders identified realistic challenges and issues that impact most organizations: funding and institutionalizing innovation and effective programs and services. How to operationalize and sustain those innovations and transformations beyond grant funding concerned several of the presidents. They also recognized the need to address individual students and to infuse and scale effective practices to all students, not just AAPIs.

Their role and responsibility in being advocate, cheerleader, connector, and communicator with internal and external diverse communities were challenges discussed by the interviewees. Solutions such as professional development and curricular reform were mentioned. And, they shared questions such as how to get people on the same page, and how to find and build partners to sustain effective practice, and how *lessons learned* from AANAPISIs can complement other minority groups. For example, one leader discussed building a "mega" coalition group that included African American, Native American, Latino, and AAPI clubs so they can share and advocate for and with each other on common agendas and similar needs.

Especially for naysayers and those who were resistant to change, having AAPI leaders, employees, or students share stories and discuss commonalities and differences was significant. For example, taking the time to relate to people unfamiliar with AAPI challenges and differences and stories helped to deter stereotypes, assumptions, misunderstandings, and misperception. Building awareness and understanding takes time, but is a long-term investment in establishing social change. A leader must understand and should be willing to provide the space and time for deeper and more difficult dialogues.

Addressing the questions and concerns of other minority groups is important when resources and attention may appear to be focused on one particular group. For instance, often internal or community members, who are not as knowledgeable about AAPIs or who believe unknowingly in the model myth, will inquire about why AAPIs need support. The leader must respond with clear and accurate knowledge about the impact and implications of AANIPISI programs and services, not just for AAPIs, but also for all students and the community as a whole.

Professional development in diversity, equity, and inclusion was a common practice. Whether they brought in speakers or sponsored regular or consistent events and activities, each leader fostered change and transformation with employee and student development. Investing in professional development is not always easy and the return in investment may not occur quickly. However, leaders need to plan for and include appropriate time and resources to actuate the significance of professional and leadership development to enhance and improve the college culture, programs, and services offered and provided, especially to decrease myths and false assumptions about the diversity of different population groups and subgroups.

Another aspect of professional development is the need for leaders themselves to experience and expand their learning and renewal of their knowledge and understanding of AAPIs. For example, delving into disaggregated data and more finite characteristics of different AAPI subgroups helps the leader comprehend the nuances of various cultures and their actions. Sponsoring and participating in panels and seminars about and for AAPIs can provide learning opportunities within the college community as well as for the AANAPISI leader.

In order to assure that the college culture is transformed, leaders also discussed the nature and nurturing of their college faculty and staff, especially related to the hiring process. The recruitment, hiring, and retention processes require intentional and strategic actions focused on cultural competence and understanding. For example, the leader must set and foster the standard for hiring culturally competent individuals across the college, not just for AANAPISI-funded programs and services, but also throughout the institutional organization and structure.

Collaboration and partnership building were stated as necessary skills for success. Working with other colleges, business and community members as partners and collaborators who supported their efforts was significant in the scalability and sustainability programs and services. Having successful students as advocates, cheerleaders, advisors, and mentors helped students, but also, program developers, faculty, and administrators.

Having exemplary relationships with different AAPI groups and subgroups can help the leader and the college, not at the superficial level of cultural events, but as more refined and significant actions that can change mindsets and behaviors. For example, having a Japanese American internee and a Filipino Muslim on a panel would be enlightening for the college to learn about the impact and implications of racial prejudice, the potential of registering immigrant/refugee populations, and coalition building and other actions framed by social justice.

Implications for Practice

Therefore, the authors' findings and analyses, though somewhat limited in scope, suggest that the development of the following leadership competencies be added to the design of leadership programs:

1. The development of cultural awareness and competence
2. A broad and deep understanding of diversity, including issues of inclusion, equity, and social justice

3. Institutional structures and practices that promote the hiring, retention, and success of organizational leadership teams comprised of diverse faculty and staff
4. The development of effective and culturally sensitive communication and team building skills
5. Strategies for developing innovative partnership and collaboration
6. Focus on advocacy and institutional development with community partners and national organizations

Implications for Future Research

When defining *Leadership* for ANNAPISIs, it is clear that more research and reflection are needed. Several of the respondents and interviewees did not respond to all the questions. Therefore, the authors need to examine more closely and determine if they need to be refined or clarified. Also, it would be beneficial to get responses from more AANAPISI leaders so that we can validate our initial findings.

The authors have just touched the surface of determining and distinguishing specific leadership competencies, values, and philosophies that are essential to lead AANAPISI community colleges. How, then, do we inform or design leadership development institutes to move from treating leadership as a checklist to one that involves a series of relevant experiences and activities?

As the fastest growing student population in higher education, especially in community colleges across the country, AAPIs have often been misunderstood or misperceived because of the Model Minority myths and stereotypes. It is essential that leadership not just address this extremely diverse population with cultural competence and commitment that allows them to flourish as individuals, but also as an integral part of the larger population and social fabric of the United States.

Sun Tzu stated that "The Commander" must possess the five virtues (wisdom, sincerity, benevolence, courage, and strictness) to lead well within the context of war. Those virtues appear to be similar to those that are significant in leading a higher education institution. In this inquiry, the authors touched the surface of the meaning and embodiment of such virtues by sharing several perspectives and examples of current AANAPISI leaders' competencies and values. Furthermore, AANAPISI institutions require leaders who are wise, with curiosity about AAPIs and their uniqueness; who are sincere and benevolent in their caring for all students; and who have the courage and discipline to build and sustain meaningful experiences and to inspire teams who are culturally competent.

References

AACC (August, 2013). *AACC competencies for community college leaders*, second edition. American Association for Community Colleges. Retrieved from www.aacc.nche.edu/newsevents/Events/leadershipsuite/Documents/AACC_Core_Competencies_web.pdf aapi nexus (Spring 2016). *Asian Americans & Pacific Islanders policy, practice and community.* Special Issue on AAPIs 2040. UCLA Asian American Studies Center, 14(1).

ACT & APIASF (2016). *The condition of college & career readiness 2015: Pacific Islander students.* ACT and Asian & Pacific Islander American Scholarship Fund. Retrieved from http://equityinlearning.act.org/wp-content/uploads/2016/06/2015-pacific-islander.pdf

Adrian, L. (2004). *Asian American leaders in higher education: An exploration of a dynamic constructivist approach to leadership.* Doctoral Dissertation for Claremont Graduate University and San Diego State University,

Adrian, L. (April 9, 2016). Summary notes from leading and sustaining an inclusive organization: Be the bold community college leader! AACC Preconvention Workshop sponsored by NAPIC, NCBAA, and NCCHC, Chicago.

American Community Survey (ACS) (2013). U.S. Department of Commerce, Census Bureau, Digest of Education Statistics 2014, Table 302.62.

APIASF (2016). *Invisible financial barriers to college access for Asian Americans and Pacific Islanders.* Asian & Pacific Islander American Scholarship Fund. Retrieved from www.apiasf.org/research/ARC_Report_2016.pdf

CARE (2010). *Federal higher education policy priorities and the Asian American and Pacific Islander community.* The National Commission on Asian American and Pacific Islander Research in Education (CARE). Retrieved from http://care.gseis.ucla.edu/wp-content/uploads/2015/08/2010_CARE_Report.pdf

Gee, H., & Yamagata-Noji, A. (July, 2016). *MIA: missing in administration – Asian Pacific Islanders and the bamboo ceiling.* Presented at Leadership Development Program for Higher Education, Kellogg West Conference Center, CA.

Kahneman, D. (2011). *Thinking, fast and slow.* New York: Farrar, Straus and Giroux.

Nakanishi, D. (2015). *Asian American leadership: A reference guide.* Santa Barbara, CA: Mission Bell Media.

Solley, A., & Story, Naomi O. (February, 2015). Diversity & leadership in the 21st century, *Hispanic Outlook*, 25(9), pp. 21–24.

Teranishi, R.T. (October, 2016). Measuring the impact of MSI-funded programs on student success: Findings from the evaluation of AANAPISIs. Presentation at MSI-Convening, Dallas, TX.

U.S. Department of Education (n.d.). *Asian American and Native American Pacific Islander-Serving Institutions programs.* Retrieved from www2.ed.gov/programs/aanapi/index.html

Zentner, A. (2016). Leadership interview matrix, Coastline Community College.

12

AANAPISI LEADERSHIP

Perspectives from the Field

Robert T. Teranishi, Cynthia M. Alcantar and
Robert A. Underwood

The changing demography of our nation means that our system of higher education must realize a fundamentally different approach to teaching and learning. Responding to this twenty-first century challenge is the Asian American and Native American Pacific Islander-Serving Institution (AANAPISI) federal program, which is a competitive grant process for institutions that serve high concentrations of low-income Asian American and Pacific Islander students. The AANAPISI program, which is one of the most significant investments ever made for the AAPI college student population by the federal government, is notable for a number of reasons. First, it acknowledges the unique challenges facing AAPI students relative to college access and completion (Teranishi, 2010), Second, it represents a significant commitment of much-needed resources to improve the postsecondary completion rates among low-income AAPI students. Finally, it recognizes that campus settings are mutable points of intervention – sites of possibilities for responding to the impediments encountered by AAPI students (National Commission on Asian American and Pacific Islander Research in Education [CARE], 2010).

The study of AANAPISIs is important for improving what we know about the unique needs and challenges of low-income AAPI college students and the institutions that serve them, as well as contributing to the body of knowledge of MSIs overall. This chapter focuses on leadership in AANAPISIs. We begin with an overview of what are AANAPISIs, who they serve, the unique challenges they face, and their unique role and function in higher education. We then place this discussion in the context of what effective leadership does or should do to attempt to remedy such challenges and maximize their potential contribution to higher education and society. We conclude with a discussion about advice, recommendations, and strategies regarding what leadership in AANAPISIs could do to improve their leadership efficacy.

Who Are AAPI Students and What Are Their Unique Needs?

The rise of AANAPISIs has been driven by changing trends in the demography of the U.S.A., which has had profound implications for the makeup of our student enrollment in higher education. Thus, our discussion of AANAPISIs is predicated on the unique demographic characteristics of AAPIs in higher education, which is a large and growing sector of higher education enrollment. AAPI college enrollment, for example, grew five-fold between 1979 and 2009, from 235,000 to 1.3 million (National Center for Education Statistics, 2011). And while college enrollment is projected to increase for all racial groups, AAPIs are projected to experience a particularly high proportional increase of 30% between 2009 and 2019.

It is not only important to note how the AAPI population is increasing in its size and proportionality; it is critical to understand that the ethnic sub-groups that comprise the larger AAPI racial category have a wide range of demographic characteristics. This is because the AAPI racial category consists of 48 different ethnic groups that vary widely with regard to language backgrounds, immigration histories, and religious backgrounds. AAPI ethnic sub-groups occupy positions along the full range of the socioeconomic spectrum. Thus, while much attention about AAPIs has focused on more affluent, educated, and high-income workers, there are also large sectors of the population that are poor, less educated, and underprivileged. Take, for example, the poverty rate among the Hmong (37.8%), Cambodians (29.3%), Laotians (18.5%), and Vietnamese (16.6%), which is much greater than is found among Filipinos (6.3%), the Japanese (9.7%), and Asian Indians (9.8%). This has a number of implications for the generalizations that are made about AAPIs in the aggregate, including what we know about their access to and success in higher education. This is critical for educational assessment, which often drives high-stakes decisions in education, as well as the perception that leadership has and how that informs the development and evaluation of educational programs and services.

Leadership in higher education, AANAPISIs notwithstanding, must recognize that differences in the backgrounds of AAPI students have a number of implications for their educational participation and attainment. Despite high rates of educational attainment for AAPIs in the aggregate, large sectors of the AAPI population suffer from high secondary school drop-out rates, low rates of college participation, and low two- and four-year college completion rates. Consider that 55 to 65% of Southeast Asian and Pacific Islander adults have never enrolled in postsecondary education of any kind. Indeed, 40% of Southeast Asians do not even complete high school. Among Southeast Asian and Pacific Islander students that do attend college, more than half will leave college without earning a degree, which is three to five times the likelihood that East Asians and South Asians will drop out (CARE, 2011). Unfortunately, these differential outcomes among AAPIs are concealed by aggregated data and result in the vulnerable sub-groups being overlooked and underserved.

A key factor in the differential postsecondary outcomes for AAPI students is the wide variation in the different types of institutions they attend, which vary by type (two-year and four-year), control (public and private), and selectivity (open access to highly selective). This is a critical point considering that educators, policy-makers, and the general public have mainly focused on AAPI students in highly selective institutions, while AAPI students in other sectors of higher education, such as community colleges, receive little or no attention. Yet lower tuition, open admissions, and proximity to home are all important factors in the decision to attend a community college for a sizeable proportion of AAPI college students, like they are for many other students. In fact, in 2010 nearly half of all AAPI college students could be found in community colleges (Teranishi, Martin, et al., 2015). While AAPIs made up less than five percent of the national population, they represented nearly seven percent of all community college students.

The perception of high achievement and attainment among AAPIs is a generalization that conceals the fact that large sectors of AAPI college students enroll as part-time students, have dependents, and work while attending college. There are large proportions of AAPI students that are the first in their families to attend college and many that come from low-income backgrounds (CARE, 2010; Chang et al., 2007). They are also more likely to have recently immigrated to the U.S.A., have a history of foreign schooling, face barriers related to language background, and have a higher rate of needing remediation in English than other students (CARE, 2010; Chang et al., 2007).

Beyond these differences, studies have found that AAPI students face a variety of challenges on college campuses in terms of engagement, including a reluctance to use support services such as academic tutoring centers, career services, and counseling; difficulty finding supportive classroom environments; a lack of culturally relevant curricular and extra-curricular activities; a perception of pervasive discrimination on campus; and the challenge of resisting insidious stereotypes of AAPI students (Kiang, 1992; Kotori & Malaney, 2003; Osajima, 1995; Teranishi, 2010). These findings underscore the importance of higher education leaders to transcend stereotypes and false assumptions that often drive the perception and treatment of AAPI students.

What Are AANAPISIs and What Are Their Unique Challenges?

There are important lessons to be learned about leadership in higher education by understanding what are AANAPISIs, the unique challenges they face, and their unique role and function in higher education. As other chapters in this book note, the federal government's investment in Minority-Serving Institutions (MSIs) is an important sector of higher education for the changing demography of American college students, which is also true for the large and growing AAPI student population. The Asian American and Native American Pacific Islander-Serving Institution (AANAPISI) federal program, initially authorized by the

College Cost Reduction and Access Act of 2007, is a competitive grant process for institutions with at least a 10% enrollment of AAPI students and a minimum percentage of low-income students similar to that in Hispanic-Serving Institutions (Santiago, 2006). As of 2016, there were 105 institutions with the AANAPISI designation, 26 of which have received federal funding through the program.

The AANAPISI program is one of the most significant investments the federal government has made for the AAPI college student population. The federal program is an acknowledgement of the unique challenges facing AAPI students in college access and completion. It also represents a significant commitment of much-needed resources to improving the postsecondary completion rates of AAPI and low-income students. Finally, the federal program acknowledges how campuses can be sites for responding to the impediments AAPI students encounter.

The composition of AANAPISIs is similar to other MSIs. They are pre-dominantly comprised of low-income minority students, have a lower average per student expenditure, and have a critical mass of two-year versus four-year institutions. By 2016, 62% of funded AANAPISIs have been community colleges. Two-thirds of AANAPISIs are located in the western states of California and Washington, there is a critical mass in the Pacific region in places like Hawai'i, American Samoa, the Federated States of Micronesia, Guam, Marshall Islands, Northern Marianas, and Palau.

Enrollment trends for AAPIs have implications for policy strategies that target these students. AAPI undergraduates are highly concentrated in a small number of colleges and universities where nearly two-thirds of the student population is concentrated in only five percent of all postsecondary institutions (CARE, 2010). Combined, AANAPISI campuses enroll 40.5% of all AAPI undergraduates, while they constitute only 3.4% of the nation's colleges and universities.

In sheer numbers, AANAPISIs are conferring degrees to a significant concentration of AAPI students. In 2016, for example, AANAPISIs conferred 43.5% of all associate's degrees and 28.8% of all bachelor's degrees to AAPI students. These students are mostly low-income AAPI students who otherwise have lower levels of college participation and completion. Evidence for the composition of these students can be found in a study by the Congressional Research Service (2009), which found that institutions that met the criteria for AANAPISI funding enrolled 75% of the low-income AAPI students in U.S. higher education.

What is critical about what AANAPISIs are doing with their designation and funding is their effort to engage in a range of initiatives to increase access to and success in college for AAPI students. The federal funding is being used for the development of student learning communities, first-year experience programs, academic and personal counselors and advisors, and tutoring programs. These programs are improving the quality of students' experiences during college, increasing persistence, and connecting students with student services that they may not have utilized without the resources.

Funding is being used for program development as well, which includes improving academic quality, increasing the quantity and variety of courses being offered, and boosting student participation in certain academic programs. AANAPISI funding is also being used to provide students with increased access to leadership development and mentorship opportunities aimed at increasing their academic experience during college and career success after graduation. Other uses of the funding include new research about the AAPI population; staff-development opportunities to help administrators, faculty, and staff better understand the complexities of the AAPI population; and infrastructure development.

What Are the Implications for Leadership in Higher Education?

Now that we have established the unique role and function of AANAPISIs in higher education, we will discuss what effective leadership does or should do to attempt to remedy the challenges and maximize their potential contribution to higher education and society. A fundamental premise to this discussion is the fact that leadership in MSIs, and other institutions that are serving large concentrations of low-income minority students, must recognize and place greater emphasis on the importance of equity mindedness in their work. This has been pointed out in previous studies, which have found that the key components to organizational and institutional response to address inequities in higher education is having responsive, supportive, and engaged leaders with a vision and mission for transformative change and a commitment to serving diverse students (Kezar, 2001; Núñez, Hoover, Pickett, Stuart-Carruthers, & Vásquez, 2013).

Serving a Unique Student Demography

MSIs are often faced with challenges that are unique to the diverse student populations and communities they serve. MSI students – including students attending AANAPISIs – are often grappling with issues of financial vulnerability, limited college-level academic preparation, English language proficiency, and first generation (or first in their families) to go to college, just to name a few (see Brayboy, Fann, Castagno, & Solyom, 2012; CARE, 2013; de los Santos & de los Santos, 2003; Kim & Díaz, 2013; Núñez et al., 2013; Santiago, 2009; Teranishi, Alcantar, & Nguyen, 2015; Teranishi, Suárez-Orozco, & Suárez-Orozco, 2011). For these students to succeed, institutions must respond to their unique needs (CARE, 2011; Cortez, 2015; Espinoza & Espinoza, 2012; Gasman, Baez, & Turner, 2008; Santiago, 2009). For example, a needs-based assessment conducted by administrators at a four-year-"Hispanic Serving Institution" revealed that a large proportion of their students had dependents (Cortez, 2015). Rather than turning a blind eye to this information, the administrators developed a child care center so students can bring their children to campus (Cortez, 2015).

The lessons learned through this unique use of inquiry to guide practices and policies on campus have also occurred in AANAPISIs, including campuses that participated in the Partnership for Equity in Education through Research (PEER), which was a project led in part by the National Commission on Asian American and Pacific Islander Research in Education (CARE). Through funding from the Kresge Foundation, Lumina Foundation, USA Funds, and Walmart Foundation, PEER was formed as an effort to support AANAPISIs to more fully realize the degree-earning potential of AAPI students. Through a participatory action research approach, PEER engaged in co-investigative research to identify promising practices, implement targeted interventions, and mobilize campus leaders to support greater institutional effectiveness.

Through this research we gained a deeper understanding of the demography and unique needs of low-income AAPI students. For example, one of the PEER partner AANAPISI community colleges found that although they had a relatively high transfer rate for AAPI students in the aggregate, disaggregated data revealed a high proportion of Southeast Asian and Pacific Islander students were not transferring. They also found that a disproportionately high concentration of these students were placing in developmental English and few ever transitioned into college-level English, which was a contributing factor in their low transfer rates. To address this need, they used their AANAPISI grant to develop a culturally responsive learning community, pairing a developmental English course with an Asian American Studies course. Through the work of PEER we found this was an effective approach to improving the English transition and transfer rates of AAPI students placed in developmental education at this institution.

In another line of inquiry through PEER, we examined the lived experiences of low-income AAPIs at the three AANAPISI community colleges. Through interviews and surveys with students we found that many of these students are experiencing various financial hardships that affect their academic and social engagement with school (Teranishi, Alcantar, & Nguyen, 2015). In fact, a majority were working over 40 hours a week, had family responsibilities such as dependents, and were first-generation college students (Teranishi, Martin et al., 2015). These collaborative efforts were made possible through the political will that was leveraged by the leadership of each institution with whom we worked, which was critical for generating buy-in among key administrators, faculty, and other key constituents on campus we engaged in this co-investigative research process.

Institutional Priorities

Various national associations and scholars have developed lists of skills and competencies that are essential for individuals and institutions to effectively lead institutions serving large proportions of students of color in the twenty-first century, including community colleges and MSIs. These competencies, many of which stem from the list developed by the American Association of Community Colleges (AACC, 2013), include: a) organizational strategy; b) institutional finance, research, fundraising, and resource management, including utilizing data to understand your students and make informed decisions; c) communication to internal and external constituents and in "diverse venues," such as social media (Freeman, Commodore, Gasman, & Carter, 2016, p. 574); d) collaboration; and e) advocacy of their institution type and mission as community colleges and/or MSIs (Cortez, 2015; Esters et al., 2016; Freeman et al., 2016; Santiago, 2009; Williams, 2013). Furthermore, leadership in community colleges and MSIs requires an understanding that successful leadership is more than a list of skills and qualities: "there is no single way for successful leaders to operate" (Eddy, 2010, p. 139), it is ever evolving, requires lifelong learning, and is fluid in the sense that in certain situations and/or particular contexts, one quality may override others.

In addition to these competencies and understanding, researchers have found a number of other skills, qualities, or competencies needed to be an effective leader at institutions serving racial/ethnic minority students. These include being "dedicated to service" (Freeman et al., 2016, p. 584). A president at a land-grant HBCU described these institutions as "the people's university" (as cited in Esters & Strayhorn, 2013, p. 125). As leaders of diverse students in diverse communities, service is an important component of community colleges and MSIs (Cortez, 2015; Freeman et al., 2016; Garcia, 2016). These institutions are often critical to providing college access, knowledge and information, and support to the surrounding communities (Santiago, 2009). Thus, leaders must be engaged with the community on and off campus. However, Santiago (2009) cautions that leaders at MSIs must be aware and recognize that, "At times, this [serving and educating the community] may not align with priorities to be nationally ranked for research, faculty, or selectivity" (p. 3). Moreover, leaders must also be aware of the historical and contemporary issues affecting college access and inequality for diverse students in their institutional context (Esters et al., 2016; Williams, 2013).

Finally, leaders at MSIs must be politically aware and strategic about communicating with local, state, and federal policymakers (Esters et al., 2016; Freeman et al., 2016). Various higher education policies related to MSIs, public colleges, and financial aid directly impact the livelihood and success of these institutions, therefore leaders must be politically aware and engaged in this arena. To facilitate this, leaders should deliberately partner with professional and advocacy organizations such as APIACU to help foster these networks and to ease communication.

Diversity in Leadership = Diverse Leadership

While student diversity on college campuses has drastically changed over the last two decades, the diversity amongst college leaders has yet to shift. In 1990, 20% of college students were racial/ethnic minorities, in 2009 they represented over a third (34%) of the student population (Cook, 2012). In contrast, in 1986 eight percent of college presidents were racial/ethnic minorities; 25 years later this rate rose by a meager five percent (13% in 2011; Cook, 2012). The underrepresentation of racial/ethnic minorities in college leadership positions is alarming given the overrepresentation of racial/ethnic minority students in community colleges and MSIs. While an estimated 86% of community college presidents are White, a mere 13.7% are racial/ethnic minorities (Weisman & Vaughan, 2002). While still underrepresented, many of the few leaders of color are presiding over MSIs and community colleges (de los Santos & Vega, 2008; Perna, Gerald, Baum, & Milem, 2007; Perna, Li, Walsh, & Raible, 2010).

The literature on leaders of color in higher education has found that their representation in college settings greatly influences the success of diverse students (Castellano & Jones, 2003). Researchers have found leaders of color are not only "culturally relatable" (Asian American and Asian Research Institute, 2016) to the students and communities they serve, but they also often take a culturally sensitive and responsive approach to leadership (Cortez, 2015; Espinoza & Espinoza, 2012). Culturally responsive leadership is an asset-based approach to leading diverse institutions. Cortez (2015) writes, "The role that institutional leaders play in becoming cultural translators, mediators, and facilitators can advance the bicultural development and understanding of the students they serve" (p. 142). In the case of AANAPISIs, culturally competent and responsive leaders are important to understanding the ethnic, cultural, and linguistic heterogeneity among the AAPI student population rather than be driven by model minority and foreigner stereotypes (CARE, 2013).

However, a point that is often overlooked is the overwhelming underrepresentation of AAPIs in leadership roles. In fact, the percentage of college presidents who are AAPI is even more appalling at only 1.5 percent (ACE, 2013); in the two-year sector they represent one percent of all community college presidents (Weisman & Vaughan, 2002). In fact in 2003, there were only 33 AAPI college presidents; nine of whom were in community colleges (CARE, 2010). Additionally, many of the AAPI presidents are at federally designated AANAPISIs. AAPIs face a number of barriers to achieving leadership roles in higher education (and in other sectors of society), some of which are unique to the AAPI population; among those are negative stereotypes of AAPIs, the model minority myth, and being perpetually seen as a foreigner, all of which influences racial bias and discrimination in hiring practices, including the exclusion of AAPIs in diversity recruitment efforts, and lack of mentoring into leadership positions, just to name a few (ACE, 2013; Asian American and Asian Research Institute, 2016). These barriers are often similarly faced by AAPI students in pursuit of a college education. For this reason representation of AAPIs in college leadership roles is important (Alcantar, Bordoloi Pazich, & Teranishi, forthcoming). CARE (2010) reports:

A lack of AAPI high-level administrators often means fewer opportunities for bringing attention to the needs of the AAPI student population, especially among networks of high-level administrators who discuss institutional priorities and how to respond to the emerging trends in higher education overall.

(p. 11)

Advocacy Beyond their Own Institutions

It is also important to note the important role that leadership in AANAPISIs – and other MSIs – plays in a broader advocacy about the importance of equity and diversity in higher education. Institutional membership organizations, research centers, and advocacy organizations that support MSIs are critical to advancing greater support for low-income minority students and the institutions that serve them. One example of this work is the Hispanic Association of Colleges and Universities (HACU). HACU is an advocacy and professional association representing over "470 colleges and universities committed to Hispanic higher education success in the U.S., Puerto Rico, Latin America, and Spain," many of which are HSIs (HACU, n.d.). HACU is critical in providing advocacy, professional development, and support to HSIs. Similar to HACU, the Asian Pacific Islander Association of Colleges and Universities (APIACU) has been a key driving force leading advocacy efforts for AANAPISIs and other institutions committed to serving low-income and underrepresented AAPI students. One of APIACU's (2017) missions is to "increase the capacity and capabilities of member colleges and universities, especially AANAPISIs, to serve the diverse needs of all AAPIs along the spectrum of achievement" (APIACU, n.d.). Together, the 34 institutional members of APIACU (as of 2012), many of which have been designated AANAPISIs, are a united front in advocating for AANAPISIs and other policies which impact low-income AAPI students. The collective advocacy efforts led by APIACU have been critical in bringing greater awareness of AANAPISIs and the diverse needs of AAPI students.

Through our own work with PEER, we have collaborated with AANAPISIs in the policy arena by increasing visibility about the program and the impact it has on the educational mobility of low-income Asian American and Pacific Islander students. This collaboration with institutional leaders has provided higher education policymakers, practitioners, and educational researchers with a deeper understanding of AANAPISIs and the students that they serve. More specifically, PEER has demonstrated the extent to which being an AANAPISI positions campuses to more effectively serve their AAPI students, studied the ways in which campuses leverage their funding and/or status to gain access to more information and resources, and empirically examined the effectiveness of programs and services funded by the AANAPISI grant. The institutional leadership in AANAPISIs has helped raise the national visibility of the AANAPISI program and has linked AANAPISIs to the larger role and function of all MSI programs, which is critical given their collective effort to increase college access and success for underserved students.

Conclusion

While AANAPISIs have made great gains in their short history, it is important to recognize the critical role that institutional leadership has played in their progress. With that said, there is much more work to be done and more institutions that need to get involved. More AANAPISI leaders should educate themselves and institutional members (i.e., administrators, staff, faculty, students) about the demography, the heterogeneity, and the needs of their AAPI student population. The unique demography of these students should be considered in the context of the surrounding communities where their students live because the success of students at MSIs is very much impacted by the conditions of the communities from which they come. To this point, it is also important to recognize, reach out to, and collaborate with community organizations and advocacy groups that are familiar with the needs of their communities.

Within institutions, data-driven processes are critical for overcoming the use of stereotypes and assumptions for making decisions about how to work with particular student groups. To raise awareness and to effectively address the needs of diverse students, MSI leaders must use data to learn about their students' needs, such as developing needs assessments. For example, working closely with the institutional research office to examine administrative data and examine equity in educational outcomes among students. Also, partnering with research organizations that can provide research capacity to the organization. In addition to establishing research partnerships, it is important for AANAPISIs to connect with and engage advocacy organizations, such as APIACU, which is essential for connecting leaders with a larger network of MSIs, as well as state and federal policymakers. This is critical for advocating for their institutions, as well as establishing partnerships to advocate for groups of institutions.

References

Alcantar, C.M., Bordoloi Pazich, L.M., & Teranishi, R.T. (forthcoming). Meaning-making about becoming a Minority-Serving Institution: A case study of Asian-serving community colleges.

American Association of Community Colleges (AACC) (2013). *AACC competencies for community college leaders* (2nd ed.). Washington, DC: Author. Retrieved from www.aacc. nche.edu/newsevents/Events/leadershipsuite/Pages/competencies.aspx

American Council on Education (2013). *ACE brief examines scarcity of Asian Pacific Islander American leaders in higher education*. Washington, DC: Author. Retrieved from www. acenet.edu/news-room/Pages/ACE-Brief-Examines-Scarcity-of-Asian-Pacific-Islander-American-Leaders-in-Higher-Education.aspx

Asian American and Asian Research Institute (2016). *Asian American leadership in CUNY and higher education: Findings, recommendations, and accountability*. New York: Author, The

City University of New York. Retrieved from www.aaari.info/notes/16-05-09CAA LIReport.pdf

Asian Pacific Islander Association of Colleges and Universities (APIACU) (n.d.). Retrieved from www.apiacu.org/

Brayboy, B.M.J., Fann, A.J., Castagno, A.E., & Solyom, J.A. (2012). *Postsecondary education for American Indian and Alaska Natives: Higher education for nation building and self-determination.* Hoboken, NJ: Wiley Periodicals.

Castellano, J., & Jones, L. (Eds.) (2003). *The majority in the minority: Expanding the representation of Latina/o faculty, administrators, and students in higher education.* Sterling, VA: Stylus.

Chang, M., Park, J., Lin, M.H., Poon, O.A., & Nakanishi, D.T. (2007). *Beyond myths: The growth and diversity of Asian American college freshman: 1971–2005.* Los Angeles, CA: UCLA Higher Education Research Institute.

Congressional Research Service (2009). *Memorandum regarding the number of institutions potentially eligible to receive grants under the assistance to Asian American and Native American and Pacific Islander-serving institutions program.* Washington, DC: Library of Congress.

Cook, B.J. (2012). *The American college president study: Key findings and takeaways.* Washington, DC: American Council on Education. Retrieved from www.acenet.edu/the-presidency/columns-and-features/Pages/The-American-College-President-Study.aspx

Cortez, L.J. (2015). Enacting leadership at Hispanic-Serving Institutions. In A.-M. Nunez, S. Hurtado, & E. Calderon Galdeano (Eds.), *Hispanic-Serving Institutions: Advancing research and transformative practice* (pp. 136–152). New York: Routledge.

de los Santos, A.G., Jr., & de los Santos, G.E. (2003). Hispanic-Serving Institutions in the 21st century: Overview, challenges, and opportunities. *Journal of Hispanic Higher Education,* 2(4), 377–391.

de los Santos, A.G., Jr., & Vega, I.I. (2008). Hispanic presidents and chancellors of institutions of higher education in the United States in 2001 and 2006. *Journal of Hispanic Higher Education,* 7(2), 156–182.

Eddy, P.L. (2010). *Community college leadership: A multidimensional model for leading change.* Sterling, VA: Stylus.

Espinoza, P.P., & Espinoza, C.C. (2012). Supporting the 7th-year undergraduate: Responsive leadership at a Hispanic-Serving Institution. *Journal of Cases in Educational Leadership,* 15(1), 32–50.

Esters, L.L., & Strayhorn, T.L. (2013). Demystifying the contributions of public land-grant Historically Black Colleges and Universities: Voices of HBCU presidents. *The Negro College Review,* 64(1–4), 119–135.

Esters, L.L., Washington, A., Gasman, M., Commodore, F., O'Neal, B., Freeman, S., & Jimenez, C.D. (2016). *Effective leadership toolkit for the 21st-century Historically Black College and University president.* Philadelphia, PA: Penn Center for Minority Serving Institutions. Retrieved from www2.gse.upenn.edu/cmsi/sites/gse.upenn.edu.cmsi/files/MSI_Ldrshp Rprt_R3.pdf

Freeman, S., Jr., Commodore, F., Gasman, M., & Carter, C. (2016). Leaders wanted! The skills expected and needed for a successful 21st century Historically Black College and University presidency. *Journal of Black Studies,* 47(6), 570–591.

Garcia, G.A. (2016). Complicating a Latina/o-serving identity at a Hispanic-Serving Institution. *The Review of Higher Education,* 40(1), 117–143.

Gasman, M., Baez, B., & Turner, C.S.V. (Eds.) (2008). *Understanding Minority-Serving Institutions.* Albany: State University of New York Press.

Hispanic Association of Colleges and Universities (HACU) (n.d.). HACU 101. San Antonio, TX: Author. Retrieved from www.hacu.net/hacu/HACU_101.asp

Kezar, A. (2001). Organizational models and facilitators of change: Providing a framework for student and academic affairs collaboration. In A. Kezar, D.J. Hirsch, & C. Burack (Eds.), *Understanding the role of academic and student affairs collaboration in creating a successful learning environment* (pp. 63–74). San Francisco, CA: Jossey-Bass.

Kiang, P.N. (1992). Issues of curriculum and community for first generation Asian Americans in college. In L.S. Zwerling & H.B. London (Eds.), *First-generation students: Confronting the cultural issues* (pp. 97–112). San Francisco, CA: Jossey-Bass.

Kim, E., & Díaz, J. (2013). *Immigrant students and higher education.* Hoboken, NJ: Wiley Periodicals.

Kotori, C., & Malaney, G. (2003). Asian American students' perceptions of racism, reporting behaviors, and awareness of legal rights and procedures. *NASPA Journal,* 40(3), 56–76.

National Center for Education Statistics (2011). *Integrated postsecondary educational data system fall enrollment survey.* Washington, DC: US Department of Education.

National Commission on Asian American and Pacific Islander Research in Education (CARE) (2010). Federal higher education policy priorities and the Asian American and Pacific Islander community. New York, NY: Author.

National Commission on Asian American and Pacific Islander Research in Education (CARE) (2011). The relevance of Asian Americans and Pacific Islanders in the college completion agenda. New York, NY: Author. Retrieved from http://care.gseis.ucla.edu/wp-content/uploads/2015/08/2011_CARE_Report.pdf

National Commission on Asian American and Pacific Islander Research in Education (CARE) (2013). *Partnership for equity in education through research (PEER): Findings from the first year of research on AANAPISIs.* New York: Author. Retrieved from http://care.gseis.ucla.edu/wp-content/uploads/2015/08/2013_CARE_Report.pdf

Núñez, A.-M., Hoover, R.E., Pickett, K., Stuart-Carruthers, A.C., & Vásquez, M. (2013). *Latinos in higher education and Hispanic-Serving Institutions: Creating conditions for success.* Hoboken, NJ: Wiley Periodicals.

Osajima, K. (1995). Racial politics and the invisibility of Asian Americans in higher education. *Educational Foundations,* 9(1), 35–53.

Perna, L.W., Gerald, D., Baum, E., & Milem, J. (2007). The status of equity for Black faculty and administrators in public higher education in the South. *Research in Higher Education,* 48(2), 193–228.

Perna, L.W., Li, C., Walsh, E., & Raible, S. (2010). The status of equity for Hispanics in public higher education in Florida and Texas. *Journal of Hispanic Higher Education,* 9(2), 145–166.

Santiago, D.A. (2006). *Inventing Hispanic-Serving Institutions: The basics.* Washington, DC: Excelencia in Education and the Institute for Higher Education Policy.

Santiago, D.A. (2009). *Leading in a changing America: Presidential perspectives from Hispanic-Serving Institutions.* Washington, DC: Excelencia in Education. Retrieved from www.edexcelencia.org/gateway/download/25900/1483694084

Teranishi, R.T. (2010). *Asians in the ivory tower: Dilemmas of racial inequality in American higher education.* New York: Teachers College Press.

Teranishi, R.T., Alcantar, C.M., & Nguyen, B.M.D. (2015). Race and class through the lens of the Asian American and Pacific Islander experience: Perspectives from community college students. *AAPI Nexus Journal,* 13(1 & 2), 72–90.

Teranishi, R.T., Martin, M., Bordoloi Pazich, L., Alcantar, C.M., Nguyen, B.M.D., Curammeng, E.R., Nguyen, M.H., & Chan, J. (2015). *The impact of scholarships for Asian American and Pacific Islander community college students: Preliminary findings from an experimental design study*. Los Angeles, CA: National Commission on AAPI Research in Education. Retrieved from www.apiasf.org/research/2015_CARE_Report.pdf

Teranishi, R.T., Suárez-Orozco, C., & Suárez-Orozco, M. (2011). Immigrants in community college. *Future of Children*, 21(1), 153–169.

Weisman, I.M., & Vaughan, G.B. (2002). *The community college presidency 2001*. Washington, DC: American Association of Community Colleges. Retrieved from www.aacc.nche.edu/Publications/Briefs/Documents/06242002presidency.pdf

Williams, D.A. (2013). *A matter of excellence: A guide to strategic diversity leadership and accountability in higher education*. Washington, DC: American Council on Education. Retrieved from https://facweb.northseattle.edu/bwilli/Diversity_Resources/Diversity_HiringResources/A%20Matter%20of%20Excellence%20A%20Guide%20to%20Strategic%20Diversity%20Leadership%20and%20Accountability%20in%20Higher%20Education%20-%20313004.pdf

13

SETTING THE STAGE FOR CHANGE

Emerging Knowledge on Leadership at MSIs

Andrew T. Arroyo, Dina C. Maramba, Robert T. Palmer, Tiffany Fountaine Boykin and Taryn Ozuna Allen

The contributors to this book have explored many opportunities and challenges for effective leadership at Minority-Serving Institutions (MSIs). In this final chapter we distill salient themes from the book in order to stimulate further discussion. The themes are: (1) the importance of racial self-determination or self-authorship, (2) the need for new models, (3) complicated missions, (4) non-traditional pathways to MSI leadership, and (5) lessons for PWI leadership. We encourage readers to consider how these themes might apply to their institutional contexts, and also to identify other themes not highlighted here. Moreover, we encourage readers to engage in conversations regarding what themes unite MSIs as a group and themes that might distinguish MSIs from each other. Probing these questions is necessary to advance the field of MSI research, policy, and practice, which is consistent with the overarching purpose of the current book.

Theme: The Importance of Racial Self-Determination or Self-Authorship

The first theme is the importance of racial self-determination or self-authorship. Several chapter contributors express the need for alignment between a senior leader's race and the MSI's classification (e.g., Native American leadership for Tribal colleges and universities [TCUs]). Underlying this theme is the notion that racial alignment between MSI classification, senior leadership, the faculty, and the student body is an indispensable key to success. Although racial alignment does not preclude the contribution of other races such as Whites, and although racial alignment is no guarantee that the senior leader is culturally aware or culturally centered, racial self-determination is a generally important principle.

To illustrate the importance of this principle, authors Kofi Lomotey and Megan Covington make an impassioned call for same-race, self-determined leadership in the context of historically Black colleges and universities (HBCUs). They issue the challenge that Black people "must [re-develop HBCUs] for ourselves, for our children and for our grandchildren." The authors express the historical observation that "people do not have revolutions staged for them; they must stage them themselves." According to these researchers, self-determination is the only sure way to achieve culturally responsive institutional cultures that differentiate HBCUs from other sites of higher learning by educating and empowering Black students. Culturally aware Black leaders are needed to take the reins and guide HBCUs as only they can.

In the context of TCUs, Cheryl Crazy Bull states that TCU presidents "must be warriors ... so their [Native American] people may prosper and their tribes can thrive." TCUs are "contextually and physically place-based and culturally rooted," making it necessary that their leaders have insider knowledge and credibility. Native American leaders share a unique "ancestral responsibility to lead in a manner that ensures the survival of their people." Also writing about TCUs, Ginger Stull and Marybeth Gasman affirm Crazy Bull's sentiments by stating, "Native Americans are the most capable people to lead Tribal education efforts." All authors state unequivocally that Native American leadership is a self-authored act of resistance against forced assimilation and for the advancement of Native American ideals and rights.

Addressing the context of Hispanic-Serving Institutions (HSIs), Magdalena de la Teja makes an urgent call for self-determined leadership that is culturally aware, responsive, and emancipatory. Enrolling high percentages of Hispanic students does not automatically mean an institution is serving the students (see theme on "Complicated Missions"). As a means of self-determined leadership for HSIs, she describes the importance of employing "counterstory." In the tradition of Critical Race Theory and LatCrit Theory, counterstory is a way to dismantle racially oppressive practices by foregrounding and affirming the agency of Latino/a students and leaders. By challenging dominant narratives with culturally grounded narratives, a marginalized group's strengths are harnessed and released.

Notably, de la Teja's description of her journey as a dedicated HSI leader suggests that she has personalized the call for self-determined leadership. We can surmise that many MSI leaders do the same. A sign of culturally centered self-determined leadership is personal investment with a sense of greater purpose. She writes that her own decision to work at an HSI community college "aligned with my professional and personal value of making higher education attainment accessible to Latinos, other people of color, and those from low-income families." The reader gains the sense that she would remain at an HSI community college from a sense of cultural service even if recruited to go elsewhere.

Self-determination is also reflected in Adrian, Hiyane-Brown, and Story's chapter on AANAPISI community colleges. All three of the authors are of Asian

American descent and have held or currently hold upper administrative community college leadership positions. Their insight and perspectives on AANAPISI leadership are indispensible as research in this area is severely limited. As mentioned in their chapter, "how to apply, balance, and transcend cultural influences is significant for AAPI leaders." Their study on the need for cultural leadership competencies and their findings are important towards increasing our knowledge about the diversity of AAPIs in higher education institutions.

Finally, Joseph Castro and Isaac Castro's chapter offers another insight on self-determination. Not only is Joseph Castro a Latino president of an institution that is classified as both an HSI and AANAPISI, but also he is a native of the region in which the institution is located. The combination of his race and local roots enables him to provide leadership that is culturally centered and also that speaks to residents of the region at-large. Even the research focus of the institution is intentionally focused on regional concerns.

Theme: The Need for New Models

The chapter contributors also affirm the need for new models and approaches to leadership. Approaches to leadership are continuously evolving to meet modern challenges across all types of institutions, including at PWIs. This reality not-withstanding, MSIs require fresh models due to special challenges and opportunities they face compared to PWIs as well as the diverse populations they serve.

For example, Crazy Bull advances a leadership framework appropriate for the TCU context. The framework contains seven functions, with each function connecting to tribal worldviews and being centered in tribal identities. The leader (i.e., TCU president) should serve as: (1) visionary, (2) hunter/gatherer/grower, (3) translator/interpreter, (4) orator/advocate, (5) warrior, (6) story teller, and (7) spiritual and physical leader. Crazy Bull carefully nuances her seven identified functions to show how they reflect and apply to the dual imperative of the TCU president to build the institution while influencing the direction of their tribe. She explicitly clarifies that attempts to understand them through a non-tribal prism, such as a Eurocentric lens, will diminish their complexity. Each function is tethered to Native American communities. The essence of Stull and Gasman's chapter concurs with Crazy Bull's paradigm. Stull and Gasman posit that Native leaders practice at least five principles that are relevant for a Native leadership framework: (1) a dedication to serving the community; (2) the importance of knowledge, both of their Tribal culture and the people they serve; (3) decentralized leadership and collective decision making; (4) leading and learning by example; and (5) persisting through difficult circumstances.

Persisting and emerging stronger is a leadership paradigm that cuts across many MSIs. Broussard and Hilton describe the need for disruptive leadership in HBCUs. For their dual-designated institution (i.e., an HSI and AANAPISI), Castro and Castro sketch a highly practical example of bold leadership with a strong theme of empowerment. President Castro has set forth an ambitious agenda for his institution, Fresno State University. Of his bold leadership paradigm, the authors write, "This unique style of leadership calls on everyone, especially the President, to set aside personal agendas and preferences and focus on how to strengthen the university so that it can better serve the needs of its students and the community." In many ways, Castro and Castro's bold leadership paradigm dovetails with the model of servant leadership described by Gasman, Washington, and Esters in their chapter about President Michael J. Sorrell and Paul Quinn College. Both Presidents Castro and Sorrell practice a "WE Over Me" ideal that combines authentic engagement, relationship management, and shared power. Upon this foundation, each president is able to make strong decisions because he has secured the buy-in of key stakeholders. Trust, in the spirit of community, is a core operating principle of bold, empowering leadership and servant leadership.

The role of the community in creating a holistic context of service deserves attention. We see this point made throughout Stull and Gasman's chapter as they emphasize Native leadership as emerging from the community rather than a hierarchy. Moreover, although de la Teja does not speak directly of servant leadership in the context of senior administrators at HSI community colleges, her chapter addresses the notion of service in the context of faculty. She refers to the relatively larger number of Latino/a faculty at these institutions as having the ability to serve as role models and mentors to students. This type of action can also be an example of servant leadership. When faculty, staff, and likeminded administrators go above and beyond their contractual obligations in united fashion, the ultimate demonstration of servant leadership is displayed.

Finally, Edward M. Willis and Andrew T. Arroyo advance a model of highly effective student affairs leadership at HBCUs. Their chapter shares the emphasis on bold, servant leadership expressed in other chapters, but recontextualizes the discussion with a conceptual model that current and aspiring chief student affairs officers (CSAOs) at HBCUs can draw from to understand the significant aspects of the job, along with knowledge, skills, and abilities necessary for success. Moreover, the authors posit the model as applicable for current and aspiring HBCU presidents due to the intersections between the fast-paced, 24/7 nature of student affairs and the presidency. Although Willis and Arroyo's model is not race-based, it does appraise and account for some of the special demands of senior leadership in the Black college context. Leaders of other MSIs can find value in the model as well, particularly as new senior leaders should be evaluated on whether they can effectively balance emergent needs and strategic needs, not on whether they come through the academic ranks according to tradition. Of note, a close examination of skill sets demonstrated by the most progressive CSAOs reveals acumen in the sort of "disruptive" leadership many MSIs need in order to define a niche in a saturated higher educational market (see chapter by Broussard and Hilton).

On another note, the lack of scholarship and research on leadership about AAPI leaders and AANAPSIs poses a challenge to our understanding of how to effectively serve AAPI students. However, Adrian, Hiyane-Brown, and Story state that "the notion that good leadership [at AANAPISIs] can be determined or assessed with a generic checklist of competencies and experiences is naïve and shortsighted." Instead, they challenge us to go beyond our understanding of basic organizational leadership competencies. They emphasize that the complex needs of AAPI students are often ignored and if college leadership "is not sensitive to them or lacks the knowledge or understanding about their differences and dynamics, then neither the students nor the organization can thrive or succeed." They identify critical qualities, predispositions, and values that leaders should possess in order to address the diverse AAPI student populations.

Along similar lines, Teranishi, Alcantar, and Underwood encourage us to consider the role of leadership organizations in working towards successful AANAPISIs and leadership. They cite that advocacy for effective AANAPISI leadership can be heavily attributed to the efforts of APIACU (Asian American, Pacific Islander Association of Colleges and Universities). This association advocates for AANAPISIs and low income, underrepresented AAPI students, thus bringing more awareness and accurate information about AAPIs and connecting leaders associated with other MSIs. On another level, Adrian, Hiyane-Brown, and Story mention the importance of addressing the underrepresentation of AAPI leadership as a whole. LEAP (Leadership Education for Asian Pacifics, Inc.), is yet another organization that helps to increase the number of AAPI administrators in higher education through a series of leadership development opportunities and services to support AAPIs.

Theme: Complicated Missions

As the prior theme suggests, a distinguishing feature of MSIs is the complicated nature of their work. Nowhere is their work more complicated than in how they frame and execute their missions. Insightful, intentional, and careful leadership is needed to tackle the difficult question of how to serve all populations without discrimination, while embracing unapologetically their special focus on a given minority student group.

Lomotey and Covington argue convincingly that HBCUs must improve in their service to Black Americans. The authors state that HBCUs are not functioning optimally to the benefit of Black students. Nonetheless, when compared to PWIs, the prevailing research literature is clear that HBCUs still provide unique, positive environments for Black students in conjunction with their federal definition. Although improvements are needed, the case can be made that HBCUs are doing good work for Black students. Where HBCUs overall lack leadership is in the area of racial diversification – that is, serving Black students well, while embracing other races in a culture of inclusivity (Arroyo, Palmer, & Maramba, 2016; Arroyo,

Palmer, Maramba, & Louis, 2016; Palmer, Arroyo, & Maramba, 2016). Leadership is needed to navigate this complicated mission landscape.

HSIs are another example of institutions with complicated missions. Laura J. Cortez incisively notes that many HSIs are "perpetuating a closeted identity." She advances the need for administrators and leaders, as advocates, to boldly (re)align their institutions around service to Hispanic students. Cortez also underscores the need to nuance the HSI classification. Although an institution must demonstrate 25% Hispanic enrollment for an HSI status, there is a qualitative difference between enrolling 25% and 85% Latino/as. Some institutions are also emerging as HSIs (i.e., eHSI), meaning they are on the cusp of receiving the designation. They, too, require special consideration from researchers and practitioners.

Similarly, Magdalena de la Teja notes the complete absence of a Latino/a agenda in many HSI mission statements and other publications such as printed materials and websites. (We can assume a similar situation at many AANAPISIs.) Because of this disconnect, she writes, "There is immense need to work toward transforming HSI community colleges to truly serve Latino students and improve overall outcomes no matter the complexity of doing so." Part of this transformation is clear *self-definition*. Having greater numbers of Latino faculty may provide an informal infrastructure of support or a curriculum with some cultural relevance, but that is not enough. Only after self-defined institutional documents such as mission statements reflect HSI status or service to Latino/a students can administrators foster real responsibility and accountability for equitable outcomes on their campuses. And only then can other stakeholders hold their leaders responsible and accountable for outcomes and the allocation of resources to achieve those outcomes. Without concrete language to solidify an institution's structural commitment to a given minority student population, dedication to that population could be tenuous at best. For de la Teja, the challenge is "to have courageous dialogue with faculty and administrators about what institutional changes in policy and practice need to be made" for Latino/a student success at HSIs.

Similar to the dilemmas in HSIs, AANAPISIs face the challenge of finding ways to ensure that AAPI students are included in the mission of higher education institutions to effectively address their needs. Teranishi, Alcantar, and Underwood share the importance that administrators and staff who work at AANAPISIs must be aware of the diverse AAPI populations. For example, the research conducted by PEER (Partnership for Equity in Education through Research) emphasized that AANAPISIs can work more effectively if their leaders use their funding sources to provide access and more accurate data about AAPIs and provide resources and programs to address the needs of AAPI students. With more accurate knowledge about underserved and underrepresented AAPIs, institutions can work closer toward serving a large part of their student population.

Stull and Gasman point out that TCUs face complicated missions as they maintain a dual focus on meeting accreditation standards and serving their tribal communities. The challenge is more than ideological. Real questions about whether courses in tribal history and culture will transfer to meet degree requirements at a traditional institution, among other policies, have to be considered. Amidst this challenge, Stull and Gasman identify an opportunity "for TCUs to become national leaders in developing curriculum on Native American history and culture."

Certainly, the existence of complicated missions demands new models of leadership. Leaders are needed who will take seriously Willis and Arroyo's challenge to focus on strategic needs, rather than subsisting in an endlessly reactionary posture. Leaders also must adopt Castro and Castro's mantra of bold leadership. Tackling the legal and ethical thicket of serving diverse student populations in a society fraught with racial challenges is not for the faint of heart.

Theme: Non-Traditional Pathways to MSI Leadership

The next salient theme found in this book is that there are many pathways to effective MSI leadership. Although leaders may follow the traditional academic trajectory by starting their careers in the professoriate, strong evidence suggests that leaders may arrive at their positions via non-traditional routes. These avenues can include student affairs leadership or leadership experience outside the academy altogether.

Willis and Arroyo's chapter challenges the traditional trajectory of the HBCU presidency by highlighting the connection between highly effective student affairs leadership and the requirements of an effective presidency. The authors offer a new model of the highly effective CSAO that current or aspiring presidents could use to inform their work. Alignment between these leadership roles is evident in their joint emphasis on responsiveness to emergent or urgent needs, as well as their need to plan strategically. Student affairs practitioners' familiarity with crisis management and how to serve students on the frontlines provide these leaders excellent preparation for key requirements of the HBCU presidency. Other successful CSAOs-turned-presidents, such as Walter M. Kimbrough, bear out this connection.

As indicated, presidents also come from outside academe. President Michael J. Sorrell, who is featured in Gasman, Washington, and Esters' chapter, is one such individual. Although his professional background is not the subject of their chapter, the authors discuss his entrepreneurial talent and impact on Paul Quinn College and the Dallas region. President Sorrell enjoyed numerous successes in the private and public sectors prior to his college leadership role, providing a foundation for college leadership with distinction.

Importantly, none of the authors disparage the traditional pathway to MSI leadership (via academic affairs). The authors do, however, enrich the discussion by offering robust alternatives that broaden the field. Search firms and hiring boards should not hesitate to broaden their search into multiple sectors when looking for the right individual to chart the course. Moreover, proactive succession planning and leadership sourcing, rather than reactionary appointments made in haste, are important for building strong MSI leadership teams. Broussard and Hilton's chapter makes this point effectively. To the degree leadership teams are formed deliberately, the institution will be positioned for enduring success that disrupts and redefines higher education.

Theme: Lessons for PWI Leadership

Another theme of this book is that MSIs and MSI leaders have much to teach PWIs and PWI leaders. It goes without saying that MSI leaders should draw on best practices wherever they are found, including PWIs. To ignore lessons from PWI models would be institutional malpractice. And yet, not only should MSIs develop best practices for their own institutional contexts as a matter of self-determination, but also PWIs should be looking to MSIs for lessons.

Stull and Gasman offer several lessons from TCUs for leaders of other institutions, especially those that serve students who "have endured years of systemic social and economic inequality." The authors point out that Native Americans have been miscast as assimilated subjects. While it is true that conformity to Eurocentric norms was one outcome of the interaction between Native Americans and Europeans, it is equally true that Native Americans contributed "much to the culture and leadership of the United States." The authors cite the influence of the Iroquois Confederacy's Great Law of Peace on the founding fathers and the Constitution as a historical example. More specific to higher education, Stull and Gasman identify six recommendations for non-Native leaders in non-TCU contexts, based on the Native leadership paradigm. A clear thread connects their six recommendations, while speaking to the non-Westernized manner in which Native Americans view themselves in connection to one another: interconnectedness and its corollary, interdependence.

PWIs can also learn a great deal from the practices and the values that AANAPISIs hold regarding the AAPI population. Both AANAPISI chapters (Teranishi, Alcantar, & Underwood; Adrian, Hiyane-Brown, & Story) underscore the urgency to recognize the diversity within the AAPI sub-populations. It is acknowledging the complexities of the over 48 ethnicities that can bring a better understanding and awareness to the diverse needs of AAPI students. Teranishi, Alcantar, and Underwood call for "culturally competent and responsive leaders [who … understand] the ethnic, cultural, and linguistic heterogeneity among the AAPI student population rather than be driven by the model minority and foreigner stereotypes." Closeted HSIs and emerging HSIs, which typically still function as PWIs, also should look to HSIs that are effectively embracing the Latino/a student populations to learn what does and does not work for fostering equitable environments of success (see Cortez's chapter).

Leaders who epitomize the best of Willis and Arroyo's model of the highly effective CSAO leader (or president) can also teach leaders at PWIs. Learning to hold in constant tension the need to be responsive to emergent needs, while also being forward thinking and methodical over the long term, is a challenge for most leaders. By applying the model — that is, becoming visionaries, risk-takers, team builders, advisors, guides, and collaborators — leaders at PWIs will meet the task.

Conclusion

MSIs can and must weather many storms en route to success. The fact that MSIs do more with less is affirmed time and again throughout this book. Now more than ever, effective leadership at MSIs is a critical factor to ensure struggling MSIs emerge strong, and strong MSIs become stronger.

Overall, the superordinate theme of this book is the need for MSI leaders to navigate change. We touch on opportunities and challenges related to change throughout the current chapter. Although change can be uncomfortable, it need not be viewed negatively. Change is an essential part of organizational life cycles. Change is an invitation to improve, with benefits accruing to diverse student populations across our unique society.

References

Arroyo, A.T., Palmer, R.T., & Maramba, D.C. (2016). Is it a different world? Providing a holistic understanding of the experiences and perceptions of non-Black students of historically Black colleges and universities. *Journal of College Student Retention: Research, Theory, & Practice*, 18(3), 360–382.

Arroyo, A.T., Palmer, R.T., Maramba, D.C., & Louis, D.A. (2016). Exploring the efforts of HBCU student affairs practitioners to support non-Black students. *Journal of Student Affairs Research and Practice*, 54(1). Online.

Palmer, R.T., Arroyo, A.T., & Maramba, D.C. (2016). Understanding the perceptions of HBCU student affairs practitioners toward non-Black students. *Journal of Diversity in Higher Education*. Online.

AFTERWORD

Twenty-first Century Leadership at Minority-Serving Institutions

Ivory A. Toldson

Minority-Serving Institutions (MSIs) produce a significant number of diverse professionals that materially strengthen the fabric of the United States. MSIs have successfully graduated millions of students of color, many of whom come from economically disadvantaged communities, where most have never attended college or earned a degree or credential. Yet, MSIs often lack adequate resources to put structures in place to graduate more students of color (Godreau et al., 2015). In 2014, four Traditionally White Institutions (TWIs) received more revenue from grants and contracts than all four-year Historically Black Colleges and Universities (HBCUs) combined. In total, 89 four-year HBCUs collectively received $1.2 billion for grants and contracts from the federal, state, and local governments, as well as private foundations. By comparison, Johns Hopkins University received $1.6 billion alone (Toldson, 2015).

On average, each HBCU receives $11 million from the federal government, $1.3 million from state governments, and a little more than $504,000 from local governments and private foundations, for a total average of $12.8 million for grants and contracts annually. The total annual average for all institutions of higher education is $27.7 million. In perspective, the annual revenue total for grants and contracts for the average TWI, would rank in the top-10 among HBCUs (Toldson, 2015).

Strong leadership can go a long way toward helping MSIs and their students achieve success. *Effective Leadership at Minority-Serving Institutions: Exploring Opportunities and Challenges for Leadership* underscores the exigency of dynamic institutional leadership during dynamic social transformations. According to the Institute for Higher Education Policy–IHEP's February 2014 *Issue Brief, Minority-serving Institutions: Doing More with Less*, MSIs are an important part of the higher education landscape as institutions (Cunningham, Park, & Engle, 2014). Results of prior research indicate that MSI students are significantly more likely to have better relationships with faculty and to have a higher sense of "belonging" (Toldson, 2013). Among HBCUs that have a Carnegie Classification of "Doctoral Granting Research University," 67% of the faculty is Black or African American. By contrast, only 4% of the faculty at doctoral granting TWIs is Black (Toldson, 2015).

MSI leaders are key to driving success across a broad cross-section of traditional institutional variables including: admissions, size, and growth; graduation, retention, and financial aid; fiscal resources and assets; and capacity, administration, and human capital. However, today, the United States of America is experiencing unprecedented changes that are forcing institutions of higher education (IHE) to adapt new strategies to remain successful. IHEs that are refractory to change will not adequately prepare students for the twenty-first century economy of knowledge, and will eventually cease to exist. This Afterword describes some of the societal transformations for which IHE leaders must prepare.

First, the White minority is imminent. For three years in a row, White deaths have outpaced White births. The millennial population, now larger than the baby boomers, is the most racially diverse adult population in U.S. history. By the mid-2040s, the U.S.A. will be majority people of color (Sanburn, 2015). Parallel to the nation, MSIs are rapidly becoming the norm, rather than the exception among institutions of higher education in the United States. The United States of America has 4,658 Title IV eligible, degree-granting IHEs. Among them, 1,905 have a student population that is less than 50% White. In total, more than 11.8 million students in the United States are enrolled at an IHE that is majority minority. As we verge closer to this reality, xenophobic hysteria promulgates throughout regressive aspects of our society. However no young person in the U.S.A. has a future, who cannot relate to people of other races.

Second, globalism is an enduring reality. The centuries-old geopolitical mandate that each person on Earth should declare allegiance to one nation, and depend on that nation for their livelihood and well-being is fading. People from nations with fewer resources cannot afford to buy into this concept, so they emigrate. Large multinational corporations are too acquisitive to buy into this concept, so they exploit opportunities beyond their national borders. Regressive aspects of our society want to stop the ambitions of immigrants and corporations, when they really should be following their leads. Today, all IHE should be thinking about opportunities beyond national borders to develop their institutions culturally, financially, and socially.

Third, automated technologies and artificial intelligence will transmute the traditional labor market and create new learning imperatives for higher education consumers. *The Economist* cited a 2013 study by Frey and Osborne which found that 47% of workers in America had jobs at high risk of automation in the foreseeable future. Over the last eight years, more U.S. jobs have been lost to automation than outsourcing. The future learning imperative of the nation will not be tied to a perennial industrial labor force, but interdisciplinary learning for collective knowledge and innovation, rather than the production of goods and services. Progressive MSIs should not simply acquiesce to corporations' dependence on human labor. MSIs should contribute to the inevitable redefinition of employment, advance STEM education, and fight for vulnerable segments of our society that might lose traditional means of capital as technology advances.

MSIs serve a vital role in educating low income and first generation college students in our nation, which is becoming increasingly more diverse. Even with limited resources, MSIs are among the top producers of higher education institutions that are the baccalaureate origin of Black students who receive Ph.D. in science and mathematics (Toldson & Esters, 2012). I have personally sat in a race car engineered by students at Alabama A&M, took a virtual mission to Mars on the campus of Tennessee State University, saw a NASA satellite mission led by Hampton University, and witnessed many other scientific feats at HBCUs. However, the true promise of MSI innovation will never be fully realized without visionary leadership and sincere investment from the federal, state, and local governments, as well as private foundations. Unleashing the potential of MSIs could open new channels of opportunity to millions of students, leading to a stronger higher education marketplace, more income equality and new scientific discoveries.

References

Cunningham, A., Park, E., & Engle, J. (2014). *Minority-Serving Institutions: Doing more with less.* Retrieved from www.ihep.org/sites/default/files/uploads/docs/pubs/msis_doing_more_w-less_final_february_2014-v2.pdf

Frey, C. B., & Osborne, M.A. (2013). *The future employment: How susceptible are jobs to computerisation.* Retrieved from http://www.oxfordmartin.ox.ac.uk/downloads/academic/The_Future_of_Employment.pdf

Godreau, I., Gavillán-Suárez, J., Franco-Ortiz, M., Calderón-Squiabro, J. M., Marti, V., & Gaspar-Concepción, J. (2015). Growing faculty research for students' success: Best practices of a research institute at a minority-serving undergraduate institution. *Journal of Research Administration, 46*(2), 55–78.

Sanburn, J. (2015). U.S. steps closer to a future where minorities are the majority. Time.com. Retrieved from http://time.com/3934092/us-population-diversity-census/

Toldson, I.A. (2013). Historically Black Colleges and Universities can promote leadership and excellence in STEM. *Journal of Negro Education, 82*(4), 359–367.

Toldson, I.A. (2015). Weeding out v. building up: Why Justice Scalia was wrong about Black scientists (Editor's Commentary). *Journal of Negro Education, 84*(4), 517–518.

Toldson, I.A., & Esters, L.L. (2012). *The quest for excellence: Supporting the academic success of minority males in science, technology, engineering, and mathematics (STEM) disciplines.* Retrieved from www.aplu.org/library/the-quest-for-excellence/file

CONTRIBUTORS

Biographies of Editors

Robert T. Palmer is currently Interim Chair and associate professor in the Department of Educational Leadership and Policy Studies at Howard University. He is also a faculty affiliate for the Center of Minority-Serving Institutions (CMSI) at the University of Pennsylvania. His research examines issues of access, equity, retention, persistence, and the college experience of racial and ethnic minorities, particularly within the context of historically Black colleges and universities. Dr. Palmer's work has been published in leading journals in higher education, such as *The Journal of College Student Development, Teachers College Record, Journal of Diversity in Higher Education, Journal of Negro Education, College Student Affairs Journal, Journal of College Student Retention, The Negro Educational Review*, and *Journal of Black Studies*, among others. Since earning his Ph.D. in 2007, Dr. Palmer has authored/co-authored well over 100 academic publications, including authoring or editing over 20 books. Dr. Palmer was named an ACPA Emerging Scholar in 2012 and an ACPA Senior Scholar in 2017. Furthermore in 2012, he was awarded the Association for the Study of Higher Education (ASHE)–Mildred García Junior Exemplary Scholarship Award. In 2015, Diverse Issues in Higher Education recognized Dr. Palmer as an Emerging Scholar. Later that year, he also received the SUNY Chancellor's award for Excellence in Scholarship and Creative Activities. This prestigious award is normally given to a full professor. Dr. Palmer earned his Ph.D. in Higher Education Administration from Morgan State University in 2007, M.S. in Counseling with an emphasis on Higher Education at West Chester University of Pennsylvania in 2003, and the B.S. in History at Shippensburg University of Pennsylvania in 2001.

Dina C. Maramba is an associate professor of Higher Education in the School of Educational Studies at the Claremont Graduate University. She is also a faculty affiliate and mentor for the Center of Minority-Serving Institutions (CMSI) at the University of Pennsylvania. Prior to her faculty positions, she worked in higher education and student affairs administration for over 10 years where she held director roles in residence life, Upward Bound, and TRIO Student Support Services. Her research focuses on equity, diversity, and social justice issues within the context of higher education. Her interests include the influence of educational institutions and campus climates on the access and success among students of color, underserved, and first generation college students; the experiences of Filipina/o Americans and Asian American/Pacific Islanders students, faculty, and administrators in higher education institutions. She has received awards from the American College Student Personnel Association (ACPA) – Outstanding Contribution to Asian/Pacific Islander American Research in Higher Education and the National Association of Student Personnel Administrators (NASPA) – Distinguished Contribution for research on Asian Americans in Higher Education. Recently, she was also recognized as an ACPA Diamond Honoree and ACPA Senior Scholar for her contributions to Student Affairs. In addition, she was awarded the prestigious State University of New York (SUNY) Chancellor's Excellence in Teaching Award. She has published a number of journal articles and co-authored monographs, which include *Charting New Realities: Asian Americans in Higher Education* (2014, Jossey-Bass) and *Racial and Ethnic Minority Students' Success in STEM Education* (2011, Jossey-Bass). Her co-edited books include *The "Other" Students: Filipino Americans, Education and Power* (2013, Information Age Publishing); *Understanding and Supporting Asian Pacific Islander Desi Americans in College* (2017, upcoming); *Fostering Success of Ethnic and Racial Minorities in STEM: The Role of Minority-Serving Institutions* (2014, Routledge); *The Misrepresented Minority: New Insights on Asian Americans and Pacific Islanders and their Implications for Higher Education* (2013, Stylus); and *Understanding HIV and STI Prevention for College Students* (2014, Routledge). Having presented her research nationally and internationally, her work includes publications in the *Journal of Higher Education, Journal of College Student Development, Journal of College Student Retention, Review of Higher Education,* and *Journal of Diversity in Higher Education and Educational Policy.*

Andrew T. Arroyo is associate professor of interdisciplinary studies, co-director for learning communities, and program director for the career pathways initiative at Norfolk State University, a public HBCU. He is also an affiliate and mentor with the Penn Center for Minority-Serving Institutions, based at the University of Pennsylvania. Andrew's efforts have contributed (as PI or co-PI) to over $2.15 million in external funding. His research has appeared in journals such as the *Journal of Diversity in Higher Education, American Journal of Education, Journal of Student Affairs Research and Practice, Journal of College Student Retention, Learning Communities Journal, Spectrum: A Journal on Black Men, Journal of Transformative Education,*

Online Journal of Distance Learning Administration, and *Teaching Theology & Religion*, among others. He is co-author of *The African American Student's Guide to STEM Careers* (Greenwood Press, 2017) and *Black Female College Students: A Guide to Student Success in Higher Education* (Routledge, forthcoming). Prior to becoming a faculty member, Andrew spent 13 years in the non-profit and for-profit sectors, holding a variety of executive leadership roles.

Taryn Ozuna Allen is an assistant professor in the Department of Educational Leadership & Policy Studies at the University of Texas at Arlington (UT Arlington). Dr. Allen's research interests focus on the educational experiences of traditionally underrepresented student populations, particularly Latino students, as they access, transition, and enroll in higher education. She is also interested in how dual credit programs influence students' college experiences, especially in Science, Technology, Engineering, and Mathematics (STEM) fields. She has published her research in the *Journal of Higher Education, Journal of Diversity in Higher Education*, and *Journal of School Leadership*, among others. Dr. Allen is affiliated with the Center for Mexican American Studies (UT Arlington), Penn Center for Minority-Serving Institutions (University of Pennsylvania), and Project Mentoring to Achieve Latino Educational Success (MALES) (UT Austin). She earned her doctorate in higher education administration, with a concentration in Mexican American Studies, from the University of Texas at Austin (2012). She received her Master's degree in Student Affairs Administration (2005) and Bachelor's degree in General Family and Consumer Sciences (2003) from Baylor University in Waco, Texas.

Tiffany Fountaine Boykin is the Assistant Dean of Student Services at Anne Arundel Community College in Arnold, Maryland. Dr. Boykin engages in strategic planning and promotes creative ideas that enable student support services programs and the College to be more innovative, productive, and efficient. She also interprets, articulates, and monitors institutional compliance with appropriate laws, regulations, and policies. Prior to her current role, Dr. Boykin was an assistant professor of higher education and held teaching assignments at historically Black and community college campuses. Currently, she maintains adjunct teaching assignments in the Community College Leadership Doctoral Program at Morgan State University. Dr. Boykin's research examines Black graduate student experiences, the role of historically Black colleges and universities, and legal aspects of higher education. A noted author and presenter, Dr. Boykin has numerous publications and proceedings to her credit. She's has also been recognized by the American Education Research Association for her efforts in producing scholarship which advances multicultural and multiethnic education, and for her continued commitment to underserved communities. Dr. Boykin is a member of many professional and civic organizations including the National Council on Student Development, Southern Association of College Student Affairs, American College Personnel Association, American Education Research Association, Council for the Study of Community Colleges, and the National Council on Black American Affairs. She was recently named as Director of Legal Counsel for the Center for African American Research and Policy. She also serves as an editorial reviewer for the *Journal of College Student Retention* and the *Journal of Negro Education*. Dr. Boykin earned a BA in Communication from the University of Maryland, College Park, an MS in Communications Management from Towson University, a Ph.D. in Higher Education from Morgan State University, and a J.D. from the University of Baltimore School of Law.

John Michael Lee, Jr. currently serves as Vice Chancellor for University Advancement at Elizabeth City State University. John has more than a decade of leadership experience in advocacy, outreach, and engagement. John previously served as the Assistant Vice President for Alumni Affairs and Advancement at Florida Agricultural and Mechanical University. He also served as the Vice President for the Office of Access and Success at the Association for Public & Land-grant-Universities. John is an accomplished researcher and scholar. He has published several peer-reviewed journal articles, policy reports, a book, numerous articles, and paper presentations at various conferences on topics ranging from diverse student populations to student access and success. John earned a Ph.D. in Higher Education Administration from the Steinhardt School of Culture Education and Human Development at New York University, an M.P.A. with a concentration in economic development from the Andrew Young School of Policy Studies at Georgia State University, and a Bachelor of Science in Computer Engineering from the FAMU–FSU College of Engineering at Florida A&M University.

Biographies of the Contributors

Loretta (Lori) P. Adrian became the sixth president of Coastline Community College on July 1, 2010. Coastline is an Asian-serving institution that is committed to serving students from diverse backgrounds. Dr. Adrian has been an educational leader for over 25 years. She is sharply focused on student success and the practice of a "students first" philosophy. Prior to joining Coastline, she served as the vice president of student services at Skyline College in the Bay Area from 2005–2010. From November 1992 to August 2005, Dr. Adrian worked as dean of student affairs, interim dean of student development and matriculation, and acting vice president of student services at San Diego Mesa College. Dr. Adrian spent 10 years of her career working with international students from around the world, both at the University of the Pacific (a private four-year university) and at San Joaquin Delta College (a community college), in Northern California. Her experiences at both the university and two-year community colleges give her a well-rounded perspective in higher education and a deep understanding of the experiences of students. In addition to her United States higher education background, Dr. Adrian worked as an intercultural trainer/project director for the

U.S. Peace Corps for six years. Dr. Lori Adrian holds a Doctor of Philosophy (Ph.D.) in Education from Claremont Graduate University, jointly with San Diego State University; a Master's degree in Communication Theory from the University of the Pacific; and a Bachelor's degree in Philippine Studies from the University of the Philippines, with a minor in linguistics.

Cynthia M. Alcantar is a Doctoral Candidate in Social Science and Comparative Education, and Research Associate for the Institute for Immigration, Globalization, and Education and the National Commission on Asian American and Pacific Islander Research in Education (CARE) at the University of California, Los Angeles (UCLA). Additionally, she currently serves as a Visiting Professor of Sociology at Pitzer College. Her research broadly focuses on issues of college access and degree attainment for underrepresented student populations. Prior to joining UCLA, Cynthia earned her master's degree in Higher Education from Claremont Graduate University (CGU) and her bachelor's degree in Psychology with a minor in Sociology from the University of California, Riverside (UCR). She also worked as a Coordinator and Interim Director of Upward Bound at Norco Community College and as a Graduate Advisor and Faculty for the McNair Scholars Program at CGU. Her research centers on college access, persistence, and completion of underserved and underrepresented populations, especially as it relates to higher education policy and practice.

William J. Broussard is an Assistant Professor of English/Assistant to the President for Institutional Advancement at Southern University. Broussard is considered an advancement expert with considerable fundraising and executive success. At Southern, the athletic department set total revenue and private fundraising records, set consecutive graduation success rate records, and won 16 SWAC divisional, tournament, and regular season championships from 2012 to 2015. With a career fundraising attainment of nearly $20 million, he secured the first $1 million+ gift in the history of Northwestern State University in 2010, has delivered talks on fundraising and branding at the National Association for Collegiate Directors of Athletics, and has twice served on the faculty Council for the Advancement and Support of Education Athletic Fundraising Conference. His research interests include athletic administration, writing program administration, and HBCU leadership. He has presented plenary and keynote lectures at dozens of national conferences and published editorials, book reviews, and articles in newspapers, trade magazines, and academic journals including *Community Literacy Journal, Louisiana Progress, Journal of English Language and Literature, HBCU Journal of Research and Culture, Education Dive,* and *HBCU Digest.*

Isaac M.J. Castro is a graduate student in Higher Education, Administration and Leadership at California State University, Fresno (Fresno State). He serves as a Graduate Research Assistant for the Fresno State Foundation. Mr. Castro received a B.A. in Sociology from the University of California, Berkeley. He has professional experience with diversity initiatives, graduate admissions, program administration, and student affairs from his service at UC Berkeley's Richard and Rhoda Goldman School of Public Policy. A passionate social justice advocate, Mr. Castro has been actively involved since 2005 with Hermanos Unidos, a support group for Latino males in higher education.

Joseph I. Castro was appointed as the eighth president of California State University, Fresno (Fresno State) in 2013. Dr. Castro is also Professor of Educational Leadership in the Kremen School of Education and Human Development. Prior to his appointment at Fresno State, he served as Vice Chancellor, Student Academic Affairs, and Professor of Family and Community Medicine at the University of California, San Francisco (UCSF). Earlier in his career, he held faculty and/or administrative leadership positions at four other University of California campuses – Berkeley, Davis, Merced, and Santa Barbara. He received a B.A. in Political Science and M.P.P. in Public Policy from the University of California, Berkeley, and a Ph.D. in Higher Education Policy and Leadership from Stanford University. Dr. Castro is the grandson of farmworkers from Mexico. He is the first person in this family to graduate from a university.

Laura J. Cortez serves as Director of Strategic Initiatives and Program Faculty at Texas State University. She has served as a scholar-practitioner at both private and public institutions for the past 15 years. Cortez graduated from the University of Texas at Austin, earning a Ph.D. in Educational Administration and a certificate in Mexican American Studies. She holds a Master of Business Administration from St. Edward's University and a Bachelor of Science in Environmental Science and Policy from Drake University. Cortez's research agenda is greatly influenced by her personal experience of growing up along the Texas–Mexico border. Her work more specifically examines the organizational context of Hispanic-Serving Institutions and how these structures impact the persistence and completion of first-generation Latino students.

Megan Covington is a second year Master's candidate in the Higher Education Student Affairs program at Western Carolina University. She holds a Bachelor's degree in Psychology with a minor in Child Development and Family Studies from North Carolina Agricultural and Technical State University. She currently serves as a Graduate Research Assistant at Western Carolina University in the Department of Human Services. She has also held internships in the Office of the President at Harris–Stowe State University and in the Department of Intercultural Affairs at Western Carolina University. Megan is a budding scholar in the area of diversity in higher education who is honing a content expertise in the relevance of historically Black colleges and universities (HBCUs), the experiences of African American women in higher education, the persistence of ethnic/racial minority students in Science, Technology, Engineering, and Mathematics (STEM), and the experiences of graduate students of color at predominantly White institutions (PWIs).

Cheryl Crazy Bull serves as President and CEO of the American Indian College Fund, a national non-profit that supports tribal college students and tribal colleges and universities. Her 35 year career includes serving as a faculty member, dean, development officer and Vice President of Administration at Sinte Gleska University and as Chief Educational Officer of St. Francis Indian School, both on her home reservation in SD. She served 10 years as the President of Northwest Indian College headquartered at the Lummi Nation in WA. Cheryl has extensive leadership experience with the American Indian Higher Education Consortium, the membership association of the tribal colleges, and through service on various national and regional boards. She has published articles and chapters about tribally controlled education, tribal colleges, and community development as well as leadership. Cheryl is a citizen of the Sicangu Lakota Oyate and is from the Rosebud Reservation.

Magdalena H. de la Teja earned a Ph.D. (1980) and J.D. (1986) from UT Austin and began in February 2009 as Vice President for Student Development Services at Tarrant County College (TCC), Northeast Campus. Former Positions: started in 1989 as a Director and was promoted to a Dean of Student Services at Austin Community College and served until February 2009; practiced law as an Attorney with the Texas Legislative Council from 1986 to 1989; and previously served as an administrator at UT Austin for a total of eight years. Dr. de la Teja is a published author and has presented at state and national conferences. Selected current and past service: NASPA Community Colleges Division Board member and Latina/o Task Force Chair; NASPA Foundation Board; NASPA Escaleras Faculty; NASPA Board of Directors; Texas Association of Chicanos in Higher Education (TACHE) President; TCC TACHE founding President. Selected recognition: 2017 NASPA Latino/a Knowledge Community Outstanding Senior Student Affairs Officer Award; 2016 Phi Theta Kappa (PTK) International Distinguished College Administrator Award; 2015 PTK Transfer Initiatives Award; 2014 NASPA Pillar of the Profession; 2014 NASPA National Community College Professional Award; 2014 TACHE Lifetime Achievement Award.

Levon Esters is an Associate Professor in the Department of Youth Development and Agricultural Education at Purdue University and Director of the Mentoring@Purdue (M@P) Program. The aim of the M@P Program is to enhance graduate education, especially among women and underrepresented minorities, by improving the quality of mentoring relationships. Dr. Esters also serves as a Senior Research Associate at the Center for Minority-Serving Institutions. His research interests focus on issues related to the educational access and equity of racial and ethnic minorities with a majority of his work comprising three areas: (1) STEM career development of underrepresented minorities, (2) mentoring of females and underrepresented minorities in Science, Technology, Engineering, Agriculture & Math (STEAM) disciplines, and (3) the role of Historically Black Land–Grant Colleges and Universities in fostering the STEM success of women and underrepresented minorities.

Marybeth Gasman is a Professor of Higher Education in the Graduate School of Education at the University of Pennsylvania. She holds secondary appointments in History, Africana Studies, and the School of Social Policy and Practice. She also directs the Penn Center for Minority-Serving Institutions. Dr. Gasman's areas of expertise include the history of American higher education, historically Black colleges and universities (HBCUs), minority-serving institutions, African American leadership, and fundraising and philanthropy. Her research also explores the role education has in the development, growth, and journey of students seeking a college degree. She has written or edited 21 books. Eight of Dr. Gasman's books have won research awards. Dr. Gasman's articles have been published in the *American Education Research Journal*, *Educational Researcher*, *Teachers College Record*, the *Journal of Higher Education*, the *Journal of Negro Education*, *Research in Higher Education*, the *Journal of College Student Development*, among others. Dr. Gasman is the principal or co-principal investigator on seven major grants from funders such as The Helmsley Trust, The Kellogg Foundation, The Kresge Foundation, The Mellon Foundation, Educational Testing Service, and the National Institutes for Health. Her research has been featured in the *New York Times*, the *Washington Post*, the *Wall Street Journal*, *Time*, *Newsweek*, USNEWS, CNN, and on National Public Radio. In 2015, Dr. Gasman received Penn's Provost Award for Distinguished Ph.D. Teaching and Mentoring and the Association for the Study of Higher Education's Leadership Award. Dr. Gasman serves on the boards of trustees of Paul Quinn College (Texas) and The College Board (New York).

Adriel Hilton is director of the Webster University Myrtle Beach Metropolitan Extended Campus. As the chief administrative officer, he is charged with implementing programs and policies to achieve Webster University's overall goals and objectives at the extended campus. Dr. Hilton's most recent positions include chief of staff and executive assistant to the president at Grambling State University and assistant professor and director of the Higher Education Student Affairs program at Western Carolina University. Dr. Hilton was the inaugural assistant vice president for inclusion initiatives at Grand Valley State University. He honed his expertise in higher education administration and teaching at Upper Iowa University (UIU) as executive assistant to the president and assistant secretary to the board of trustees. He was the school's first chief diversity officer and an adjunct faculty member at both UIU and the University of Northern Iowa. Dr. Hilton is a noted scholar. Previously, he had served as the first public policy fellow at the Greater Baltimore

Committee, a leading regional organization comprised of civic and business leaders, where he worked closely with advisors to research, develop, and advocate a public policy agenda to advance the organization's work in various areas, including access to health care. Dr. Hilton is a prolific author and researcher. His research is published in refereed journals, such as *Teachers College Record, Journal of College Student Development*, and the *Journal of the Professoriate*.

Kathi Hiyane-Brown is the President of Whatcom Community College, Bellingham, WA. A nationally recognized advocate of community college education and diversity and leadership, she conducts training and workshops on leadership and diversity in venues locally, nationally, and internationally. She is committed to supporting leadership development initiatives with underrepresented groups and is a mentor to many aspiring leaders. She is a member and immediate past chair of the American Association of Community Colleges (AACC) Presidents Academy Executive Committee (PAEC); and on the board of the National Asian Pacific Islander Council (NAPIC), an affiliate council of AACC. Additionally, she is a past director on the AACC Board of Directors, and past chair of the Commission on Diversity, Inclusion and Equity for the organization. As a member of the Washington Association of Community and Technical Colleges (WACTC), Kathi serves as chair on the WACTC Strategic Visioning Committee, serves as member on the WACTC Executive Committee and has served as chair of the Educational Services Committee and Critical Issues Committee and on the Legislative Committee. Her local leadership experience includes serving on the Boards of the Northwest Economic Council (NWEC) and past board member of Whatcom Alliance for Healthcare Advancement (WAHA). In addition to statewide committees focused on the work of the two-year college system, she is a member of the Governor's Taskforce on Adult Education Advisory Council and serves on the board of The Association (the Washington Community and Technical College Administrative Training Association). Dr. Hiyane-Brown's national involvement with professional development includes her experiences as a member of the National Council for Staff, Program, and Organizational Development (NCSPOD), having served in numerous leadership positions, including President for that organization. Dr. Hiyane-Brown holds a Bachelor of Arts in Anthropology, Grinnell College; a Master of Arts in Instructional Design and Technology, University of Iowa; and a Doctor of Education in Community College Leadership, Oregon State University.

Amanda Washington Lockett is a Ph.D. student at the University of Pennsylvania's Graduate School of Education and a research associate for the Center for Minority-Serving Institutions. She completed an M.A. in Education Policy at Teachers College Columbia University, an M.A. in TESOL at American University, and received a B.A. in English from Spelman College. Previously, Amanda served as a Teach for America corps member and worked for the Center for International Education Exchange in Adra, Spain. She has completed graduate internships with the White House Initiative on Educational Excellence for African Americans and the White House Initiative for Historically Black Colleges and Universities. Her research interests focus on education leadership and the correlation between students' P-12 academic preparedness and their postsecondary outcomes.

Kofi Lomotey is the Bardo Distinguished Professor of Educational Leadership at Western Carolina University. He received his Ph.D. from Stanford University and has previously taught at SUNY–Buffalo and LSU. He has served as Chancellor at Southern University–Baton Rouge, President at Fort Valley State University, Provost at Medgar Evers College–CUNY, and Provost at Fisk University. His research and publications focus on urban education, Black students in higher education, African-centered schools and Black principals. His research has been published in such journals as *Educational Administration Quarterly*, *Urban Education*, *The Journal of Negro Education*, *Education & Urban Society*, and *Educational Policy*. He has authored, edited, or co-edited more than a dozen books on race in higher education, urban education, and the education of Black people.

Naomi Okumura Story has devoted over 35 years of her professional career to being an educator, instructional innovator, and academic leader. Prior to her retirement from the Maricopa Community College system, Naomi was the Faculty Director of the Mesa Community College Center for Teaching and Learning, where she supported and led college efforts to infuse strategic planning, learning initiatives, innovative pedagogies, curricula and evaluation transformation, and community-based partnerships. As a district administrator, Dr. Story led and supported Maricopa's major directions in teaching, learning, assessment, and curricula reform.

Naomi has published and presented on topics related to leadership and professional development, pedagogical and curricular transformation and reform, and the advocacy for AAPI leadership development in higher education. Naomi was a founding board member and President of NAPIC, the National Asian Pacific Islander Council, an affiliated council of the American Association for Community Colleges. She is currently NAPIC's Executive Director. She has her Ph.D. in Educational Technology/Instructional Design and an M.A. in Instructional Media from Arizona State University. Her B.A. is in Creative Writing/English from Coe College.

Ginger C. Stull is a Ph.D. student at the University of Pennsylvania, and Program Coordinator for the Executive Doctorate in Higher Education Management program at Penn, an accelerated doctoral program for senior level higher education leaders. Her research interests include Tribal Colleges and Universities (TCUs), Hispanic-Serving Institutions (HSIs), performance funding, public policy, and funding inequities in higher education. As a former Pell student and HSI graduate, Ginger has a deep commitment to the ideal that higher education is a basic human right. She believes all people are entitled to education that reflects their culture, values, and goals, and promotes their political, economic, and existential freedoms. As a researcher she hopes to bring attention to funding inequities in higher education, and help reverse current public policies that disproportionately benefit wealthy campuses and students.

Robert T. Teranishi is Professor of Social Science and Comparative Education, the Morgan and Helen Chu Endowed Chair in Asian American Studies, and co-director for the Institute for Immigration, Globalization, and Education at the University of California, Los Angeles. He is also a senior fellow with the Steinhardt Institute for Higher Education Policy at New York University and principal investigator for the National Commission on Asian American and Pacific Islander Research in Education. In 2011, he was appointed by Secretary of Education, Arne Duncan to the U.S. Department of Education's Equity and Excellence Commission. In 2015, he was appointed by President Barack Obama to serve as a board member for the Institute for Education Sciences. He has also served as a strategic planning and restructuring consultant for the Ford Foundation. Teranishi was formerly a National Institute for Mental Health postdoctoral fellow at the University of Pennsylvania's W.E.B. Du Bois Research Institute. He received his B.A. from the University of California Santa Cruz in Sociology and his M.A. and Ph.D. from the University of California Los Angeles in Higher Education and Organizational Change.

Ivory A. Toldson is the president and CEO of the QEM Network, professor at Howard University and editor-in-chief of *The Journal of Negro Education*. Previously, Dr. Toldson was appointed by President Barack Obama to be the executive director of the White House Initiative on Historically Black Colleges and Universities. He also served as senior research analyst for the Congressional Black Caucus Foundation and contributing education editor for *The Root*, where he debunked some of the most pervasive myths about African Americans in his *Show Me the Numbers* column.

Robert A. Underwood is a former Member of the U.S. Congress and is currently the President of the University of Guam. As an educator, he has served as a high school teacher, curriculum writer, administrator, Dean of the College of Education and Academic Vice President. He is a distinguished scholar with many publications to his credit on educational issues, regional political matters, and language change. He served as the Congressional Delegate from Guam in the 103–107th Congresses (1993–2003) during which he sponsored major legislation for Guam, played an active role in Department of Defense authorization bills and was a forceful advocate for political development for insular areas and the extension of educational and social opportunities for Asian Americans and Pacific Islanders. In 2003, he helped create the Asian Pacific Islander American Scholarship Fund and served as the first Chairman of the Board. He has worked on several research projects with the East West Center, the University of Hawaii, and the Asian Pacific Center for Security Studies. Robert received Bachelor's (1969) and Master's degrees in History from Cal State University, Los Angeles. He holds a Doctor of Education degree from the University of Southern California.

Edward M. Willis has 35 years of diverse student affairs experience in a variety of higher education settings. His university experiences include tenures at Norfolk State University, Florida A&M University, University of Michigan–Ann Arbor, University of Missouri–Columbia, Rutgers University, and The University of Toledo. His student affairs administrative portfolio has included the following areas of responsibility: enrollment management, student housing, multicultural student affairs, Greek life, student conduct, orientation, accessibility services, women's center, veteran affairs, student unions, student activities, leadership programs, career services, and student development/tutorial services.

INDEX

Italic page numbers indicate tables.

AACC Competencies for Community College Leaders, Second Edition (AACC) 176

AANAPISs. *see* Asian American and Native American Pacific Islander-Serving Institutions (AANAPISIs)

Aboh, S. 25, 39

abroad, studying (Fresno State University) 116–17

accountability at Paul Quinn College 82

accreditation for Tribal Colleges and Universities (TCUs) 156–7

activism: HBCUs 38; at Paul Quinn College 85

Adrian, L. 173, 176

advising structure at Fresno State University 115

advocates: beyond the institution 194–5; leaders as 157–8

Alabama State University (ASU) 4

Alexander, L. 35

alumni, academic, focus on at HCBUs 38

American Association for Community Colleges (AACC) 175, 176

American Council on Education 175–6

American Indian Higher Education Consortium (AIHEC) 141, 142, 146, 152, 157, 160

Anderson, Jim 24

Applied Critical Leadership (ACL) 102

Arnett, A. 69

Arroyo, A.T. 49

Asian American and Native American Pacific Islander-Serving Institutions (AANAPISIs): AAPI students and their needs 187–8, 190–1; AAPIs as leaders 192–4; advocacy beyond the institution 194–5; Asian American and Native American Pacific Islander Serving Institutions Program 171–2, 186, 188–9; Asian American and Pacific Islander Serving Institutions Act 11; challenges and issues for leaders 175, 178; classification as 11; cultural sensitivity 173–4; degrees conferred 189; differences among communities 169, 174, 187–8; dual mission and worlds 173; educational attainment for AAPIs 170, 171; enrollment for AAPIs 170, 187; ethnic/racial diversity 10–11; funding 171–2, 172, 186, 188–90; future research 184; importance of 11–12; innovation 182; institutional priorities 191–2; leadership at 172–7; location of 189; minority groups, concerns of other 182; misperceptions about AAPIs 169–70, 188; Model Minority Myth 10–11; MSIs comparison 173–4; non-AAPI leaders 174; Partnership in Equity in Education through Research (PEER) 191; partnerships 182, 183, 192; personal background of leaders 181; preparedness of AAPI students 170–1; presidents, AAPIs as 171; professional development 182–4; recruitment and selection of senior-level staff 174–7, 183; research on leadership as limited 12; skills, qualities and competencies of leaders 174–84, 191–2; student composition 189; survey of leaders of 177–84; transformative leadership, need for 172; values, leadership 182; workforce participation for AAPIs 170. *see also* Fresno State University

Asian American and Native American Pacific Islander Serving Institutions Program 171–2, 186, 188–9

Asian American and Pacific Islander Serving Institutions Act 11

Asian Pacific Islander Association of Colleges and Universities (APIACU) 194

automation, and work 209–10

Badwound, E. 153

Bensimon, E.M. 106, 108

Bethune, Mary McCloud 22–3

Black Studies, aims of 22–3

Blyden, Edward Wilmot 40

boards: appointments to 34; micromanagement by 32; training for 34; turnover of Presidents of MSIs 34–5. *see also* leadership; Presidents of MSIs

bold leadership (Fresno State University) 120–1, 122–3

Bordas, J. 104

Border HSIs 129

Boyd, Gwendolyn 4

branding: attraction of talent 77; Paul Quinn College 82–4

Brawer, F.B. 100

Brooks, David 123

Bukoski, B.E. 101

Calderon Galdeano, E. 96–7, 101–2

California State University, Fresno. *see* Fresno State University

Carruthers, Jacob 40

Castro, Joseph 113, 114, 118

Cave, M. 74

Ceja, M. 100

Chavez, A.F. 105

Chenault, Vernida 150

Cheyney University 3

chief student affairs officers (CSAOs): academic affairs, contrast with 55; competencies needed 48; complexity of work 49; crisis aspect of 56–7; day-to-day work 48–9; diversity, leadership in 49; emergent needs, responsiveness to 56–7; expertise, use of other people's 53–4; future studies 61; leadership 47–9; limitations: time and capacity 53; master's/doctoral education 49; model of highly effective 53, **54,** 55–61, **58**; Norfolk State University **58**, 58–9; on-call status 56; as pathway to presidency 46–7, 50, 59–61; proactivity 56; responsiveness of 56–9; strategic needs, responsiveness to 57–9; team-building 53–4, 60; traits and roles 56–7, 59; unpredictable ethos of arena for 55–6. *see also* Presidents of MSIs

civic engagement. *see* community engagement

clarity of role 36

Clay, P.L. 68

Closson, R.B. 27

Cohen, A.M. 100–1

Cohen, R.T. 29

collective leadership by Native Americans 146

Colon, A. 25

Commodore, F. 51

communication 61, 179, 182

community, caring for by Native American leaders 145

community based participatory research (CBPT) 30

community colleges: author's connection to 94–5, 103; diversity of students 95; history 93–5; junior colleges 94; number of 95; skills, qualities and competencies of leaders 174–84. *see also* Asian American and Native American Pacific Islander-Serving Institutions (AANAPISIs); Hispanic-Serving Institutions (HSIs); Tribal Colleges and Universities (TCUs)

Community Conversations, Fresno State University 120

community engagement: Fresno State University 114, 115, 122; Historically Black Colleges and Universities (HBCUs) 29–30; Paul Quinn College 82, 84–6; service-learning programs 115 competencies of leaders: Asian American and Native American Pacific Islander-Serving Institutions (AANAPISIs) 174–84, 191–2; chief student affairs officers (CSAOs) 48; framework of leadership for TCUs 152–60; qualifications/experience 162–3

Conrad, C.F. 26

contracts, multi-year, performance indicators 73–4

Contreras, F.E. 107

Conversation on Inclusion, Respect and Equity initiative, Fresno State University 119–20

Cooper, G. 34

Cortez, L.J. 193

counterstories 104

crisis aspect of student affairs administrators 56–7

Critical Race Theory 103–4, 104

Cross-Cultural Center at Fresno State University 115–16

cultural sensitivity of leaders 173–4, 193

culturally responsive education: aims of 21–3; defined 21–3; Historically Black Colleges and Universities (HBCUs) 29; leadership in 102–7

culture, courses on 6–7

curricula: assessment of at HBCUs 37–8; cultural empowerment through 29; ethnic courses 6–7; as flawed at HBCUs 30–1, 33

customer service at HBCUs 33, 38–9

Davila, B. 106

decision-making: for benefit of campus and students 38–9; collective, by Native Americans 146; involvement of others in 35–6

DeGregory, C. 72

delegation 53–4

Developing Hispanic-Serving Institutions Program 129–30. see also funding; Title V funds

Dine College 7

disaggregation of data at HSIs 107, 108, 129

DISCOVERe 116, 121

disruption, embracing 74–6

diversity: AAPIs as leaders 192–4; advocacy beyond the institution 194–5; cultural sensitivity 173–4, 181; leadership in 49; professional development 182–4. see also ethnic diversity

dual mission and worlds: Asian American and Native American Pacific Islander-Serving Institutions (AANAPISIs) 173; Tribal Colleges and Universities (TCUs) 142–3

DuBois, W.E.B. 30–41

Edmonds, Randolph 24

Ehrenberg, R. 74

emergent needs, responsiveness to 56–7

emigration 209

employee engagement 178

empowerment: cultural 29; of others at Paul Quinn College 87

enrollment: Asian American and Native American Pacific Islander-Serving Institutions (AANAPISIs) 170, 187; shifts in as impetus for HSIs 96

entrepreneurship for opportunity creation 83, 85, 86–7

equity: advocacy beyond the institution 194–5; mindedness 190; Partnership in Equity in Education through Research (PEER) 191; professional development in 182–4; TCU presidents, focus on by 163–4

Espino, M.M. 104

Esters, L.T. 5

ethnic courses 6–7

ethnic diversity: AAPIs as leaders 192–4; Asian American and Native American Pacific Islander-Serving Institutions (AANAPISIs) 10–11; community colleges 95; faculty 28; Fresno State University 113; Hispanic-Serving Institutions (HSIs) 97–9, 98; Historically Black Colleges and Universities (HBCUs) 3, 27, 28; Predominantly Black Institutions (PBIs) 9

example, leading and learning by 146

exit interviews 78

expertise, use of other people's 53–4

faculty: collegial environment for 28; ethnic/racial diversity 28; Hispanic 106; satisfaction with HSIs 131; support from at HBCUs 27; teaching styles 29

Fanon, Franz 40

Felix, E.R. 108

Figueroa, J.L. 101

financial management: expertise, using other people's 54; faculty/administrative salaries, gap between 36; fundraising 36;

at HBCUs 32, 36; improvement opportunities 36; unpredictability 55–6. *see also* funding

Fleming, J. 26

Florida A&M University 4

for-profit colleges 75

Forkenbrock, J. 153

forums, campus (Fresno State University) 119

Freeman, Jr., S. 4, 5, 49–51, 52–3, 69

Freeman, K. 29

Freire, P. 103

Fresno State University: abroad, studying 116–17; advising structure 115; 'Be Bold' message 120–1; bold leadership 120–1, 122–3; Cabinet changes 120; Community Conversations 120; community engagement 114, 122; Conversation on Inclusion, Respect and Equity initiative 119–20; Cross-Cultural Center 115–16; DISCOVERe 116, 121; DISCOVERe Program 121; ethnic diversity 113; feedback page 118–19; forums, campus 119; graduation rate 117; high-impact programs 114–17; history 112–13; inclusiveness, programs for 118–21; information gathering by new President 114; infrastructure, updating 122; international study 116–17; leadership style 118; location, students from 113; national recognition 117–18; President Joseph Castro 113, 114, 118; problems inherited by new President 113–14; recruitment and support of faculty and staff 121–2; results from high-impact practices 117–18; service-learning program 115; social media 119; Strategic Plan 2016-20 114, 121–2; student borrowing 117; teaching and learning programs 116, 121; technology-based teaching and learning 116, 121

From Capacity to Success: HSIs, Title V, and Latino Students (Santiago, Taylor and Calderon Galdeano) 96–7

funding: Asian American and Native American Pacific Islander Serving Institutions Program 171–2, 186, 188–90; entrepreneurship for opportunity creation 86–7; grant funding 144; Hispanic-Serving Institutions (HSIs) 6, 129–30; Historically Black Colleges and Universities (HBCUs) 31; Minority-Serving Institutions (MSIs) 1–2; Predominantly Black Institutions (PBIs) 9–10; President's role regarding 68–9; Tribal Colleges and Universities (TCUs) 8, 143–4; TWIs comparison with 206; unpredictability 55–6

fundraising 36

Gallup-USA Funds Minority College Graduate Report (2015) 26

Garcia, G.A. 99, 107

Gasman, M. 2, 4, 27, 49–51, 68, 69, 96, 102

Gee, Henry 172–3, 174, 179

gender of Presidents of MSIs 4, 5

globalism 209

graduation rates: analysis of resources 37; low, at HBCUs 32–3

Grambling State University 4, 26

grant funding 144; Asian American and Native American Pacific Islander Serving Institutions Program 11, 12, 171–2, 182, 186, 188–9, 191; Hispanic-Serving Institutions (HSIs) 6, 7, 107, 112, 115, 130; Historically Black Colleges and Universities (HBCUs) 3; Predominantly Black Institutions (PBIs) 9; Tribal Colleges and Universities (TCUs) 7, 8, 142, 143–4

Gray, J. 108

grooming of future leaders 51

Hagedorn, L.S. 101, 106

Hall, B. 27

Hampton-Tuskegee model 24

Hanson, D. 108

Harper, S.R. 49

Hart, A.W. 72

Hart, J. 153

Hawaiians, Native, educational attainment of 171. *see also* Asian American and Native American Pacific Islander-Serving Institutions (AANAPISIs)

HBCUs. *see* Historically Black Colleges and Universities (HBCUs)

Hernández, E.A. 96, 100–1

Herring, P.M. 52

Hetherington, K. 54

high-impact programs at Fresno State University 114–17

Higher Education Act (HEA): amendment re. AAPI students 11; Title V 6. *see also* funding hiring process. *see* recruitment and selection of senior-level staff

Hirt, J.B. 48

Hispanic Association of Colleges and Universities (HACU) 194

Hispanic-Serving Institutions (HSIs): access/success of Latino students 99, 100–2; Applied Critical Leadership (ACL) 102; attraction for students 100–1; author's connection to 94–5, 103; Border HSIs 129; change as continuous 125–6; complexity around identity of 130–1; Critical Race Theory 103–4, 104; culturally responsive leadership 102–7; defining, challenges in 128–9; definition in federal law 125; designation as 96; Developing Hispanic-Serving Institutions Program 129–30; disaggregation of data 107, 108, 129; education about HSI designation 131–2; enrollment shifts as impetus for 96; ethnic courses 6–7; ethnic diversity 97–9, 98; evolution of 126–8; faculty, Hispanic 106; faculty satisfaction 131; funding 6, 129–30; future possibilities 130–1; future research 132–3; growth of 128–9; Higher Education Act (HEA) 6; historical designation 132; importance of 6; LatCrit Theory 104; Latino population, growth in 131; Latino Students 98, 99; Latino students' success at 128; leadership 34–6, 131–3; legislation regarding 125; location of 97, 128, 129; male students, Latino 101; mission statements/websites 87–8; MSIs comparison 127; numbers of 6, 96–7, 97, 128–9; origin of 5–6; Peace Corps volunteers 30; policies and practices supporting Latino students 106–7; policy, national-level 132; post-traditional students 127–8; recruitment of faculty 131; research, focus of recent 126; research on leadership as limited 7; student characteristics 100–2, 127–8; student needs, understanding of 7; student numbers 6; Title V funds 96, 98, 101, 107, 129–30, 132; two/four-year institutions 97. *see also* Fresno State University

Historically Black Colleges and Universities (HBCUs): activism on campus 38; alumni focus on academics 38; appointments to boards 34; assessment of curricula 37–8; autocratic leadership 32; challenges for 30–3, 34; collegial environment for faculty 28; community and civic engagement 29–30; credentials and experience of senior-level staff 72; culturally responsive education 21–3, 29; curricula as flawed 30–1, 33; customer service 38–9; customer service, poorness of 33; disruption, embracing 74–6; ethnic/racial diversity of 3, 28; exit interviews 78; faculty, support from 27; faculty/administrative salaries, gap between 36; financial management 32, 36; firing of incompetent staff 37; founding of 2–3; funding 31; fundraising 36; high turnover of Presidents 3–4; high turnover of senior-level staff, impact of 65, 66–7; importance of 3; inequality in early institutions 23; key performance indicators (KPIs) 73–4; leadership 34–6, 72–3; leadership experiences for student s 38; marketing 76–7; micromanagement by boards 32; Morrill Act 1890 3; motives of White philanthropists 23–5; multi-year contracts 73–4; negative experiences of senior-level staff 67; nepotism 32, 37; new leaders, challenges faced by 68–9; numbers of 3; opportunities and strategies for 34–9; peers, support from 27–8; positive environment for Black students 26–7; power of students and faculty 34; power relations 33–4; Presidents 49–53; protection from impacts of high turnover 70; recruitment and selection of staff 32, 37, 66–7; research focus 65–6; research on leadership, paucity of 2; responsiveness to all views 39; retention rates 32–3, 37; revolution in higher education for Blacks 39–41; sourcing of staff 77–8; strengths 25; student numbers 3; student outcomes 26; succession planning and sourcing 77–8; support systems 26; teaching styles 29; tenure negotiations 71; training for boards 34; turnover of Presidents 34–5; as uncompetitive 31; as unhealthy 30; White students at 27; women presidents 4, 5. *see also* Paul Quinn College; student affairs administrators

HSIs. *see* Hispanic-Serving Institutions (HSIs)

Hubbard, S.M. 126
hunter/gather/growers, leaders as 154–5
Hurtado, S. 96

immigration 209
inclusion: professional development in
    182–4. *see also* equity
Indigenous self-governance and
    identity 151
Indigenous students. *see* Native Americans;
    Tribal Colleges and Universities (TCUs)
Indigenous Ways of Knowing 140
infrastructure at Fresno State
    University 122
innovation 74–6, 182
international study at Fresno State
    University 116–17
intersectionality 104

Jackson State University (JSU) 4

Kahneman, D. 173
Kellogg MSI Leadership Initiative 155
key performance indicators (KPIs) 73–4
Kim, M.M. 26
Kimbrough, W.M. 49, 53
Klingsmith, L. 108
knowledge, indigenous 140
Krumm, B.L. 153

Laden, B.V. 101
Larkin, Willie 4
LatCrit Theory 104
Latino faculty 106
Latino leadership 102–4
Latino students: Fresno State University
    113; at HSIs 98, 99, 100–2; male 101;
    policies and practices supporting 106–7;
    success at HSIs 99, 100–2, 128
leadership: at AANAPISIs 172–7; AAPIs as
    leaders 192–4; advocacy beyond the
    institution 194–5; Applied Critical
    Leadership (ACL) 102; Asian American
    and Native American Pacific Islander-
    Serving Institutions (AANAPISIs)
    190–5; autocratic, at HBCUs 32; bold
    120–1, 122–3; clarity of role 36;
    collective leadership by Native
    Americans 146; communication 179;
    culturally responsive education 102–7;
    decision-making, involvement of others
    in 35–6; employee engagement 178;
    entrepreneurial 85, 86–7; Fresno State

University 118; growth in capacity for
    178; at HBCUs 34–6; Hispanic-Serving
    Institutions (HSIs) 131–3; hunter/
    gather/growers, leaders as 154–5;
    importance of 72–3; innovation 182;
    knowledge of the institution 36;
    modelling behavior 35; Native American
    practices 140; negotiation skills 161;
    networking 179; new models of, need
    for 201–3; non-traditional pathways to
    205–6; orators/advocates, leaders as
    157–8; partnerships 182; paucity of
    research on 2; personal background of
    leaders 181; philosophy 178; political
    and public scrutiny 160–1; professional
    development 179, 182–4; qualifications/
    experience of leaders 162–3;
    responsibilities and expectations of
    150–1; servant 81–2; storytellers, leaders
    as 159–60; student affairs administrators
    47–9; styles 51–2, 60, 81–2, 118; survey
    of leaders of AANAPISIs 177–84;
    TCUs, challenges for 142–6; team
    building 181; translators/interpreters,
    leaders as 155–7; values 178, 182;
    warriors, leaders as 158–9
Leadership Development Program for
    Higher Education Summer Institute 173
Lewis, E.F. 69
Lincoln University 3
Littlebear, R. 155
Lomotey, Kofi 22, 25, 39
Long, D. 47–8
Lu, C. 101

Malcolm, L.E. 106
Mangum, Elmira 4
Maramba, D.C. 2
marketing 76–7
Martinez, A.Y. 103–4
mentorship: of future leaders 51; high
    turnover of senior-level staff, impact of
    69; as part of leadership 73
messaging 61
Meyers, Carolyn 4
*MIA: Missing in Administration - Asian Pacific
    Islanders and the Bamboo Curtain* (Gee and
    Yamagata-Noji) 173
micromanagement by boards 32
Minority-Serving Institutions (MSIs):
    challenges facing presidents 12–13;
    common threads shared 1–2; lessons for
    PWIs from 206–7; as the norm 209;

number of currently 1; research on leadership, paucity of 2; resources/achievements 1–2; student numbers 1. *see also* Asian American and Native American Pacific Islander-Serving Institutions (AANAPISIs); Hispanic-Serving Institutions (HSIs); Historically Black Colleges and Universities (HBCUs); Predominantly Black Institutions (PBIs); Presidents of MSIs; Tribal Colleges and Universities (TCUs)

mission: Asian American and Native American Pacific Islander-Serving Institutions (AANAPISIs) 173; complexity of 203–5; Hispanic-Serving Institutions (HSIs) 87–8; Tribal Colleges and Universities (TCUs) 142–3

Model Minority Myth 10–11

Moore, T. 76

Morrill Act 1890 3

motives of White philanthropists 23–5

MSIs. *see* Minority-Serving Institutions (MSIs)

multi-year contracts 73–4

Nakanishi, D. 172

Native Americans: American Indian Higher Education Consortium (AIHEC) 141, 142, 146; assimilation, forced 139, 151; collective leadership 146; community, caring for the 145; contribution to US culture and leadership 139–40; example, leading and learning by 146; failure of leadership in colonial and federal education 140–1, 151; Indigenous Ways of Knowing 140; knowledgeable, leaders as 145–6; language 158; leadership practices 140, 144–7; learning, approaches to 151; self-governance and identity 151. *see also* Tribal Colleges and Universities (TCUs)

Native Hawaiians, educational attainment of 171. *see also* Asian American and Native American Pacific Islander-Serving Institutions (AANAPISIs)

Navajo Community College 7. *see also* Tribal Colleges and Universities (TCUs)

negotiation skills 161

Nehls, K. 49

nepotism at HBCUs 32, 37

networking 77–8, 155, 179, 182

Nobles, W.W. 33

non-traditional pathways to leadership 205–6. *see also* student affairs administrators

Norfolk State University **58,** 58–9

Nunez, A.-M. 96, 97–8, 100–1

Okhidoi, O. 99

Olivas, M.A. 95

orators/advocates, leaders as 157–8

Pacific Islanders: educational attainment of 171. *see also* Asian American and Native American Pacific Islander-Serving Institutions (AANAPISIs)

Pak, Y. 11

Palmer, R.T. 2, 27, 49

Partnership in Equity in Education through Research (PEER) 191, 194

partnerships and networks: Asian American and Native American Pacific Islander-Serving Institutions (AANAPISIs) 182, 183, 192; Tribal Colleges and Universities (TCUs) 155

Paul Quinn College: academic excellence 83–4; accountability 82; activism 85; attraction of students 88; branding 82–4; community engagement 82, 84–6; Dallas Symphony concerts 86–7; empowerment of others 87; entrepreneurship for opportunity creation 83, 85, 86–7; servant leadership 81–2; student leadership 88; WE Over Me Farm 83, 85, 86–7; WE Over Me motto 81, 83

PBIs. *see* Predominantly Black Institutions (PBIs)

Pease, Janine 158, 160

Pedagogy of the Oppressed (Freire) 103

peers, support from at HBCUs 27–8

Perez, P.A. 100

performance indicators 73–4

Perrakis, A. 101, 106

personal background of leaders 181

philanthropists, motives of White 23–5

philosophy, leadership 178

political scrutiny 160–1

Ponjean, L. 101

positive environment for Black students at HBCUs 26–7

power: relations at HBCUs 33–4; of students and faculty 34

Predominantly Black Institutions (PBIs): challenges faced by leaders 10; creation

of 9; ethnic/racial diversity 9; funding
9–10; student numbers 9
Predominantly White Institutions (PWIs:
funding comparison with MSIs 206–7;
lessons for from MSIs 206–7
Presidents of MSIs: administrators, impact
on after CEO departure 66; alternative
pathways to 50–1; commitment to
future generations 51; communication
by 61; CSAO role as pathway to 46–7,
59–61; differentiated from PWI
presidencies 52; funding, role regarding
68–9; gender of 4, 5; HBCU 49–53;
leadership styles 51–2, 60; mentoring of
future leaders 51; new policies,
introduction of 69; pace of work 60; as
past faculty members 50; protection
from impacts of high turnover 70;
requirements of 52–3; sector-crossing
50; skills needed for leadership 4–5; time
management 52; turnover of 3–4, 12,
34–5; understanding of 49–50; work-life
balance 51. *see also* leadership
professional development 179, 182–4
public scrutiny 160–1

qualities of leaders: Asian American and
Native American Pacific Islander-
Serving Institutions (AANAPISIs)
174–84, 191–2; framework of leadership
for TCUs 152–60; qualifications/
experience 162–3

racial alignment, MSI classification/senior
leadership 199–201
racial diversity: AAPIs as leaders 192–4;
Asian American and Native American
Pacific Islander Serving-Institutions
(AANAPISIs) 10–11; community
colleges 95; faculty 28; Fresno State
University 113; Hispanic-Serving
Institutions (HSIs) 97–9, *98*; Historically
Black Colleges and Universities
(HBCUs) 3, 27, 28; Predominantly
Black Institutions (PBIs) 9
racial self-determination 199–201
recruitment and selection of senior-level
staff: ability to do the job 37; Asian
American and Native American Pacific
Islander-Serving Institutions
(AANAPISIs) 174–7, 183; background
checks 37; as challenge 66–7; credentials
and experience 72; disruption,

embracing 74–6; exit interviews 78;
Fresno State University 121–2; at
HBCUs 32, 37; Hispanic-Serving
Institutions (HSIs) 131; key performance
indicators (KPIs) 73–4; leadership team
35; marketing 76–7; multi-year contracts
73–4; negative experiences of
senior-level staff 67; new leaders,
challenges faced by 68–9; protection
from impacts of high turnover 70; skills,
qualities and competencies of leaders
174–84; sourcing of staff 77–8;
succession planning and sourcing 77–8;
tenure negotiations 71
Red Bird, Snr., Stanley 154
Reilly, M. 74
research on leadership: as limited 2, 7;
paucity of current 2, 7, 12
responsiveness to all views at HBCUs 39
retention rates: analysis of resources 37;
low, at HBCUs 32–3
revolution in higher education for Blacks
39–41
Robinson, P. 69
Rodriguez, S. 101

Saenz, V.B. 101
salaries, faculty/administrative, gap
between 36
Sampson, Tom 158–9
Sanlo, R. 105
Santamaria, A.P. 102, 105
Santamaria, L.J. 102, 105
Santiago, D. 96–7, 101–2, 192
scrutiny, political and public 160–1
sector-crossing by Presidents of MSIs 50
self-determination, racial 199–201
senior staff. *see* leadership; Presidents of MSIs;
recruitment and selection of senior-level
staff; turnover of senior-level staff
servant leadership 81–2
shadowing 51
skills needed for leadership 4–5; Asian
American and Native American Pacific
Islander-Serving Institutions
(AANAPISIs) 174–84, 191–2;
framework of leadership for TCUs
152–60; qualifications/experience 162–3
social activism on HBCU campuses 38
social justice: advocacy beyond the
institution 194–5; professional
development in 182–4; TCU presidents,
focus on by 163–4. *see also* equity

social media (Fresno State University) 119
Society for College and University
    Planning (SCUP) 77
Society for Human Resource Management
    (SHRM) 77
socio-economic conditions 161–2
Solley, Anna 174–5
Sorrell, Michael: community engagement
    84–6; empowerment of others 87;
    entrepreneurial leadership 85, 86–7;
    recruitment of students 88; servant
    leadership 81–2; student leadership 88
sourcing of staff 77–8
Sparks, J.P. 96, 100–1
Spring, J. 33
St. Pierre, Nathanial 155
Stage, F.K. 126
Stein, W. 160
Story, Naomi 174–5
storytelling 104, 159–60
strategic needs, responsiveness to 57–9
Strickland, Haywood 35
student affairs administrators: academic
    affairs, contrast with 55; competencies
    needed 48; complexity of work 49; crisis
    aspect of 56–7; day-to-day work 48–9;
    diversity, leadership in 49; emergent
    needs, responsiveness to 56–7; expertise,
    use of other people's 53–4; future studies
    61; leadership 47–9; limitations: time
    and capacity 53; master's/doctoral
    education 49; model of highly effective
    53, **54**, 55–61, **58**; Norfolk State
    University **58**, 58–9; as pathway to
    presidency 46–7, 50, 59–61; proactivity
    56; responsiveness of 56–9; strategic
    needs, responsiveness to 57–9;
    team-building 53–4, 60; traits and roles
    56–7, 59; unpredictable ethos of arena
    for 55–6. see also Presidents of MSIs
student borrowing (Fresno State
    University) 117
student numbers: Historically Black
    Colleges and Universities (HBCUs) 3;
    Minority-Serving Institutions (MSIs) 1;
    Predominantly Black Institutions (PBIs)
    9; Tribal Colleges and Universities
    (TCUs) 8
student outcomes at HBCUs 26. see also
    graduation rates
students: needs of at AANAPISIs 187–8,
    190–1; under-resourced students 144. see
    also Latino students

succession planning and sourcing 77–8
support systems at HBCUs 26

Taylor, M. 96–7, 101–2
TCUs. see Tribal Colleges and Universities
    (TCUs)
teaching styles 29
team-building 53–4, 60, 181
teamwork 53–4
technology, and work 209–10
technology-based teaching and learning:
    DISCOVERe 116; Fresno State
    University 116, 121
tenure negotiations 71
Teranishi, Robert 172
Tierney, W.G. 153
Tijerina, K.H. 155
time management by Presidents of MSIs 52
Title V funds: Higher Education Act
    (HEA) 6; Hispanic-Serving Institutions
    (HSIs) 96, 98, 101, 107, 132. see also
    funding
Toldson, I.A. 34
training for boards 34
translators/interpreters, leaders as 155–7
Treadwell, K.L. 56
Tribal Colleges and Universities (TCUs):
    accreditation 156–7; adaptability 154;
    American Indian Higher Education
    Consortium (AIHEC) 142, 146, 152,
    157, 160; as centers of community 155;
    collective leadership by Native
    Americans 146; community, caring for
    by leaders 145; creation of 7–8; dual
    mission and worlds 142–3; early 141–2,
    152; employment opportunities 162;
    equity and social justice, focus on by
    presidents 163–4; example, leading and
    learning by 146; framework of
    leadership 152–60; funding 8, 143–4,
    156; future of 156–7; grant funding 144;
    grow-your-own programs 155; hunter/
    gather/growers, leaders as 154–5;
    indigenous self-governance and identity
    151; Indigenous Ways of Knowing 140;
    knowledgeable, leaders as 145–6;
    leadership challenges today 142–6;
    learning, tribal approaches to 151;
    mainstream/tribal balance 142–3; Native
    American leadership practices 144–7;
    Navajo Community College 141;
    number of 8, 139, 141; orators/
    advocates, leaders as 157–8; partnership

and networks 155; political and public
scrutiny 160–1; presidents of 152–64;
programs offered 8; qualifications/
experience of leaders 162–3;
recommendations from leadership at
147; resources, attracting and allocating
154–5; responsibilities and expectations
of leaders 150–1; socio-economic
conditions 161–2; storytellers, leaders as
159–60; student numbers 8, 139;
translators/interpreters, leaders as 155–7;
Tribally Controlled Community College
Assistance Act (TCCCAA) 1978 8, 143;
trust obligations, unfulfilled 143; tuition
fees 8; under-resourced students 144;
vision 153–4; warriors, leaders as 158–9;
World Indigenous Nations Higher
Education Consortium (WINHEC) 157.
see also Native Americans
*Tribal Colleges Contributions to Local Economic
Development* (IHEP) 162
*Tribally Controlled Colleges: Making Good
Medicine* (Stein) 160
Tribally Controlled Community College
Assistance Act (TCCCAA) 1978 8, 143
tuition fees for TCUs 8
turnover of senior-level staff:
administrators, impact on after CEO

departure 66; impact of high 65, 66–7;
mentorship, impact on 69; new leaders,
challenges faced by 68–9; new policies,
introduction of 69; Presidents of MSIs
3–4, 12, 34–5; protection from impacts
of high 70; recruitment and selection
hampered by 67

Underwood, Robert 11

Valdez, P. 96
values, leadership 178, 182
vision 153–4

Warner, L.S. 155
warriors, leaders as 158–9
Watkins, William 24–5
WE Over Me Farm 83, 85, 86–7
WE Over Me motto 81, 83
White philanthropists, motives of 23–5
Wiggins, U. 71
women presidents 4, 5
work-life balance 51
workforce participation for AAPIs 170
World Indigenous Nations Higher
Education Consortium (WINHEC) 157

Yamagata-Noji, Audrey 172–3, 174, 179